SHAKTI
POWER IN THE CONCEPTUAL STRUCTURE
OF KARIMPUR RELIGION

Susan Snow Wadley

The University of Chicago Studies in Anthropology
Series in Social, Cultural, and Linguistic Anthropology, No. 2

Published by the Department of Anthropology,
The University of Chicago

1975

Library of Congress Cataloging in Publication Data

Wadley, Susan Snow, 1943-
    Shakti: power in the conceptual structure of Karimpur
religion.
    (Series in social, cultural, and linguistic anthropology)
(The University of Chicago studies in anthropology; no. 2)
    Bibliography: p. 217-22.
    1. Hinduism--Rituals. 2. Hinduism--Karimpur, India.
3. Karimpur, India--Religious life and customs. 4. Religion
and language. I. Title. II. Series. III. Series: Chicago.
University. Dept. of Anthropology. The University of Chicago
studies in anthropology.
BL1226.2.W3   294.5'514'095414
ISBN 0-916256-01-4
76-37612

The University of Chicago Studies in Anthropology
are available from:

Department of Anthropology
The University of Chicago
1126 East 59th Street
Chicago, Illinois 60637
    Price: $5.00 list; $4.00 series subscription

ACKNOWLEDGMENTS

This monograph is the outcome of the support and encouragement of many individuals and institutions. First, I would like to thank the National Science Foundation for supporting the research itself. Additional financial support was given by the Department of Anthropology, University of Chicago, both before and during fieldwork, in the form of a National Defense Educational Act, Title IV Grant. The South Asia Committee of the University of Chicago contributed further funds, first a National Defense Educational Act Title VI (Hindi) Grant and later grants-in-aid for living and translating expenses.

This monograph is the result of research conducted from December 1967 to March 1969 in Karimpur, a village in western Uttar Pradesh, India. Karimpur was first studied in the 1920s by William H. Wiser and my major debt is to the people of Karimpur and Mrs. Charlotte Wiser. While I was preparing for fieldwork, Norvin Hein of Yale University gave me a collection of folksongs and stories collected by the Wisers in Karimpur in the 1920s. Later, Mrs. Charlotte Wiser, then still living in Karimpur part of each year, offered me her hospitality, introductions, and the use of her house for the period of my research. To her, I owe many thanks, particularly for her home and "her" village.

My stay in Karimpur was particularly successful because of my cook, Bashir Khan, who not only fed me but also was guardian, mentor, and teller of tales for fifteen months. But most of all I must thank my Karimpur family, belonging to the house of Bajreng Prasad Pandey, who welcomed me happily and provided me with the unusual and unforgettable opportunity to know intimately an Indian family and eventually, as much as an outsider can be, to be part of that family. I am also grateful to other Karimpur friends, particularly Januki, Raghubar, Jageshvar Dube and his wife, and the women of the House of Asha Ram Dube for introducing me to the complexities of Karimpur religion and oral traditions. My many research assistants included Umesh Chandra Pandey and Nanhe Khan. To the many others of Karimpur who put up with me and gave me their assistance, I must give a general thanks.

iii

I must also express my gratitude to Richard and Martha Alt, who took me into their Delhi home when illness struck and allowed me to become physically and mentally revived in their care periodically for nine months.

This monograph could never have been written without the guidance and inspiration of my professors and fellow students at the University of Chicago. In particular, I wish to acknowledge the help of Milton Singer and Paul Friedrich, who guided me on my first anthropological endeavors, waited patiently for the results of this one, and provided encouragement and support along the way. My many talks with Ronald Inden in 1969-70 have proved invaluable to the formulation of the problem presented here and I am grateful to him for his provocative insights. Above all, I must thank my "guru," McKim Marriott.

To the many other people who contributed in various ways to this work, I must single out my parents, Ellen and Chester Wadley, who without protest allowed me to spend my junior year at Delhi University in 1963-64 and have given me encouragement when needed in later years. In the past two years my husband, Bruce W. Derr, has provided support while I completed this manuscript.

The results are mine. But they belong equally to the people of Karimpur. I hope that I have done them justice.

CONTENTS

ILLUSTRATIONS

TABLES

NOTE ON ROMANIZATION

In the transcription of Hindi words, proper names have been left unmarked, unless used in a Hindi-language context, e.g., Krishna instead of *kriShNa*; so have geographical names. Occasionally a common
word has been retained in the anglicized form.

      The standard conventions have been followed for representing
long vowels ($\bar{a}$, $\bar{\imath}$, $\bar{u}$); *e* and *o* are long unmarked. Retroflex conso-
nants are represented by capital letters (*D*, *T*, *N*). Aspiration is
indicated by an *h* following the consonant; *ch* as in "church" is unas-
pirated; *chh* is aspirated. *sh* and *Sh* represent the palatal and retroflex variations of *sh* respectively. Current scholarly conventions
have been employed elsewhere.

Chapter I: INTRODUCTION

This monograph is based on the hope that comprehension of rural Hindu religious behavior can be furthered by analyzing the structure of the verbalized beliefs of its practitioners. There has been little previous work on the structure of the concepts of Hindu villagers and almost no attention has been paid to little-traditional or local-level "texts." Yet despite the visible complexity and apparent chaos present in village religious behavior, the conceptual system of the practitioner is systematically organized, even if often unself-consciously, and provides a conceptual reality for his ritual activity. In his songs, myths, ritual sayings, and comments on his religious behavior, the Hindu villager reveals the organization of this belief system. By analyzing the oral traditions of a North Indian village, we can identify the principal categories in which religious action takes place.

I have attempted to apply analytic methods, as initiated primarily by linguists and developed by the structuralists, to the religious literature, both oral and written, of a North Indian village. My primary purpose is to define some of the conceptual categories which underlie village Hindu religious behavior. In conjunction with this analysis, I have dealt with the relationship of conceptual categories to specific types of ritual behavior. Those aspects of the belief system described in the following pages are centered on the natives' beliefs about the nature of their deities, the various deities' relationships to each other, and the deities' relationships to men.

In addition, understanding the principles and categories of people's beliefs about their rituals and their deities allows us to augment the literature on the importance of some basic principles which underlie Indian society--in particular, to perceive in the religious system the working of the principles of power and purity. Specifically, the evidence presented here concerning religious belief systems emphasizes the importance of the idea of power in Hinduism and Indian society.

1

Orientation

More generally, this study is concerned with some aspects of the
North Indian peasant's cultural system, that is, of the system of
symbols which defines his world or universe.[1] Symbols are "vehicles
for the conception of objects" (Langer 1951:61). When we conceive
of an object, we do not act toward it overtly, we are not aware of
the actual presence of that object. Rather, we are aware of ideas
and attitudes about that object--conceptions of it--and it is these
conceptions which are the symbol's "meaning." Or, as Geertz states,
symbols are "tangible formulations of notions, abstractions from ex-
perience fixed in perceptible forms, concrete embodiments of ideas,
attitudes, judgements, longings or beliefs" (1966:5). Furthermore,
there is no intrinsic relation between a symbol and that which it
symbolizes--symbols are arbitrary. The connection between a particular stone and a given deity is imposed by man--any other stone could
be equally adequate as a "symbol," that is, as a vehicle for the conceptions associated with that deity. A cultural system, then, is the
system of the conceptions, meanings, and beliefs of a given society
embodied in its symbols.

This study is also concerned with what people say--with language. One segment of any cultural system is the language of that
culture, particularly the words of that language. Words are a common
embodiment of conceptions; they are symbols (although they can also
be signs). Words, like the stone, are based on arbitrary relations
between sounds and conceptions. And even though words may have objective referents, they are cultural constructs and are one form of
symbol. Words, as symbols in a cultural system, are important to the
anthropologist because they are one of the best sources in discovering what the conceptions of a particular culture are. However, words
seldom represent one meaning, one conception. Rather, they are poly-
semous, they are vehicles for a number of conceptions. The interrelationships of these conceptions and the relevance of one or another
in given circumstances must be discovered for each "word" symbol.
Thus language is a part of culture, although it is not the only possible system of meanings and symbols which makes up culture.

Another aspect of a cultural system is religion. According
to Geertz, a religious system is a symbolic system,

> . . . a system of symbols which acts to (2) establish powerful,
> pervasive, and long-lasting moods and motivations in men by
> (3) formulating conceptions of a general order of existence and
> (4) clothing these conceptions with such an aura of factuality
> that (5) the moods and motivations seem uniquely realistic
> (1966:4).

Like all elements of cultural systems, religious symbols belong to "society," not to individual members of that society. In other words, religious symbols are part of the "common understandings" of a given society.[2] Moreover, religious systems are a model "of" reality--they chart the physical relationships (reality) in a way that makes the world comprehensible to men. In addition, they are models "for" reality--they organize physical relationships. That is, religious systems not only make sense of the world by constructing a model of its functioning, they also provide guidelines for the way the world will function, particularly by providing guidelines for men's actions within the world. Thus religious systems are concerned with what is and what ought to be. This duality is essential to the following analysis.

This study deals with those aspects of the North Indian peasant's cultural system which are primarily embodied in words (linguistic symbols) pertaining to religion. Within the realm of religious symbols, I am concerned with those symbols by which men define their various deities and their deities' relationships to men. I am particularly concerned with those units found in man's verbal expressions that deal with his gods, goddesses, demons, etc. This monograph is then based on three premises:

    a. A cultural system is a system of symbols.

    b. Language is one major part of a cultural system.

    c. Religion is a cultural system.

Geertz suggests, in "Ritual and Social Change, A Javanese Example," a distinction between social and cultural systems that is particularly provocative.

> This contrast is between what Sorokin has called "logico-meaningful integration" and what he has called "causal-functional integration." By logico-meaningful integration, characteristic of culture, is meant the sort of integration one finds in a Bach fugue in Catholic dogma, or in the general theory of relativity; it is a unity of style, of logical implication of meaning and value. By causal-functional integration, characteristic of the social system, is meant the kind of integration one finds in an organism, where all the parts are united in a single causal web (1957:33).

If the cultural, and by implication the religious, systems are integrated in a logico-meaningful way, and language is a part of the cultural system, the techniques of the structuralists, especially those techniques based on recent developments in linguistics, potentially have a wide application. Discussions and definitions of cultural (and religious) systems as described by Geertz are similar to recent works in semantic theory, where the emphasis has been on the structural unity of sets. Borrowing methods of analysis from the lin-

guists, I shall attempt to define some of the fundamental categories
regarding religion as found in the language, particularly the lexicon,
of the North Indian peasant.

Methodology

The methodological apparatus with which I approached the oral literature collected in a North Indian village has three related aspects.
First, I have used a variant of myth analysis as detailed by Levi-
Strauss (1963a). Second, I have relied in spirit on the techniques
of structural semantics as defined by John Lyons (1963, 1968) and in
conjunction with this analysis I have borrowed and adapted from the
cognitive anthropologists, particularly Conklin (1955, 1962, 1964)
and Frake (1961, 1962). Third, I have taken a specifically structural approach, following Yalman: "'structure' is behind both thought
and behavior" (1967:7). In this connection, Chomsky's (1965) comments on competence and performance are particularly valuable. Competence represents the native's often unconscious knowledge of the
rules of his language. I should note that the rules of the linguist
are merely a model of the rules of the speaker: the linguist wishes
to provide rules which can explain and generate all grammatical speech,
but he has no guarantee that the speaker actually uses the rules
created by the linguist. In a similar fashion, the anthropologist
can suggest rules for other aspects of human behavior, rules which
are models of the native's knowledge of his society. It is possible
that the competence of the native is the "structure" which is behind
both thought and behavior.

At this point, a word about the origins of this study is useful in clarifying the application of these approaches. The never
ceasing religiosity of the village practitioner of Hinduism is well
known to most anthropologists, but not fully understood. This monograph is the result of my interest in attempting to comprehend the
cultural system underlying this religious behavior. I went to North
India interested in the content of oral traditions and specifically
in the "local-level" use of conceptual categories concerned with religious belief. In part, this concern arose from earlier work in
which religious texts were used as my primary data for a structural
analysis both of concepts of fate as found in a local tradition and
of the god with which this tradition was concerned (Wadley 1967).

Another major factor that led me to consider textual analysis
as the justifiable domain of an anthropologist interested in South
Asia was Milton Singer's repeated pointing to the gap between textual
and contextual studies and of his statement of the need to combine

them. (See Singer 1961, 1972.) My aim was to combine the textual
approach of the philosopher or theologian with the contextual one of
the anthropologist and use local-level texts as my primary data. By
analyzing the verbal statements of the villagers, I hoped to be able
to delineate the conceptual system which underlies and therefore provides meaning for their religious activity.

In recent years, anthropologists have become increasingly
aware of the need to examine the verbal components of their natives'
behavior, especially the verbal components of religious behavior,
both in statements about religious belief and in ritual itself. (See
Tambiah 1968; Freedman 1967; Goody 1962.) Gombrich (1971) in *Precept
and Practice* relied heavily on the verbal statements (statements
about religion and statements used in ritual) of his Sinhalese informants in his analysis of the relations between Pali doctrine and
ritual behavior in Ceylon. In a similar fashion (but with no concern for doctrinal texts), this study examines what a North Indian
villager says about and to his deities in relation to how he behaves
toward them.

In attempting to obtain explanations of religious behavior
from the people of Karimpur,[3] a village on the Gangetic plain in
North India, I quickly realized that personal interpretations were
seldom given. The most common response to any queries about religious behavior was, at least initially, *niyam hai*, "it's a law." If
the people of Karimpur had explanations for their religious activity,
they were seldom spontaneous; rather, they were formalized explanations. As I became more familiar with Karimpur and its inhabitants,
I realized that, although very few people were able to offer conscious interpretations of their ritual activity, they were continually providing me with explanations. Their own verbalized justifications and knowledge of religion were repeatedly stated in the form
of songs, myths, ritual sayings, etc. These verbal traditions, passed
on from generation to generation, provide the average villager with
the rudiments of his religious belief system. Very few people were
able to expand upon the formalized explanations and offer their own
interpretations of religious activity. The primary categories and
principles which give meaning to village religion are found in the
many verbalizations about religious activity. So I remain grateful
to the many people of Karimpur who said *niyam hai* and then told a
story or sang a song.

Thus my purpose in being in Karimpur was to collect data related to religious explanation: the most prominent explanations were
the public ones, those shared by a large number of the members of

the community. Since a large portion of my data was such public textual explanations, I had to develop techniques of analysis which
could be used profitably on such information.

In recent years, the study of folklore and particularly of
oral traditions has changed rapidly in the direction of a structural
and semantic anthropological approach or what Maranda and Kongäs
Maranda (1971) call structural folkloristics. This approach, radi-
cally different from that of traditional folklore studies, emphasizes
underlying rules, not texts per se. Structural analysis in anthropology began with Hubert and Mauss (1897-98, 1902-3) and Durkheim
and Mauss (1963). Later linguists provided important developments
(the Prague linguistic circle), and Propp (1968) proposed a structural model for the folktale. Modern structural linguistics provided a
catalyst for a further development in anthropological analysis, represented by Levi-Strauss (1963b), Goodenough (1956), Conklin (1964),
Frake (1962), and others. I have used the analytic methods based in
this tradition of structural anthropology.

Indian Studies

Studies of religious traditions in India have been primarily concerned
with the doctrines of the Sanskritic traditions, the great traditions
of Hinduism. Anthropologists have countered this tendency of discussing Hinduism in terms of theology and philosophy by, for the most
part, merely acknowledging formalized religious doctrine.

To a large extent, anthropologists have been correct in paying little more than lip service to the religious doctrines of the
great traditions. Although these formalized religious traditions
must be considered in any study of the Hindu people, the lack of context for texts expounding the great-traditional doctrines does not
allow the anthropologist to deal with the relations between religious
practice and practitioners and doctrinal ideas.

There is yet another problem related to the anthropologists'
lack of concern with the philosophy and ideas of the formalized religious traditions. Modern anthropology, British and American, is
based on the primacy of behavior, and ideologies must be subordinated
to actual, preferably visible (and thus empirically controlled), behavior. This viewpoint is increasingly under attack, as the influence of French anthropology (Levi-Strauss and Dumont) and the transformation of folklore studies toward a structural approach illustrate.
Yet the anthropological behavioral basis continues and is notable in
the context of Indian studies. Although studies of Hindu doctrine
by the philosopher and theologian are based almost totally on textual

material, which is usually Sanskritic, studies of the "little traditions" of Hinduism are almost never concerned with textual material-- the "standard" texts of the North Indian Hindu villager are seldom even translated.

In countering the trend toward Hindu theology, anthropologists have concentrated their studies of Hinduism in three general areas. First, they have been concerned with the interrelationships of religious and social behavior, particularly the concept of purity/pollution. Second, most anthropological works on Indian religion attempt to connect and clearly define the great and the little traditions and the processes linking them. Third, some studies are concerned with the varieties of village gods and rituals. Let me examine the results of these three approaches more carefully.

First, the relationship of the concept of purity/pollution to social structure is ubiquitous in the anthropological literature on South Asia. (See Srinivas 1952; Dumont and Pocock 1959; Harper 1964; Dumont 1970.) Harper believes that purity/pollution is fundamental to Hindu society because "society is organized around the task of caring for its gods, and a division of labor among the castes is necessary to attain this end" (1964:195). This division of labor is based on a hierarchy of purity--thus purity/pollution penetrates Hindu social organization. The argument advanced by Dumont is in its end result very similar; the conceptual process through which he arrives at it is not. Essentially, he states that the pure/impure opposition is the single true principle underlying the caste system, as all other principles are reducible to this fundamental one (Dumont 1970). Despite variations in method and approach, no author denies the importance of the concept of purity in Hindu society.

Second, we find throughout most of the anthropological literature on South Asia attempts to connect and clearly define the great and the little traditions and the processes interlinking them. (See also Marriott 1955, 1966; Berreman 1963; Harper 1959; Cohn and Marriott 1958; Mandelbaum 1964, 1966.) The relationship between the great and the little traditions is extremely complex and perhaps presents as many problems as it solves. As several authors have noted, the great tradition itself includes many diverse elements (Redfield 1955; Singer 1955; Staal 1963; Raghavan 1956) or can be construed in a variety of ways (see Miller 1966). One common accord among anthropologists is that great-traditional ideas are differentially distributed among a village social hierarchy, from Brahman to untouchable, although even here some Brahmans may be imperfectly familiar with traditional forms (Marriott 1955). In the distribution of awareness

of great-traditional forms, education and religious specialization
also crosscut caste hierarchies and have important consequences for
an individual's knowledge of great-traditional concepts. Those authors who do present data regarding the influence of great-traditional forms generally do not give a clear picture of the concepts used
and are also hindered by a bias in their informants. (See Cohn 1959;
Carstairs 1967; Beals 1962; Lewis 1965; Kolenda 1964; Mahar 1960.)

Third, students of the little traditions have investigated
the attributes and characteristics of village and local gods and rituals. Although the propitiation of the many godlings, ghosts, and
spirits found in Hindu villages tends to dominate discussions of village religion, only recently have systematic studies of gods and rituals been made. Earlier studies of Hindu deities dealt primarily
with their numbers and characteristics (Crooke 1896; Opler 1959),
while several more recent ones have attempted to describe the structure of a village pantheon (Harper 1959, 1964) and the nature of specific supernatural beings in relation to the roles which they play
(Babb 1970a; Leach 1963; Dumont 1959). Meanwhile, a concern has developed for the structure of rituals themselves (Babb 1968, 1970b;
Yalman 1964).

These works have dealt with the Hindu gods in terms of their
immediate aspect and short-range spatial and temporal contexts, with
their relationships within the pantheon of a particular locality.
In focusing their studies in this way, anthropologists have partially
circumvented the problem raised by contrasting the great and the little traditions. They have not been concerned with the relationship
of a particular god to higher deities (in a great-traditional sense)
but with its relations with all other deities of all levels of that
locality. In their studies, one can perceive connections with the
great tradition, in that the roles sometimes attributed to great-
tradition deities (e.g., Shiva or Vishnu) are distributed among "lower"-level, often regional, gods. Very often elements of the great
and of the little traditions are present, then, when certain roles
and powers conceived to be derived from a "higher" god, that is, a
great-tradition god, are attributed to a local god. Yet these connections with great-traditional gods and powers derived in some way
from them are not so important as the actual ordering or structuring
of the pantheon itself. Harper (1959) has described the structure
of a South Indian pantheon in terms of the functions of gods as partially defined by village categories of gods. Even here, he is primarily concerned with which category of god has more "Sanskritic"
(i.e., great-traditional) characteristics and which is more pure or

impure. He also argues for a man-god continuum of purity and impur-
ity: here the highest gods are generally higher than the highest
men, whereas the lowest gods are generally lower than the lowest
men--"highness" and "lowness" are defined in terms of purity or im-
purity. This argument does not convincingly prove that men and the
gods are "the same" except for their relative states of purity, but
it does assert that the principle of pure/impure is considered critical to the role and place of a given deity in the pantheon of a certain locality.

Those studies which analyze the "semantics" of local-level
gods, that is, the characteristics of various deities in terms of the
roles which they play in a given pantheon, provide further insight
into the nature of Hindu supernatural beings. We know, for example,
that female deities without consorts are more likely to be malevolent
than female deities with consorts (Babb 1970a; Beck 1969). And Leach
(1963) has shown that, as one moves from South India to Ceylon, Ganesh
(Pulleyar) changes in characteristics and attributes, because of his
associates in the pantheons of the two areas. Pulleyar is a god concerned with fertility when found in the Ceylonese context of Buddhism
where the ascetic character of the Buddha predominates. Ganesh is
an ascetic god not concerned with fertility when he is found in South
India in conjunction with Shiva, a god definitely concerned with fertility. Studies delineating the relationship of special characteristics to the functions of various deities have augmented our previous
knowledge of the "semantics" of village Hinduism.

Investigations of the structure of ritual are primarily concerned with the nature of the transactions and communication between
men and the gods. They emphasize the separation of man and god, the
mundane and the divine, in their concern for purity in the approach
to the deity involved. Yet such studies do not examine--or answer--
the question about the characteristics of the ultimate transaction
between man and god which the ritual represents, although the characteristics of the ritual transaction are clearly defined (see Babb
1970b).

This question and others are related to the lack of studies
of the conceptual system of the Hindu villager and to the lack of
little-traditional or local-level "textual" studies. Some authors
have used or mentioned conceptual material in substantiating their
theses; however, none of them has attempted to explore the help that
non-great-traditional texts could provide for understanding village
religious behavior.

My purpose here is to begin filling this gap in our knowledge about Indian religion, that is, to analyze in detail aspects of the conceptual belief system relating to the religious behavior of a North Indian villager. I wish to present the ideas and beliefs, the order of reality, which give meaning to North Indian peasant's religiosity. The primary question asked is what there is in the belief system of the Hindu villager that makes the performance of rituals necessary. A corollary to this question is, what is the nature of those many beings to whom and for whom rituals are enacted. These two questions, essentially *why* and *who*, interlock at the level of social action, where both are used to define situations and lead to certain courses of actions. A secondary aim is to relate these two questions, dealing specifically with belief systems, to actual ritual behavior--to define the ideas which organize and give meaning to ritual behavior and to demonstrate the points at which religious categories of thought and categories of action interact.

Most anthropological studies of Indian religious systems have begun with ritual behavior and have attempted to derive from it aspects of the conceptual system of the participants. This study proceeds in the opposite direction--from a careful delineation of aspects of the conceptual system, as inferred from verbal texts, to a concern for its manifestation in religious action. I have not attempted to define how men will act, according to their beliefs, in given situations. This essay is not an exercise in defining the ideas capable of making one behave (religiously) as a member of a North Indian village society. I hope by not doing so to avoid the pervasive problem of cognitive anthropology. My primary aim is to delineate the major conceptual categories which give meaning to actual behavior and which define the major constraints and boundaries in which a member of the society may act. As Lehman states, "Knowledge does not generate behavior. It only gives it meaning and at most constrains whatever generates actual behavior within broad limits of interpretability" (1972:374).

NOTES

1. I am following Schneider and Geertz in this definition of culture, as well as Parsons, Kluckhohn, and Kroeber. Schneider (1968) and Geertz (1957, 1958, and 1966) have been especially useful.

2. The complaint may be made that religious symbols have different meanings for different members of that society and that there are therefore no "common understandings." However, if we treat symbolic systems as linguists have been treating language in the past decade, individual competence is not our primary concern. Rather, we are concerned with what the meanings and conceptions of a given symbol are if a member has full "competence" of his cultural system.

3. "Karimpur" is the name given this village by William H. Wiser (1933, 1958); for the sake of continuity in the literature, I have retained it.

Chapter II: THE VILLAGE SETTING

Karimpur, where the research for this study was conducted, is a village in both the District and the Tahsil of Mainpuri, Uttar Pradesh.
Aspects of life in Karimpur have been described elsewhere--it is the
village "behind mud walls" presented in the works of William and
Charlotte Wiser (Wiser 1933, 1958; Wiser and Wiser 1971).[1] Karimpur
is even now a farming community, remarkably little affected by the
increased urbanization and progressive farming techniques so talked
about in the literature on India today. District Mainpuri as a whole
has a reputation for being backward in comparison to other sections
of U.P. and North India. Although one can readily identify elements
of change, the changes have not yet fundamentally altered the routines
of life. Urban migration remains minimal, whereas ties to land and
village are still potent. Karimpur can still be described as a con-
servative North Indian Hindu village.

The Locality

Located in the so-called Hindu heartland of Northern India on the
Gangetic plain between the Ganges and Jamuna rivers, Karimpur is approximately 150 miles southeast of Delhi and 95 miles northwest of
Kanpur. (See figure 1.) A paved road through the village links it
to Mainpuri, the district headquarters 7½ miles south, and Kuraoli,
a small market town 7½ miles north. A dirt road also runs to the
east, meeting the Grand Trunk Road at Bichhwan 2 miles away. (See
figure 2.)

Karimpur people travel mainly to Mainpuri, both because the
civil authority is there and because it has a thriving bazaar. Trans-
portation to Mainpuri and Kuraoli is easily obtained. There are six
or seven public buses per day and one or two private ones. There are
also *ikkas*, the traditional horse-drawn carriages of U.P.; lorries
which take passengers; and cycle rickshaws. If a villager has no
money for paid transport, he walks, rides a bicycle, or drives a bullock cart. Contact with Mainpuri is frequent--many families have a
man going there almost daily to work, to attend to a court case, to
sell grain or milk, to see a doctor, or more rarely just to shop or

11

Fig. 1.   India

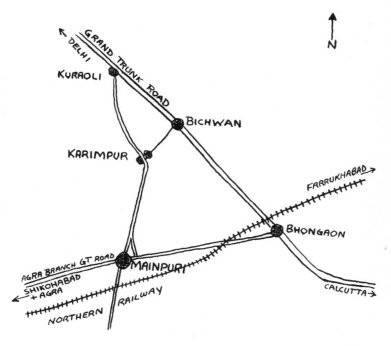

Fig. 2.   Road map of Mainpuri District

to see a movie. All the high school students but one attend school in Mainpuri. Less frequently, Karimpur people go north or east, primarily to visit their affinal relatives or some holy place.

From Mainpuri, one can get buses to Agra, Kanpur, Delhi, and the nearby towns, or a train to Farrukabad (on the Ganges thirty miles east), or to Shikohadbad, to the west, where there are connections to Delhi or Kanpur. However, the villagers rarely go farther than their most distant relative, who usually lives in one of the adjoining districts; and the local buses and their own bicycles are the main means of transport.

The village known as Karimpur is composed of several nucleated settlement areas. (See figure 3.) These are Karimpur *khās* (the main settlement area 100 yards east of the Mainpuri-Kuraoli road); *kāchhī kā nagalā* (or *kherā*), on the road; *chamār kā nagalā*, also on the main road; and the "bus stop" where the boys' primary school, a shop and mill, and some houses are now.[2] Although the administrative, revenue, and panchayat village is larger (including several named hamlets some distance away), these areas are considered as making up the unit called "Karimpur." (Unless otherwise specified, "Karimpur" hereafter refers to this smaller unit.)[3] The reality of Karimpur as a unit distinct from the administrative one becomes clearest both in naming ("Karimpur" refers in local parlance to only these settlements) and in ritual activity. Several village deities are considered to belong to this unit only; moreover, the rainy season ritual to cure illness is concerned with these four settlements and the fields associated with them.[4]

One thousand three hundred and eighty people belonging to twenty-two named castes (*jāti*) live in the village. (See table 1.) Of these, only *chamārs* (Leatherworkers) live in the *chamār kā nagalā*; *kāchhīs* (Farmers), *lodhī rājpūts* (Vegetable Growers), and *banyās* (Shopkeepers) live on the *kherā*; Muslim Beggars and *baRhaī* (Carpenters) live at the bus stop. Members of all castes except the *lodhī rājpūts* and *banyās* live in Karimpur *khās*. Within Karimpur *khās* the Brahmans live mostly in the southern half (with Mat-makers on the far southern edge); Sweepers are set apart by a road at the north edge of the settlement; and the other castes are scattered in caste enclaves throughout.

In 1967-69, there were the following visible characteristics of modernization in Karimpur.

Schools: a primary boys' school located at the bus stop (four masters);

a primary girls' school in the Brahman area (two masters);

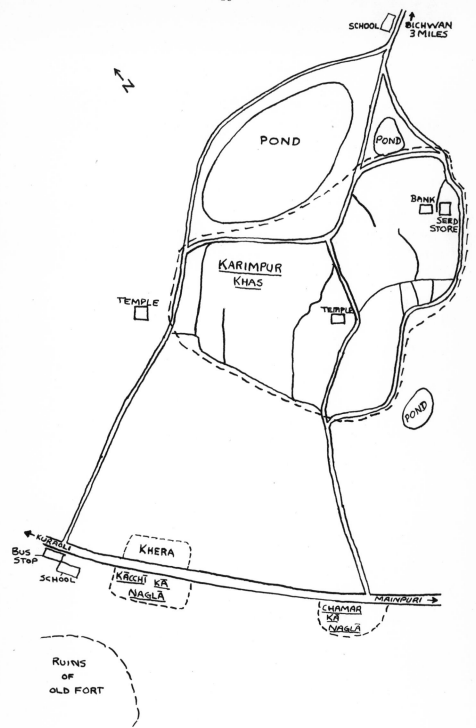

Fig. 3. Village known as "Karimpur"

Table 1

Karimpur Population by Caste and Household

Caste Name	Traditional Occupation	Number of Households	Population	Percentage of Total Population
brāhman[a]	Priest	41	306	22.4
rāy	Bard	2	12	.9
sunār	Goldsmith	2	8	.6
kāyastha	Scribe	3	22	1.6
baRhaī	Carpenter	8	56	4.1
gaDariyā	Shepherd	19	88	6.4
lodhī rājpūt	Vegetable Grower	3	18	1.3
kāchhī	Farmer	43	249	18.0
banyā (mahājan)	Shopkeeper	2	19	1.4
kahār	Water Carrier	29	174	12.6
kumhār	Potter	2	6	.4
bhūrjī	Grain Parcher	3	19	1.4
darjī	Tailor	3	15	1.1
mālī	Flower Grower/ Gardener	3	17	1.2
dhobī	Washerman	3	13	.9
telī	Oil Presser	5	36	2.6
dhānuk	Midwife/Mat-maker	16	104	7.5
chamār	Leatherworker	9	55	3.9
bhangī	Sweeper	14	87	6.3
phaqīr (Muslim)[b]	Beggar	12	45	3.2
manihār (Muslim)[b]	Bangle Seller	3	11	.8
dhunā (Muslim)[b]	Cotton Carder	4	19	1.4
Total		229	1,380	100.0

[a]I shall hereafter refer to this group by its Indian name. All others will be referred to by their traditional occupations.

[b]These three Muslim groups are castelike in structure. They are assigned individual ranks in village opinion scales and view themselves as distinct endogamous groups.

a coeducational junior school on the Bichhwan road east of the settlement (two masters).

Government agencies: a Cooperative Seed Store (serving twenty-five villages and hamlets in the area);

a Cooperative Bank (connected to the seed store: same membership);

a Post Office, run from a house by a Brahman (whose teen-age son had to deliver the English mail);

a Government-run tube well located north of Karimpur *khās* that, given the present demand, could irrigate approximately one-third of the cultivated land of Karimpur.[5]

Mills: one run by a Goldsmith, near the bus stop, for grinding grain;

one run by the Shopkeeper, next to his shop, for grain, oil pressing, cotton carding.

Shops: a large one on the road at the *kherā* run by the Shopkeeper family;

a thriving smallish one in the center of the village run by the Grain Parcher;

a small one, run by an old widowed Goldsmith, on the east edge of Karimpur *khās*;[6]

a bicycle repair shop, run by a Shopkeeper, at the bus stop.

Temples: a Shiv temple on the north road of Karimpur; a *dharamshala* is connected to it (They were built by a newly rich Water Carrier widow. The temple was completed and inaugurated in February, 1968);

a Hanuman temple, on the Bichhwan road, built by a Mat-maker widow for her personal use;

a Shiv temple, uncompleted when I left, being built in the center of the village by a Brahman widow.[7]

Vehicles: one motorcycle owned by the Goldsmith millowner;

two cycle rickshaws owned by a Brahman landlord and rented by the week to lower-class rickshaw walas whose livelihood depends on their earning more than the rent (Other rickshaws are rented by Karimpur drivers from owners in Mainpuri.);

numerous bicycles owned by the wealthier families.

Other features characteristic of modernizing villages were absent.[8] There were no working radios, no electricity (although the lines had been up since 1966 and the mills and tube well had electricity), no village center or panchayat meeting hall--in fact, a nonfunctioning panchayat.[9]

History

Using both records and legend, we can trace the outlines of the history of Karimpur back 250 years. In the mid-eighteenth century, a Muslim king named Khan Bahadur entered what appears to have been a thriving market town of thousands and allegedly destroyed part of it in order to build himself a fort. Evidence also suggests that

> [Karimpur] must be an imposing city containing some thou-
> sands of inhabitants, and perhaps a mile in circumference, with
> an inner bazaar reaching nearly to the road and a *ganj* or market
> outside. There are few remains of the old town, but the ground
> is everywhere covered with fragments of brick, while on the road
> are traces of a gateway, with some remnants of another gateway
> on the ground beyond the road. . . . Khan Bahadur is even said
> to have helped the then Raja of Mainpuri to enlarge that city,
> whose rivalry ultimately proved fatal to Karimpur (Neave 1913:
> 217).

Somewhat similar is the story told by the present-day inhabitants of Karimpur. According to the legendary history known to
many, Thakurs were in control of the area and had a fort to the west
of the present village settlement. A Brahman from Kanauj, 60 miles
to the east, came to the village and wanted to reside there. With
the help of a Muslim raja from Kas Ganj, a town 40 miles northwest,
the Thakurs were defeated and the Brahman got the right to the village lands (with the Muslim raja as zamindar). The fort of the Thakurs was destroyed by the cannon of the Muslim king.[10] The Muslim
king, known as Khan Bahadur, was buried atop the ruined fort, and
even today he continues to protect the village. As village protector,
he is still worshiped by all castes.[11] Since their defeat, no Thakur
has been allowed to live in Karimpur, because the people believe that
if a Thakur lives in the village he will become rich and the Brahmans
poor. As proof of the harmfulness of Thakurs, they cite the example
of a Thakur servant in a Brahman house who was finally chased out of
the village, as he was becoming rich while his Brahman master became
poor.

There is also some evidence in support of parts of this legend. The major Brahman lineage can be traced back ten generations
to a single man, supposedly the Brahman who was able to get rid of
the Thakurs. The other Brahmans were all brought to Karimpur at a
later date. In some way, Khan Bahadur, whoever he may have been,
did have enough influence (or legend) connected to his name to become
the village guardian. And the fort was definitely destroyed some
time before the British took over the area.

In 1801 what is now Mainpuri District was ceded to the British and a civil cantonment was constructed slightly west of Mainpuri
Town proper. The Settlement Report of 1869 states that Karimpur

> formerly belonged to the Brahman residents of Karimpur *khās*. It
> was sold for arrears about 60 or 61 years ago, bought in by Gov-
> ernment and made over afterwards to Chaudri Udai Chand in whose
> family it has remained ever since (Conaghey 1869).

By the Settlement Report of 1904, the zamindar had again changed:

> At last settlement the proprietor was the Chaudhry of Bishungarh.

When his estates were sold up some few years ago,[12] this village
of Karimpur was bought up in execution of decrees of Bannias of
Cawnpore and Farrukhabad, who have since sold 10 *biswas*[13] of the
whole to a relative of the raja of Awa, who is a Lambardar (Lupton 1904).

The village remained partitioned between these two zamindars and
their heirs until the U.P. Zamindari Abolition and Land Reforms Act,
1950. This was enacted in Mainpuri in the mid-fifties; by the mid-
sixties, the land belonged to those members of the village who could
afford the payments and the bribes. In 1966, another change in land-
ownership began to be instituted--in this case, land consolidation
whereby the many scattered plots of one farmer would be condensed
through equal exchange for one or two large (or larger) plots. The
final maps were still being drawn in 1969 and again, he who paid the
most got the most. In both the post-Independence land actions, and
even earlier under various zamindars, the Brahmans continued to act
as if they were the "real" rulers of the village--as, in fact, because of their overwhelming control of the cultivated land, they were.

Social Organization

Owning 54 percent of the cultivated land, the Brahmans dominate the
village economically and politically. In intravillage affairs they
are not, however, a united group. They are split into East Brahmans
and West Brahmans. Two *khāndāns*, lineages, of Pandeys form the poles
for these two groups. The Pandeys are descendants of the original
Brahman settler, who had three sons: the first son's descendants
are the East Pandeys; the second son's descendants are the West Pandeys; and the third son's descendants are in a nearby village.[14]

Of the forty-one Brahman families in the village, all but
six represent descendants of the original Pandey--either direct descendants through the male line or descendants of daughters whose
husbands settled in Karimpur. Although the East and West Pandeys
recognize their common ancestor, they consider their *khāndāns* or lineages (lineages for ritual purposes, such as funeral rites) to be
separate. Lineages related to the Pandeys through a daughter align
themselves (with one exception) to the Pandey lineage into which they
married. The exception is the Chaubes (now calling themselves Dube)
who are related by marriage to the West Pandeys, but maintain a certain amount of neutrality in relations between the two larger, more
powerful Pandey lineages. In fact, the prevote *mukhiyā* (headman) of
the village was the elder of this Chaube lineage.

The two Brahman lineages which are not related to the Pandeys
are the Misras, descendants of the priest whom the Pandeys brought

to the village; and the Dubes, descendants of a tax collector sent
three or four generations ago by one of the zamindars of the village.
The Misras have little land and only one adult male now alive and
align themselves with the West Pandeys. The Dubes are aligned for
certain ritual purposes with the East Pandeys, although politically
they attempt to maintain neutrality and go their own way. They are
wealthy, with landholdings comparable to those of individual Pandey
households. However, they do not have the depth of a large *khāndān*
such as the two Pandey lineages have and thus are not truly effective
in the political arena of the village.

Most of the Brahman men are farmers. They farm what they
can themselves with the aid of day laborers and give the rest of
their cultivated land out to sharecroppers. Three men act as priests
when necessary but continue to support themselves and their families
principally by farming. One middle-aged man, not a village priest,
is a traveling lecturer ("Pandit"), but even he has kept his land
and helps his son farm it when at home. Only one Brahman has a cash
job; he runs the government tube well in the village. Only the present generation of teen-agers is seriously concerned with acquiring
education and obtaining sources of income outside of the village and
away from their family fields.

The organization of political activity in Karimpur can be
most easily seen through examining the existing social cleavages and
their representative factions. The dominant cleavage is a vertical
one between the two Pandey lineages, that is, between two structur-
ally equivalent political groups. A second important but so far
largely uneffective horizontal cleavage exists between Brahmans and
Farmers.[15]

The two Pandey lineages are approximately equal in population
and economic resources. In village-level politics, they maintain a
kind of equilibrium: since Panchayati Raj was instituted with a series of elected headmen, two headmen have come from the West Pandey
lineage and one from the East Pandey lineage.[16] However, a stalemate
has developed in the panchayat itself. Each of the two groups seldom
allows the other to act effectively, and little concrete action of
any sort is taken by the panchayat.

The next most important, influential, and numerous caste group
in Karimpur are the *kāchhī*, farmers by both traditional and real occupation. Most families in this group live in the *kherā*, a semisep-
arate hamlet on the main road. Although they are the only other
group owning sizable amounts of land, they continue to be dominated
by the Brahmans, for whom many work as either sharecroppers or labor-

ers. Nevertheless, they maintain their independence whenever possible. They are more likely to unite within themselves against their traditional enemies, the Brahmans, than they are to factionalize internally. They maintain their caste unity against the pull of their individual ties to particular Brahman families--usually their landlords. The Farmers form the only important group within the village that is relatively unaffected by the vertical cleavage formed by the dominant Brahmans.

The other caste groups are involved in politics primarily through their landlord or *jajmān* (patron) ties. In this way, the vertical cleavage found in the Brahman caste penetrates most of the rest of the village. A large percentage of non-Brahmans work as tenants or laborers for Brahman landlords. Moreover, *jajmān-kamīn* (patron-client) ties are still strong in many cases, particularly between Brahman *jajmāns* and non-Brahman *kamīns*.

The all-pervading network of *jajmān-kamīn* relationships described by Wiser has changed, however. In comparison with the situation in 1925-30,[17] there has been a significant decrease in the number of castes acting as *kamīns* and probably a corresponding decrease in the intensity of those relationships still maintained, although documenting this decrease is difficult. Of the castes present in Karimpur in 1925-30, two no longer exist. One, the Barber, has been replaced by Barbers from nearby villages; the other, the Muslim Dancing Girls, have simply died out. Of those castes remaining in the village, two no longer follow their traditional occupations and thereby have lost their client roles: the Goldsmith and the Oil Presser. The Goldsmiths left in Karimpur are "businessmen" and have themselves given up their traditional occupation. The Oil Pressers were displaced by machines at the mills in Mainpuri and forced out of business--all adult males have found other sources of income, including tailoring. Another group, the Muslim Cotton Carder, observes its traditional calling only at the time of festivals, especially Divali, the Festival of Lights, when cotton is needed for the wicks of the homemade oil lamps: the men in this group are constantly job-hunting, having no other resources or skills. The Grain Parchers are today paid only for services rendered and claim no *jajmāns*. Some Muslim Beggars still claim food at festivals, but this is the extent of their ties to a patron and their claim on him. These men are also laborers, and many drive rickshaws. The above castes have been most drastically affected by changing times and have become those from whom the Brahmans are not easily able to claim rewards for their patronage--in politics, votes.

Fig. 4. Occupations: (a) A Potter
(b) An Oil Presser turned tailor

Other castes remain more susceptible to demands from the
Brahmans, although here again the nature of the patron-client tie
has altered in the direction of reducing close connections in the
past forty years. The services given by the Sweepers, Leatherworkers, and Mat-makers have all been sharply curtailed since 1930, and
some members of all these castes have sought work outside of Karimpur, though always leaving someone behind to do the work demanded by
one's patrons. One Sweeper did so well in Calcutta that he returned
and built a brick house, much to the consternation of the village
elite. The Potters and Tailors have both suffered a loss of clien-
tele, mostly because of the increasing use of the Mainpuri market
and the concomitant desire to have "status" clothes, utensils, etc.
The Carpenter and Water Carrier castes have most closely adhered to
their traditional calling and maintain strong ties with their hereditary *jajmāns*; however, a critical factor aiding this connection is
the frequent addition of a landlord-tenant tie.

All castes that do maintain their ties to *jajmāns* through
their traditional calling do so primarily with the Brahmans, whose
families are the only ones with the resources necessary to take ad-
vantage of the services offered (which is not to imply that all Brahman families are wealthy by village standards--some are most definitely not--however, there are several wealthy Brahman families in
each major faction). Again, these *jajmān-kamīn* ties are often sup-
plemented by landlord-tenant or employer-employee ties. The castes
still strongly affected by these factors are those in which the vertical cleavages found in the Brahman community are most easily distinguished. It is these close economic ties with other caste groups,
mostly Brahman, which affect political activity in Karimpur by allowing the patrons to demand votes and support in return for employment.

The economic and political dominance of the Brahmans, added
to their traditional high ritual status, place them without question
at the top of Karimpur's hierarchy of castes. And no one in Karimpur,
except perhaps they themselves, would deny that the Sweepers are at
the bottom of the hierarchy. In the middle, there is less agreement;
nevertheless, using a synthesis of the results of opinion scales and
food transactions, we obtain the hierarchy of castes for Karimpur
shown in table 2.[18]

Education

Education is only beginning to be considered important for success
in Karimpur, although there was a primary school in the village as
early as 1921. (See table 3.) Approximately 250 children (includ-

Table 2

Hierarchy of Castes in Karimpur

	Brahman		
Bard	Goldsmith	Accountant	
Farmer	Shepherd	Vegetable Grower	Carpenter
Grain Parcher	Water Carrier	Gardener	
	Shopkeeper		
	Oil Presser		
	Tailor		
	Potter		
Washerman		Leatherworker	
	(Muslim castes)*		
	Mat-maker		
	Sweeper		

*Many informants refused to rank these castes with the others as they were of a different *dharmik* (religion). And to many villagers, all Muslims are the same, or, more truly, equally bad--but better than Sweepers and Mat-makers.

Table 3

Caste Population and Literacy* by Sex

Caste	Population		Literacy Percent (number)			
	Male	Female	Male		Female	
Brahman	159	147	78.6	(125)	29.9	(44)
Bard	7	5	71.4	(5)	60.0	(3)
Goldsmith	5	3	100.0	(5)	33.3	(1)
Scribe	10	12	100.0	(10)	25.0	(3)
Carpenter	28	28	42.9	(12)	7.1	(2)
Shepherd	47	41	23.4	(11)	2.4	(1)
Vegetable Grower	12	6	50.0	(6)	. . . . . .	
Farmer	145	104	36.6	(52)	1.9	(2)
Shopkeeper	12	7	66.6	(6)	14.2	(1)
Water Carrier	92	82	4.9	(4)	. . . . . .	
Potter	5	1	20.0	(1)	. . . . . .	
Grain Parcher	11	8	27.3	(3)	. . . . . .	
Tailor	8	7	62.5	(5)	. . . . . .	
Gardener	10	7	10.0	(1)	. . . . . .	
Washerman	8	5	. . . . . .		. . . . . .	
Oil Presser	17	19	47.6	(8)	. . . . . .	
Mat-maker	58	46	13.8	(8)	2.1	(1)
Leatherworker	30	25	20.0	(6)	. . . . . .	
Sweeper	49	38	2.0	(1)	. . . . . .	
Beggar	24	21	4.2	(1)	. . . . . .	
Bangle Seller	6	5	83.3	(5)	. . . . . .	
Cotton Carder	9	10	33.3	(3)	10.0	(1)
Total	752	628	36.9	(278)	9.4	(59)

*Literacy is defined here as having two or more years of schooling.

ing some from the administrative village) attend the three schools
in Karimpur. A small number of boys attend high school in Mainpuri
and one goes to high school in Bichhwan: the long walk each day if
one's family cannot afford a bicycle and the need for that extra labor every day mean that only rarely does a non-Brahman boy manage to
go to high school. As of 1969, no village daughter had gone on to
high school, although some wives had tenth-grade passes. One Brahman
boy had a B.A. pass and another was presently working for his B.A.
Education degrees are involved in status now, at least among the
wealthier groups, and more and more teen-age boys are proclaiming
interest in post-high school degrees. Yet despite an increasing interest in education, table 3 suggests that there are definite biases
for or against education in various caste groups and a marked bias,
also visible in school enrollments, against female education. The
girls' primary school had more than forty first-graders, whereas the
coeducational junior school had three girls in the sixth grade and
none in the seventh and eighth grades. Even the Brahman girls from
wealthier families generally drop out of school after finishing the
fifth grade. In general, the lack of education in Karimpur represents both a style of life and world view which is unsophisticated
and *dehāti*, of the country, i.e., "hickish."

The Women's World

Many of the songs, stories, and rituals discussed in the following
analysis are either rituals performed by women or songs and stories
told by women. A brief outline of the world of the Karimpur woman
should clarify the settings for these events.

In Karimpur, there are two broad patterns of life styles for
women that are correlated with economic status and therefore to a
large extent with caste status. The Brahman women represent the
"rich" pattern most prominently, along with Scribes, Bards, and some
Farmers. The other women follow what can be termed a "poor" pattern.
Within each of these two patterns, there is some variation, but the
general characteristics of each remain constant. Two factors seem
most salient: the degree to which purdah (*pardā*) is maintained, and
the amount of attention paid to formality and etiquette.

In Karimpur, as in many North Indian villages, purdah, the
seclusion of women, defines a woman's place and role in her community
and strictly limits her mobility. According to the ideal of purdah
(literally, "curtain"), the world of women should be separated from
the world of men: the seclusion of women should be maintained to
show one's respect and concern for women as well as to enhance one's

Fig. 5. Women: (a) A woman in
purdah (b) Two wives husking rice

status within the community. Women, who in Indian society are considered aggressive and potentially dangerous, should be symbolically
sheltered from themselves and others. The result is that the women
often remain within the confines of their homes and the men deal with
the outer world.

Two marriage rules affect a woman's purdah situation in Karimpur. As in many North Indian villages, there is a rule of village
exogamy--daughters are always married to men from other villages,
wives always come from other villages. Purdah, both bodily seclusion
within a house and the use of a head covering in the presence of men,
is followed only by the wives of the village. A wife must keep her
head covered whenever in the presence of older and/or higher-ranked
relatives of her husband--particularly his male relatives. In addition to village exogamy, a woman must marry a man whose family has
higher rank than her own. Therefore, all her husband's relatives,
male or female, are in some sense her superiors and, when in their
presence, she should remain secluded. Daughters of the village need
not follow purdah, although even they are not given full freedom of
movement in the village, especially the higher-caste girls. Furthermore, as a family seek higher status, they will impose more rules on
their women. Purdah is maintained by bodily seclusion or head covering, yet there is much variation in the adherence to these rules, as
will be shown below.

One factor contributing to variation in standards of purdah
is house types. The woman's world is definitely the world of the
house, and physical facilities are important components of her conduct. Two basic house types exist in Karimpur, the wealthy family
compound and the poor family hut.

The compounds of the wealthy are toally enclosed by walls
and wives rarely venture outside them (except for their daily trips
to the field "latrines"). One door leads into an outer room of each
compound; if there are any windows in the house, they are in this
outer room. It is in this room, facing the road or lane, that the
men usually sleep, entertain their friends, etc., during the cold
weather, using the verandah outside it during the hot seasons. Passing through the outer room, one comes to the courtyard, the world of
the women. The courtyard is the center of the women's daily activities and where they and the children sleep during the hot season.
Men must announce their presence before entering it, and few men other
than immediate family members are allowed in, at least for long.[19]
A corner of the courtyard contains the household "kitchen," a small
square enclosed by mud walls containing a mud stove. The kitchen is

off limits to all but the day's cook, as it must be kept ritually clean for the preparation of food.[20] Nowadays a hand pump is often found in another corner of the courtyard, and a few families even have an enclosed bathing area near it.[21] Another room, at the back of the courtyard, is used for the storage of valuables (grain, seed, clothing, jewelry, etc.). The women and children sleep there during the cold season. Larger well-off families will have immense court-yards with numerous rooms leading off them.

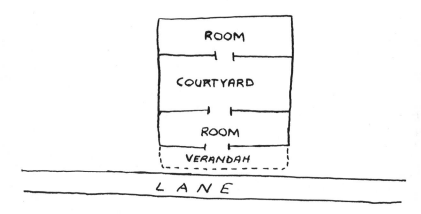

Fig. 6. A sketch diagram of a "wealthy" house

The other house type is the "poor" variant, usually a single room, perhaps with a verandah by the road or path. The "kitchen" is in one corner of the verandah and is not normally enclosed. For many of these families, the road or path serves as a courtyard. Sometimes a cluster of these single-room houses are grouped around a dead-end path, forming a natural semisecluded courtyard. Obviously women liv-ing in these types of homes cannot follow the rules of strict seclu-sion with the ease that the rich can with their enclosed courtyards. The richer women pursue their work and live their lives within their courtyards and are seldom seen outside the walls of their homes. The poor women, with one room, must engage in their daily activities be-fore the eyes of the world.

Rules of etiquette are most clearly perceived in visitation patterns, which are different for the rich and the poor. The Brah-mans and rich, who turn most visiting into an event, have a very stylized formal visiting pattern which is completely lacking among the poor except for weddings, births, and deaths. When at home, grown daughters pay many social calls; at other times, the oldest

wife does all the visiting for that family.[22] Moreover, no proper
Brahman lady would think of visiting another house without first
dressing up--a good, clean sari, jewelry, freshly plaited hair, and
cosmetics are all necessary. While the poor just "drop in" if something interesting is happening in another house, the Brahman women
either remain at home or put on finery before venturing out.

Women's dress varies from rich to poor as well. Although
everyone believes in the necessity of jewelry, the rich wear gold
and the poor wear silver. Moreover, the poor usually wear whatever
jewelry they own at all times, whereas the rich don it only for special occasions. Everyone except widows wears glass bangles. Most
women in Karimpur now wear saris, although a few still have the full
skirts and long blouses of previous times. (Girls begin wearing
saris, instead of frocks, for special events when in their early
teens.) Saris are worn so that there is a piece covering the head
that can be easily pulled over the face when necessary (see figure
5a). Various cosmetics are used--lipstick and nail polish in addition to the red line in the hair part designating marriage and the
bindī. Festivals provide an excuse for decorating one's hands and
feet with *methī* (henna) or red dyes. One last item of the Brahman
woman's toilette is essential--her *chaddar*, a shawl which must be worn
every time a wife steps out of her house. The shawl is wrapped over
the sari and pulled down over the face. Those worn in the winter are
heavy, those worn in the summer are a fine cotton that, when pulled
across the face, is still enveloping but not stifling. The availa-
bility of these items of toilette marks many differences between rich
and poor.

When the Brahman women visit another house (usually unan-
nounced), the visitors are seated according to status. Daughters of
the village take precedence over wives and the older over the younger.
A young wife will never sit on a cot unless told to by her elders,
and usually a group of young women are seated on the ground around an
older woman resting on a cot. Besides seating, status is marked by
foot-touching--each woman has her feet touched and sometimes her legs
pressed by every woman married into the village whose status is lower
than her own, with the youngest wife in the house being the lowest of
all. (Daughters rank higher than all wives of the village and never
touch each other's feet.) If a new visitor should arrive, the whole
cycle of foot-touching is repeated. Visits involve gossip and/or
singing. Food is not offered or expected aside from water or perhaps
parched grain. At the conclusion of a visit, the foot-touching is
repeated.

Special occasions, such as the events surrounding marriage
or childbirth, repeat the above pattern with additional flourishes--
more care is given to choosing clothing, singing will definitely be
part of the event, people are invited or expected, and large numbers
of women and girls will be present. These formal visitations occur
among the poorer families only on special occasions. Otherwise, the
wives, especially the older ones, are relatively free to roam the village and do not have to wear the enveloping shawls of the Brahman
women. The Brahman woman sees only those who come to her house,
whereas the poorer women are constantly visiting others and are a
major source of news and gossip.

The women's day begins at about five or six in the morning.
The first business of the day is a trip to the fields which function
as the village latrine. The married woman wraps herself in a shawl,
takes her brass pot of water, and goes off with another woman (married women, especially the younger ones and those from rich families,
are not allowed to go alone). When she returns home, the household
kitchen area must be cleansed with a new coating of cow dung and mud,
the courtyard swept, the string cots turned on their sides along the
walls to allow room for movement, the bedding stacked inside, the
cows and buffaloes milked, the milk churned and boiled, etc. Meanwhile the men have awaked, made their trips to the fields, and either
are off gossiping or have gone to the fields for work. The children
eventually awake and are put to work collecting the night's cow dung.
Later they see that the family's animals are sent off with the village herd for grazing. In addition, when school is in session (July
to April), a hurried meal must be given the school-aged children
(often bread left over from the day before, with either milk or pick-
les).

By mid-morning, the women have bathed and begun the day's
cooking. One of them will have formed the cow dung into cakes to
dry in the sun. Those women who work as servants (Sweepers and Water
Carriers) will have finished their morning rounds. The rest of the
morning is spent in various work activities--grinding grain or lentils, husking corn, rice, or wheat, etc. The poorer women may also
be helping in the fields at harvest time or be out cutting grass
along the roadsides for their animals.

The period from noon till mid-afternoon is a quiet one, especially during the hot season when many people nap. If the household and field chores are completed, it is a time for quiet gossip,
handicrafts (baskets and wicker mats are made for use within the
family or as dowry gifts, sweaters are knitted, etc.), and grooming

(including the continual hunt for lice). Visits between women of
different households usually occur during the later part of the afternoon, and dusk marks the time when they must be back home to cook the
evening meal, tether the cattle as they return from grazing, milk
them, etc. After the men and children have eaten, the women eat,
make another trip to the fields, and are ready for singing, gossip,
or sleep.

Given the restraints of purdah, a woman's strongest emotional
ties are with other women and their children. For many, their father's houses are much happier places than their husbands'--the tears
and wailing when a middle-aged woman leaves her father's village are
just as heart-rending as those of a new bride. This tie with the
natal home is repeated again and again in women's songs and rituals.

Agriculture

As in any agricultural community, the yearly cycle of crops orders
much human activity in Karimpur. There are three possible crop seasons, one during the hot season (April-June); one during the rainy
season (July-October); and one during the winter season (November-
March). However, there are only two crops for most farmers, since
few plant during the hot season.

The Hindu year, in the calendrical system used in Karimpur,
begins in April. Thus, the first crop of the year is the hot season
crop--cucumbers, gourds, and melons grown by the very industrious.
Meanwhile, the fields are prepared for the rainy season crops.

The rainy season (kharīf) crop is sown with the coming of
the monsoon in July and is harvested from September to November.
Nowadays the primary kharīf crop is makā, corn. Corn chapātīs (un-
leavened bread) are the major food item from late September until
March. Some rice is grown if the monsoon is good, but it is a rarity
in the diet of the villagers and is usually saved for special occasions. Other kharīf crops include several kinds of millet, bājrā,
jovar (planted with lentils, mungh, urad, arhar), sorghum, peanuts,
cotton (planted with sesamum), and sweet potatoes, tomatoes, and
chilis. The kharīf crop does not usually require irrigation except
for some rice fields. The corn must be irrigated only if the monsoon
is exceptionally bad. Corn and rice are harvested first, in September and October, and then the other pulses are harvested. Tomatoes
and chilis are harvested from October to November, and the sweet po-
tato harvest begins in December.

The winter crop, rabī, is sown during the fall after the monsoon has ended, beginning in October with barley and then wheat.

Wheat is the main crop of the *rabī* season, and wheat *chapātīs* are the dietary staple from March to September. Barley is usually sown in the poorer soil along with gram, peas, or mustard, whereas wheat is planted alone in better soil. Potatoes are planted in October and dug from December to February. Peas and carrots are harvested from February on, and wheat and barley are harvested in March and April.

The *rabī* crop usually requires irrigation, although it often rains in December and early January. In recent years, irrigation has become increasingly important as Mexican wheat has become more popular. Mexican wheat needs more water and more fertilizer than the old wheat. Even though it is common knowledge that Mexican wheat gives better yields, many farmers still do not plant it--and those who do usually plant some fields with the old seed for their own consumption. Another factor hindering the use of Mexican wheat is the initial capital outlays for seed, fertilizer, and water.

One other crop is important--sugarcane. Sugarcane is planted in late February and March and not harvested until December or later. Although it is a valuable cash crop, it does require ten months' growth before harvesting and is therefore planted only by farmers with excess acreage, i.e., those who have more than enough land for their families' immediate needs. Some cane is sold in Mainpuri, but most is pressed in the village. Then the juice is boiled down to make a hard brown sugar known as *guR*. Some *guR* is kept for home consumption and the rest is sold in Mainpuri. Another delicacy of the sugarcane harvest is rice cooked in the fresh juice. And the men often use the juice for their home brews.

After the *rabī* crop is harvested in April, there is little farm labor until June. The children are also on vacation from school and the many activities of the marriage season fill everyone's time. The two main harvests of the year, the *kharīf* and *rabī*, are each associated with a series of festivals which mark periods of gaiety.

Religious Activity

Religious and ritual activities in Karimpur are frequent. Ritual activity will be discussed in detail later (Chapter VIII), but a few words placing it in context are appropriate here. There are thirty-three yearly rituals or festivals in Karimpur: six during the hot season (three months); twenty during the rainy season (four and a half months); and seven during the winter season (four and a half months). The hot season is the most auspicious time for marriages (and none can occur from late June until late October--a period of four months), and the cold months of December and January are also

Fig. 7. Agricultural work:
(a) Plowing (b) Winnowing wheat

good times for marriage festivities. In addition to annual rituals,
there are some weekly rituals and life-cycle rituals.

Aside from birth, marriage, and death rituals, two other life-
cycle events are recognized in Karimpur. One is the ceremony in which
Brahman males receive their sacred threads, marking their twice-born
status. (Traditionally, only Brahmans and Bards were considered
"twice-born" and had this ceremony, although one lineage of Carpenters have recently claimed status as a Brahman *jāti* and now wear the
sacred thread.) Nowadays a boy is given his sacred thread in conjunction with his marriage, even though he may be twenty or older.
The other common life-cycle rite is the first haircut, which is usually done at a major temple on a festival day which is particularly
auspicious for the family involved. In addition to the cyclical ritual activity, there are religious occasions during crises, such as
illness, possession, or lack of rain.

Various kinds of ritual forms are found in Karimpur. Life-
cycle rituals, particularly marriage, require *havan*, sacrifice to the
sacred fire. *havan* is performed at other times (for example, at the
opening of the Shiva temple in Karimpur) but only rarely. Technically,
havan requires the aid of a Brahman priest, which limits its usage.[23]

Another common ritual form is *vrat*, actually a series of
events involving fasting, *pūjā* (worship), a ritual story (*kathā*),
and song (*ārtī*). *vrat* occur as yearly events (nine of the thirty-
three) or as weekly events and will be discussed at length later.
No ritual specialist is needed for any of the activities of *vrat*, although a priest may tell the *kathā* and do the *pūjā*.

The most prevalent ritual form is *pūjā*, worship of deities.
Briefly, the deity is treated as an honored guest in one's home--he/
she may be bathed, dressed, and/or offered perfume, incense, flowers,
food, etc. The food offered the deity is then distributed among the
community (family, friends, neighbors, or the whole village). This
food, the leftovers of the gods, is known as *prasād* and symbolizes
one's recognition of the higher status of the god involved (because,
as is well known, Hindus can take leftover food only from higher-
ranked beings). *pūjā* is in fact a daily rite in many homes: the
first food cooked each day is offered to the household fire (a small
piece of a *chapātī* is thrown into it and water is sprinkled on it),
and the rest of the *chapātī* is fed to a cow. Thus all food consumed
by Hindus in Karimpur is, in essence, the *prasād* of the gods.

All *vrat* involve *pūjā*, worship of deities, but not all *pūjā*
are associated with *vrat*. Seventeen of the thirty-three yearly rites
usually require *pūjā* alone and nine of the rites normally require

vrat. In addition, *pūjā* is performed in conjunction with some life-cycle rites (childbirth, the haircutting, and marriage) but not as part of the Vedic element of these rites. *pūjā* also occurs at times of crisis, for example, a court case, snakebite, or lack of rain. *pūjā* is generally performed by the women of a house (although some Brahman men do daily or weekly *pūjā* to the sun) and does not require the aid of religious specialists.

Two other ritual forms are found in Karimpur. One is possession, of either an oracle or a "victim," by some powerful being. Possession always requires a ritual specialist of some sort, either an oracle or an exorcist. Another form of honoring the gods is singing. Most singing in Karimpur is done to honor the gods, especially since singing the praises of the gods is one way to show devotion to them.

Various kinds of religious specialists are found in Karimpur. The most notable is the family priest (called *paNDit*[24] or *purohit*), a hereditary "servant" of each family. Because of the large number of Brahmans resident in Karimpur, not all Brahmans act as priests, and no Pandeys were priests. Instead, the men of three resident families act as priests for the village (and two brothers in one family share their portion of the labor). One requirement is that the priest must be of a higher Brahman lineage than one's own. The highest-ranked Brahmans in Karimpur are the Chaube (now Dube) lineage, and the two brothers of this group act as priests for most of the Pandey families. The Chaubes have a priest in Mainpuri who comes when they have need. Two other priests (not Pandey or Chaube) act for the rest of those villagers eligible for priestly services (the Sweepers are nominal Christians and ineligible for Brahman services in any case, and the Muslims, of course, do not partake of this service). The priests function primarily in life-cycle rites.

A variant of the priest is the educated Pandit, a man who has knowledge of the sacred texts and travels the countryside giving lectures about and readings of them. One such Pandit resides in Karimpur, and others periodically are invited to visit. Another Brahman specialist is the astrologer. I cannot say how many families in Karimpur regularly used his services, but all the Brahman families did. He lives in Mainpuri and would come to Karimpur every three or four weeks and give advice on one's horoscope, good times for journeys, etc. Yet another Brahman specialist associated with Karimpur is the low-ranked Brahman from a nearby village who has the duty of lighting the Holi fires once a year.

Another set of specialists are the oracles, *bhagat*, men who

are devotees of a particular deity. They can become possessed by
their deities and thus answer questions from other men. Oracles can
be of any caste, including Sweeper, and are approached by other men
when a question needs to be answered. Women can be oracles, but
none were in Karimpur. In addition, the oracles take part in two
yearly rites, *khappar*, "The Pot," and *nāg panchmī*, "Snake's Fifth."

Complementing the oracles are the exorcists, men who can
force malicious spirits to leave their victims alone. There was one
exorcist in Karimpur, although a group of men involved in snake possession could also be considered exorcists. In addition, the *hakīm*,
medical specialists, can be considered semireligious specialists.
The oracles, exorcists, and medical specialists are all self-chosen.
Their positions are not hereditary and they must all be trained by a
guru or other specialist. There is one other hereditary specialist
in Karimpur, the Muslim man whose job it is to perform the rituals
honoring Khan Bahadur, the Muslim guardian of the village. When the
women (of any caste) desire to worship Khan Bahadur, they call this
Muslim, who leads them up the hill and guides them in making their
offerings, says a short prayer, collects the offerings, and leaves.

Aside from these acknowledged religious specialists, there
are people who know more stories, tales, and songs than their neighbors. And everyone knows some songs and tales. Most of this "religious" lore is passed on orally; these verbal traditions provide the
data for much of the following analysis. These traditions, their
uses, and their settings require some explanation. In the following
sections, I examine them in some detail.

Verbal Traditions

Although I have no intention now of describing the verbal traditions
of Karimpur in full, a short discussion of those found in 1967-69
seems useful.[25] In reviewing the kinds of traditions of Karimpur,
we must recognize two facets of tradition--the dynamics of its trans-
mission (the "social organization of tradition," Redfield 1955), and
its cultural substance or cultural content. These two aspects of
tradition are closely intertwined in Karimpur verbal traditions.

The groups of which an individual is a member strongly influence his/her knowledge of various traditions. Both caste and sex
are critical in determining group membership, as is the neighborhood
where one resides. Most ceremonies in which verbal traditions are
used are centered around one lineage or caste group, e.g., the gath-
ering of women to roll *purīs* for a wedding feast. Sex is, perhaps,
the most pervasive factor in determining group membership, because

there are few sexually integrated religious or social activities.
Neighbors are often involved in the songfests of noncaste members
merely because of friendship--thus Brahman women from several nearby
families may attend the ceremonies connected to a Carpenter boy's
wedding, but other Brahman women living farther away would not be expected to attend.

Songs

Of the kinds of tradition which exist in Karimpur, songs are the most
common; everyone, down to three-year-olds, knows one or two and more
likely a great number. Like most village activities, singing occurs
in sexually segregated groups and there are distinct styles and categories of songs for men and women (see table 4). Literacy and stron-
ger connections to the written traditions (especially among the men)
also produce variation in the cultural content (both textually and
musically) of songs. In addition, caste membership correlates with
variation in content and music--for example, women in the village
were able to identify the castes of groups recorded on my tape re-
corder by the drum rhythms used. And Brahmans had little expertise
in *phāg*, the songs of Holi, as it was not respectable for them to
know these risque songs. An additional factor is the acknowledged
good singer: everyone knew some songs, but not everyone was considered to be good at singing them. Those who did achieve acclaim for
their ability (both men and women) developed larger repertoires and
would be the leaders in whatever groups with which they had contact.

In investigating the cultural content of songs, I found it
useful to look first at the Karimpur classification of songs. Songs
are categorized by content and by melody. Often the two coincide,
that is, the content specifies a particular melody. For example, a
group of songs are connected with Savan, the monsoon month of July-
August, when daughters return home and swings are hung in the trees.
These songs, called *malhār*,[26] are sung only at this time, their internal structure differs from that of other songs, one particular
melody is used for the whole group (and no others), and their content
allows them to be easily recognized as one of those types of song
sung during this month.

I have been able to identify thirty-one categories of songs
(each recognized by a distinctive label in Karimpur; see table 4),
some of which allow more than one melody. Also, some melodies can
crosscut categories of song, for example, between *kīrtan* and *bhajan*,
or, more interestingly, a typical *bhajan* melody used with the words
of a *philmī*.[27] It should be noted that the repertoire of melodies

Table 4

Categories of Song in Karimpur

Type/Name	Sung by Men	Women	Description/Usage
Life Cycle			
lorī (*janne*)		+	At birth of child relates events surrounding a birth and happiness of a mother; some have purely religious themes.
varnā		+	At boy's wedding; religious themes.
varnī		+	At girl's wedding; some religious themes.
bhāT		+	When MoBr. gives clothes at wedding; semireligious themes.
gālī		+	Abuse sung by women at a wedding.
jyonār		+	When *bārāt* eats at wedding, semiabuse.
Annual Cycle			
malhār	rarely	+	In Savan when swinging; secular themes concerning women.
sāvan	rarely	+	In Savan when swinging; secular themes concerning women.
phāg	+	+	At Holi; religious themes.
rasiyā	+	+	Always about Krishna; usually sung in *phāgun*.
chhand	+	+	When go to do Devi's *pūjā*.
jas	+		To cause Devi possession.
Dank	+		To cause snake possession.
ālhā	+		During rains; in honor of a mythological character.

Table 4--*Continued*

Type/Name	Sung by		Description/Usage
	Men	Women	
General Religious			
bhajan	+	+	Praise of the gods; an act of worship.
kīrtan	+	+	Praise of the gods; an act of worship.
ārtī	+	+	Sung at conclusion of *pūjā*.
pad	+		Similar to a *bhajan*; in praise of god.
General			
gānā	+	+	"Song," a category for anything not otherwise classified.
Dholā	+		Folk opera songs (Nal and Motini).
bārah māsī	+		Description of the 12 months of the year.
rangīt	+		In time of or in celebration of war.
Thumrī	+		Semiclassical short song; requires musical skill.
gazal	+	rarely	Based on an Urdu poem.
kavālī	+		Sung poems.
dādrā	+		A popular tune (beat).
shair	+		Partially Sanskrit.
vahrat	+		
jhap	+		Song to a particular beat.
khayal	+		As part of a recited story, a short piece is sung.
philmī	+	rarely	Film songs.

is very limited; many songs are sung to one melody, rather than the
1:1 relation of the West.

Two of the most important categories are *bhajan* and *kīrtan*.
bhajan, also meaning a prayer or act of worship, identifies songs in
honor of or praising the deities. To sing a *bhajan* is in itself a
form of worship. *kīrtan* means, more accurately, to recite, to com-
memorate, or to praise, and songs in this category are similar to
bhajan. One of my more sophisticated informants claims that the dis-
tinguishing factor is how they are sung. In *bhajan*, one man sings
the song alone; in *kīrtan*, one man sings a line which is then repeated by the group. Although this distinction appears to hold true for
men, I did not find this method of classification pertinent for the
women. They never sing in either style; rather, singing is a group
activity and anyone who knows the song and cares to join in may do
so. Certain other categories of songs are *varnā*, those for a bridegroom; *varnī*, for a bride; *lorī*, for the birth of a child; *phāg*, in
honor of the Holi festival; *jas*, sung at Devi *pūjā*, and so on, not
exluding the recent favorite, the *philmī*. And there is a catchall
category, the *gānā* ("song"), used when nothing else seems appropriate.
(Songs with "modern" content were always classified as mere "song,"
for example, two beginning "Uncle Nehru has died . . ." and "In Delhi
all the boys wear pants.")

Children begin learning to beat out drum rhythms at an early
age (many five- and six-year-olds can play simple rhythms and sing a
few songs) and the more proficient are quickly recognized. The importance of being able to sing well is illustrated by the fact that
one of the first tests of a new bride is her ability to sing and play
the drums--and expert singers are sought after. Various drum rhythms
are known, and there is some variation in those used by different
castes. Among the women, there is little innovation in tune and little stylistic elaboration in the singing itself. They characteris-
tically repeat a line several times before going on to the next one.
Many of the men, especially the upper-caste men, regard music differ-
ently and take pride in their innovations. In addition, the men
often use a harmonium with the drum, which allows them to play more
complex musical accompaniments. Most singing by upper-caste men is
reminiscent of "classical" Indian singing, whereas the singing of
women and lower-caste males is nonclassical in its simplicity. The
upper-caste men know different *rāga* and drumbeats (*tāl*) by name and
will consciously use them, but the women will classify melodies merely by the song types with which they are associated.

The kinds of occasions for which sungs are sung vary greatly.

Often the women in one household or compound will join together to sing, especially during Savan when married daughters are likely to be home. *bhajan* and *kīrtan* are commonly sung on any occasion along with the special songs which are connected with it. Or men and women will sing (separately) on the days of important religious festivities, e.g., Krishna's Birthday. The arrival of a daughter or daughter-in-law may be used by the women as an excuse for a songfest. The men will use the excuses of guests, little field work, etc., to have some merriment. Life-cycle rites provide another occasion when singing is usual for the women, particularly at the time of the birth of a child or of a marriage. Childbirth and marriage provide the oppor-tunity for communal songfests, when many women from different house-holds gather together to participate in the singing and other activi-ties.

Since childbirth provides one important occasion for singing, let me briefly describe the events. When a child is born, especially a male child, the friends of the mother are informed. Normally these friends are of the same caste as the mother or of one ranked close to it. Some neighbors from other castes may be informed (i.e., in-vited to the ensuing rites) but not always. These friends or compan-ions of the new mother are generally daughters of the village (wheth-er the mother is in her father's or her husband's village) and a few wives from nearby houses. Although the primary purpose of these gatherings is to honor the new mother and child with songs of joy and blessing, the songfest also provides an opportunity to gossip and show off one's newest sari and other ornaments. Everyone dresses up in an attempt to outdo her neighbors, and young girls wearing saris publicly for the first time are greeted with gaiety and laugh-ter.

During the daylight hours (usually early to mid-afternoon) of the first day after the birth, groups of young girls and women can be seen filing down the village lanes and into the house blessed by a birth. Most, being daughters of the village, will have their faces uncovered, while the few wives present will have discreetly pulled their shawls or saris over their faces. Depending upon the wealth and importance of the new mother's family, five to twenty or more women and girls may have come. It is essential, in village eti-quette, for the families informed of the birth to send at least one representative to the songfest. If a family do not participate in these events when they occur in other families, they may find them-selves without guests when their own family events require singing.

As the women gather in the new mother's courtyard, they ex-

change gossip and perform the rituals of respect (foot-touching).
The mother and new infant are secluded in a back room of the house
and are not allowed visitors. If the child is male, one of the women
of the family will have already decorated the outside walls of the
room of mother and child with auspicious symbols (*satiyā*) made of
cow dung and barley seeds (see figure 8a). After most of the invitees
are present, the singing of *lorī* begins, and the nasal, monophonic
phrases, characteristic of women's singing in this region, can be
heard throughout nearby parts of the village. One girl is singled
out to play the drum (*dholak*) (see figure 8b) and lead the singing;
she must be noted for her expertise with the drum as well as for her
singing voice and repertoire of songs. While singing *lorī*, the women
also decorate a clay pot known as the *charuā* with cow dung and barley
seeds; this pot is then used to boil water which is fed to the new
mother. There are many songs included in the classification *lorī*,
and they have varying melodies. One of the most common *lorī* is a
long rambling description of the woman's agony and trouble at birth.
This particular *lorī* has many variations and can last as long as anyone remembers another line or segment. As one segment is completed,
any woman who recalls another takes up the lead, until her knowledge
or memory fails, then another woman takes the lead--the song ends
only when everyone's memory is exhausted. Other *lorī* describe the
despair of a new mother in her husband's house (a very common theme)
or, on a more joyous note, the delight and happiness of the gods'
mothers when their sons (usually Krishna or Rama) were born. The
following *lorī*, which also describes the events surrounding childbirth, is typical of this kind.

> Jasoda gave birth to a son, bliss spread in Gokul.
> Came--came outside the call of the *dāī*.[a]
> The *dāī* cut the cord, bliss spread in the palace.
> Now the queen gave birth to a son, bliss spread in Gokul.
> Came--came outside the call of the *sāsulī*.[b]
> The *sāsulī* decorated the *charuā*,[c] bliss spread in the palace.
> Jasoda gave birth to a son, bliss spread in the palace.
> Came--came outside the call of the *nanadī*.[d]
> The *nanadī* fixed the auspicious signs [*satiyā*], bliss spread
>   in the palace.
> Came--came outside the call of the *jiṬhanī*.[e]

---

[a]Midwife, of the *dhānuk* caste.

[b]Mother-in-law.

[c]A clay pot--it is decorated with cow dung and barley.

[d]Husband's sister.

[e]Husband's older brother's wife.

Fig. 8. Childbirth rituals:
(a) Auspicious design on doorframe
(b) A woman singing

The *jiThani* did the grinding,[f] bliss spread in the palace.
The *devar*[g] shot the arrow,[h] bliss spread in the palace.
Came--came outside the call of the Pandit.
The Pandit counted the numbers,[i] bliss spread in the palace.
The companions sang blessings,[j] bliss spread in the palace.
Jasoda gave birth to a son, bliss spread in the palace.

Song #1[28]

Most *lori* celebrate the mother's joy and delight in the birth of her
child. If and when the group of women exhaust their combined knowledge of *lori*, they will go on to sing other religious songs, such as
kirtan and *bhajan*. As they eventually begin to disperse, the woman
in charge of the household distributes *batasa* (puffed sugar candies)
to all the "companions" who have performed their part in the ceremonies in honor of the new child. The women and girls then return home
to relate the doings to their more secluded female relatives.

All types of song are primarily oral traditions. The low
literacy rate (table 3) precludes any extensive use of written traditions, and many types of songs are sung exclusively by women, de-
creasing the ability to use a written work even more. Now and then
a few of the younger women (those in their teens and early twenties)
would use a bazaar-printed pamphlet (costing fifteen or twenty cents)
of *malhar* or other songs. However, it must be remembered that only
two women in Karimpur had more than an eighth-grade education; those
two daughters-in-law plus some present-day schoolgirls were the only
ones who resorted to books for inspiration.

The men, especially the better-educated Brahman men, were
more likely to use bazaar pamphlets for new songs and ideas. The
lower-caste men, most not more than semiliterate--if that--relied on
their memories, on friends, and on relatives for their repertoires.
One teen-age boy, a blind Farmer, had one of the best, purely memorized, repertoires of songs.

As can be seen, social factors influence the use of the vernacular, regional-great-tradition written works.[29] The fact of literacy and the related factors of caste and sex automatically indicate
the people and groups who are most likely to be influenced by the

---

[f]A combination of *ghi* (clarified butter), *atta* (wheat flour),
mithai (sweet), *jire* (cuminseed), *sonThi* (ginger), and *piparamul* (the
root of a pepper) must be ground together to be given to the mother
and family.

[g]husband's younger brother.

[h]On the 3d day after birth, the husband's younger brother must
shoot an arrow over the roof in all four directions.

[i]In order to name in the child.

[j]As they are doing in the ceremony described here.

various kinds of written traditions found in Karimpur. The sexual
division of most occurrences of verbal tradition, and caste and home-
site divisions within the village, prevent the flow of influence from
various written sources from one group to another. These factors are
also important in the social organization of another major grouping
of Karimpur verbal traditions, the prose tale.

Prose

Prose forms of tradition are less numerous and less common than song
forms. Moreover, there is less rigid division of sex in participation, at least for the first two types mentioned below. Here, however, expertise is rare, and any substantial knowledge of prose tales
is also rare. Individuals known for their storytelling are acclaimed
and sought after. The telling of a prose tale is always done by one
person, but the audience--unlike that for songs--may not be sexually
segregated. However, the religious tales told at rites of worship
occur with an audience of only one sex and usually with no members
of castes other than one's own present.[30]

The people of Karimpur also classify stories, or prose tales,
by content. There are three kinds of prose tales, the *kahānī*, *kissā*,
and *kathā*. *kahānī* approximates our usage of "story." They are generally rather brief and often funny, and deal with real-life (this
world) characters. *kissā* are usually long and mythological but not
rigorously connected to religious activity. Most often they are village versions of excerpts from the *Mahābhārata* or other all-India
great-tradition works or are based on mythological themes not readily
connected to the known great tradition. Both *kahānī* and *kissā* are
exclusively oral traditions in Karimpur. Although it is possible to
find some pamphlets in the bazaar in Mainpuri containing *kissā*, I
never saw or heard of these in the village itself, both because the
villagers lack reading ability and because the village storytellers
are more entertaining.

There is, however, one extensively used written tradition,
the *kathā*. In Karimpur, as elsewhere in India, one finds a series
of tales related to some of the various religious ceremonies that one
sees. These tales, distinguished from *kahānī* and *kissā*, are connected with religious observances per se and their telling is an essential part of the religious ceremony itself. If the corresponding
kathā is not told or read, the cermony is considered incomplete and
its value is lost.[31] In some cases, the *kathā* is read from a pamphlet or book bought in the bazaar; in others a knowledgeable person
will recite it. The better-known and more widespread rituals are

usually accompanied by a written *katha*, e.g., *satya Narayan vrat katha*, whereas the lesser-known, more local rituals are connected with oral *katha*, e.g., *hathi ki puja* (Worship of the Elephant).

The bazaar pamphlets containing *katha* come in several varieties. One can purchase pamphlets with the *katha* for the whole week (the religious ceremonies of each day are distinct, and the supernatural being to be worshiped, the rules to be followed, and the *katha* are all different) or individual pamphlets for each day. Each day's rules will be given initially, followed by the appropriate *katha*, and then the *arti* or song to be sung as the worship is concluded. The rules delineate foods to be eaten or avoided, the colors of offerings, the rewards for worship, etc. One persistent rule is "you have to read the *katha*." The weekly sets, called "The *katha* of the *vrat* for Seven Days" (*saptvar vrat katha*), contain less elaborate *katha* than those containing only one day, although the corresponding versions do resemble one another. The *katha* for annual rites are found less often in pamphlet form and more often in villagers' memories.

People in Karimpur used these rules and texts for their favorite weekly worship or the worship on the day appropriate for their *ishta devata* (chosen deity). Most of them were guided by their particular concerns (sons, family welfare, husbands) in choosing whom to worship. Some were fully aware of all of the implications of an *ishta devata*; others would revert to once-a-month worship. However, most disregarded anything but the major annual festivals.

katha recited by memory were rather rare. A few older Brahman women, one Water Carrier widow, the older Scribes of both sexes, a couple of middle-caste religious specialists (a Shepherd and a Farmer), and, rarely, an older man were the only people able to tell the *katha* of the various observances or to explain the different forms of these rites. As few of the men performed any rites aside from the two or three major ones, and the Brahman's daily prayer (*gayatri mantra*), I do not find the greater knowledge of the women surprising.

The men's religious observances focused on the daily rite of the twice-born (although many younger men did not perform this daily recognition of the sun) and on the reading of various longer religious works. A few of the literate men (primarily Brahman and Scribe) would periodically read the Hindi versions of the *Ramayana*, *Sukh Sagar*, or the *Bhagavad Gita*.

These longer religious works are one of the major sources of contact with verbal traditions not extensively known in Karimpur itself. Of the several sources of religious ideas and traditions which

are predominantly "outside" and nonvillage, the foremost is the sponsored *kathā*. For these events, a Pandit educated in religious texts
is brought to the village from some eminent ashram. For one to seven
days, the Pandit gives a religious discourse based on his own writ-
ings, usually developing themes found in the *Rāmāyana*, *Sukh Sāgar*, or
Bhagavad Gītā. Sponsoring such a *kathā* is considered an act of merit
and two were held in the fifteen months that I was in Karimpur. The
first was in honor of the new Shiva temple completed in February 1968:
its opening coincided with *shiv teras* (Shiva's Thirteenth), and the
kathā lasted seven days. Everyone dropped in at least once, although
the lowest castes were not admitted to the temple grounds. For many
of the women, it was a rare opportunity to get out of their household
courtyards and visit with friends and relatives. Pandemonium reigned
as women visited and children played and people constantly came and
went. Moreover, the Pandit's Hindi was far too Sanskritized for most
of the inhabitants of Karimpur to comprehend. The second sponsored
kathā was at the June *dassehra* and lasted only one day. Karimpur
does have its own educated lecturer-Pandit, but he seldom performs
officially in Karimpur itself (never in 1967-69).

Another source of contact with oral traditions were the performances of the traveling drama groups. A leader of such a troupe
resides in Karimpur and everyone is familiar with the tale acted by
his troupe. Called *Dholā*, it is a folk opera with religious-mytho-
logical themes. The story line is always that of Nal and Motini and
has some vague connections with the *Mahābhārata*. *Dholā* is, even for
the troupe, an oral tradition. Periodically (but not yearly), a *Rām
Līlā* troupe will be brought to the village, and the more enterprising
village men will attend one every fall in Mainpuri. This form of
drama is a written and nonvillage tradition.

The other two major outside sources of religious traditions
are films and fairs. For most people, the two coincide, since the
only hope the women have of seeing a film is the district fair.
Films shown at these local fairs always seem to have mythological
themes. Moreover, there are puppet shows acting out scenes of varying importance, always quasireligious (Gandhi and Mirabai are favorite characters). The younger, well-off men do frequent the cinemas,
in town, where the standard triangle-disaster themes so remarkably
perfected by the Bombay producer dominate.

The schools themselves add another source of wider contact
with ideas and values common throughout the nation. Readers contain
life histories of important historical and/or mythological figures,
have short sections on the major deities, excerpts from the *Rāmāyana*,

etc. The major influence that I could perceive was that the students
or ex-students were turned toward the bazaar pamphlets of songs.

Religious ceremonies themselves, aside from those accompanying *kathā*, are another focal point of verbal traditions. Weddings,
births, visits to one's guru or the temples in town, and the yearly
cycle of events all contribute. Within the village itself, several
major occasions involve many people and the rituals themselves con
tribute more tidbits of verbal traditions. Moreover, the oracles
and curers, all with their handed-down knowledge, function as do
Brahman priests in identifying the characters and traits of gods.
The wealth of information in one rite of possession will be explored
in a later chapter.

Summary

The verbal traditions of Karimpur belong to two major groupings. The
song forms involve a larger number of participants and, within certain limits, a wider range in caste, age, and education of participants. Prose forms have a limited number of actual participants and
a larger audience, except for the household *kathā*. All communal participation in religious rites (aside from a few major ones) is, again,
limited to one sex and one lineage. The verbal traditions which are
not "oral" and which have definite connections with sources outside
Karimpur are of three types: the bazaar pamphlets (songs and *kathā*);
"performances," e.g., the Pandit's giving a sponsored *kathā*, folk
operas such as the *Rām Līlā*, or the films and shows at fairs; and
the school, with its emphasis on all-India great-tradition Hinduism
and nationalistic values.

The belief system analyzed in the following pages is based
in large part on the content of these verbal traditions of Karimpur.
The traditions on which my analysis is based are taken from all castes
except Leatherworkers and Sweepers.[32] I shall not be using the verbal traditions of the Muslims, although the Muslim connections in
some aspects of these questions in Karimpur will be seen. For those
castes whose traditions I have, variations in education, sex, and
age are represented. It is through songs, myths, and stories that
the Karimpur resident provides a conceptual reality for his ritual
activity.

The preceding discussion is intended to provide an overview
of some relevant social facets of the Karimpur way of life and the
setting for my analysis of ritual beliefs and practices. My basic
subject of analysis is the relationships between mankind and the varieties of gods. My aim is to grasp the principles by which men order
their religious thoughts and actions.

NOTES

1. A recent addition to works on Karimpur is a filmstrip by Donald and Jean Johnson, "Looking behind Mud Walls," New York: Industrial Media Associates, 1970.

2. This settlement area did not exist in 1925-30 (see Wiser 1933). Its existence seems due to the more extensive use of the northern roadway to the village, which passes by the Sweeper enclave and remains an unpopular route, despite the temple and bus stop.

3. The other "villages" in the administrative unit are Laharipur, Singhapur, Rajpur, Nekpur, Deolpur, and Shahalampur.

4. Called *khappar*, "The Pot," this ritual involves circumambulating the village area and putting the illness thus gathered in an adjoining village's fields. The above named settlements and no others are included in the defined circle. (See Chapter VIII.)

5. When I left in the winter of '69, two privately owned tube wells were being installed.

6. These shops sold primarily small trade items: cigarettes, matches, thread, buttons, firecrackers (in season), oil (kerosene for lanterns, mustard for cooking); soaps, spices, and small amounts of foodstuffs, primarily grain and lentils. Payment was normally made in small amounts of produce. All important or large items were bought in Mainpuri.

7. Most ritual activity took place in one's home or at the old traditional trees and *sthans*. Even the village Shiv temple was not used after it was inaugurated, although I suspect that it would be activated once a year for *shiv teras* (Shiva's Thirteenth, occurring in February).

8. There seems to be no consensus about the attributes of a progressive area. I have briefly mentioned a few, both present and absent in Karimpur, which are often given as markers of progress.

9. The panchayat was in flux when I was in Karimpur. The headman, *pradhān*, was thrown in jail for embezzling government funds in August 1968, about half-way through my stay. He had abdicated responsibility long before, so that the panchayat was in disarray when I arrived and had not yet reconstituted itself as a functioning body when I left.

10. In an alternative version of the legend, the fort was built by the Muslim king and its ruin was caused by neglect.

11. *chaddar lagānā*, "to spread a sheet," a Muslim rite of honoring a saint, is used as the ritual form. A family of Muslim Beggars receives the offerings.

12. In 1899.

13. Ten *biswas* means 10 of 20 parts, or one-half.

14. The Karimpur Brahmans are Kanauji (Kanyakubja) and consider east better than west. (Their former home territory, centered at the city Kanauj, lies eastward from Karimpur.) This directional preference is today most visible in the Brahmans' marriage arrangements: wives come from the northwest (primarily Etah District) and daughters go to the southeast (primarily Farrukabad District).

15. See Nicholas (1968) for further discussion of the social ramifications of political activity.

16. A fourth panchayat election should have taken place in 1967. However, the government felt that the work then engaging the Land Consolidation Officers would be furthered by not changing the village officials.

17. See Wiser 1958 for a detailed discussion of the late '20s *jajmānī* system.

18. This version of caste ranking is noticeably different than the one Wiser gives in *The Hindu Jajmani System* (1958:xviii). To take two examples, I believe that Wiser's giving high rank to the Gardener is due primarily to his concern for the Laws of Manu: one cannot doubt that flower growing is "clean." The difference with regard to the Shopkeeper is a matter of village legend and controversy--to which the key is that they became wealthy.

19. In a humorous example of this rule, a distant relative visited the family with which I lived and settled himself in the courtyard for most of an evening. My sisters-in-law were extremely angry by the time he left, since they could not eat, put their children to bed, or sleep themselves until he left. He had clearly violated social etiquette and was called many names by the women huddling together in a back room.

20. By evening, when the food for the day has been cooked, the kitchen's sanctity is ignored (it must be cleaned again in the morning again anyway), especially during the cold weather when the whole family may gather in it to keep warm.

21. If a wealthy family do not have their own pump, they will have a Water Carrier woman come daily to fetch their water from a well outside.

22. This rule means that younger wives are seldom allowed to see their neighbors unless by chance they are the only wife in the family. Thus the younger wives see primarily the older women of other families, never their own age-mates except for visiting daughters.

23. I say technically, because the women of my house would sometimes do *havan* themselves to one of the goddesses or the *tulsī* (basil) tree.

24. *paNDit* is less frequently used and means "a wise man." *purohit* is the traditional term for one's family priest; however, it is gradually being superseded by *paNDit*.

25. I shall not discuss children's games, jokes, riddles, and proverbs--all topics on which I have almost no information.

26. *malhār* is also the name of a *rāga* of the classical music traditions.

27. My musical skill allows me to recognize only the broader implications of the use of melody in the categorization of song. I hope some day to be able to collaborate with a more qualified musicologist and explore in detail the ramifications of content versus melody.

28. Transcriptions of all songs in Hindi are found in Appendix I.

29. Certainly the Mainpuri printed and written collections of songs (and tales) cannot be classified with the "great" traditions of India. However, the standardization of what were probably little traditions into printed form takes them out of the real local (little) or village-centered tradition category. These bazaar pamphlets of various sorts probably are an example of the universalization of oral traditions. Other bazaar pamphlets are, however, probably a parochialization--for example, the weekly *kathā* (to be discussed), the *kissā* of Dropadi, or collections of songs of the poet-saints, e.g., Kabir and Mirabai. (See Marriott 1955, for the definition and usage of "parochialization" and "universalization.")

30. The one exception is the sponsored *kathā* when a Pandit from outside is brought to the village.

31. I learned this fact forcibly one Friday when I was called upon to read the Friday _kathā_ for my "sister-in-law," as I was the only literate Hindi-_wālā_ in the house. Twenty pages later, after many corrections of pronunciation, etc., my Hindi-reading ability was improved, but not my patience. Somewhat to my dismay, I was periodically called upon to repeat the performance.

32. The fact that I lived with a Brahman family made interviewing and recording with these two groups difficult. I have some data from the Sweepers, but their self-proclaimed Christian status requires that they be dealt with separately.

Chapter III: THE NATURE OF A HINDU PANTHEON

In order to comprehend religion in Karimpur, one must examine the
definitive characteristics of Hindu supernatural beings in general
and then develop a paradigm for "supernatural" action. In the following pages, I shall elaborate on the nature of Hindu supernatural
beings as a prerequisite for constructing a model of "supernatural"
action for Karimpur.

What Is a Hindu Supernatural Being?

The nature and classification of Hindu deities, demons, ghosts, etc.,
are a recurring theme in the literature on South Asia, beginning with
the classicists concerned with the multitudes of great-traditional
gods and the anthropologically oriented compendiums of the British
era (see Crooke 1896; Whitehead 1916). In a more recent discussion,
Harper has attempted "to order and classify the supernaturals affecting the inhabitants of the village of Totagadde" (1959:227). Unfor-
tunately, he does not provide information about his definition of
"supernatural" or specify the boundaries of the pantheon of Totagadde,
although he discusses the pantheon as if he had defined its boundaries. If one is going to deal with the order of a "Hindu village
pantheon" as Harper does, a necessary first step is to define what
is meant by a "Hindu supernatural being" or the characteristics of
beings who are supernatural. Unless this first step is taken--unless
the limits of the pantheon are known--any ordering becomes meaning-
less.

In an article on the goddesses of Chattisgarh, L. A. Babb
comes closer to dealing with this vital definition, although he too
manages to skirt the real issue. At one point, he says "a notion of
potential 'force' or 'power' [is] intrinsic to the very concept of
the sacred" (1970a:138). Certainly a notion of force or power is intrinsic to the concept "supernatural," although this aspect of Indian
divinity is often ignored by anthropologists. This bias in the literature has resulted in narrow, circumscribed discussions of Hindu
"pantheons," discussions which do injustice to the notion of power
or force and are not related to the reality of the pantheons of deities and demons in the villages of India.

In the following pages, I shall explore the Hindu concept of "supernatural" in an attempt to define the nature of a Hindu pantheon.[1] As will be shown, the notion of power is the defining characteristic of Hindu deities, who are in fact "powerful" beings. Explicitly recognizing that "supernatural beings are powerful beings" requires a drastic revision in our idea of a Hindu pantheon--a revision in definition that is long overdue.

Supernatural Is Powerful

The first difficulty in enumerating the members of a Hindu pantheon for village Hinduism is that there is much inconsistency between the lists of objects that any two Hindus consider to constitute the realm of religion. Potentially, all beings can be members of a Hindu pantheon; any being with powers over other beings could be, for the individual concerned, a member of his pantheon.

Second, there is no bounded supernatural spatial domain; concepts of "heavenly world" or "underworld" do not define objects of worship, because Hindu deities exist in any or all three worlds of the universe. Certainly the idea of "heavenly" does not define Hindu deities, whether good or bad. While valid to some extent, at least for "good" gods and goddesses, "heavenly" does not include the yogi, still on earth, or the snakes and others of the underworld. Three worlds are commonly recognized in Karimpur--svarg lok, the heaven world, the world above; majhlī lok, the middle world (earth); and pātāl lok, the lower world. Good and bad deities exist in all three worlds, and movement back and forth among them is considered plausible and natural. For example, Arjuna goes from majhlī lok, his home, to pātāl lok for the right kind of wood for a sacrifice. Later in the same story, he goes to svarg lok after a girl. Basuk Dev, the snake king, comes from pātāl lok to Karimpur to possess his oracle, while the goddess Devi comes from svarg lok to Karimpur to possess her oracle. Ravana, the evil ruler of Lanka, is a demon who exists in the middle world as does his antagonist, Rama, the incarnation of Vishnu on earth, representative of good divine power. Only living men and women cannot travel between the worlds--although that too is in doubt, since some claim they do so while asleep. All beings are thus intertwined; all create one huge whole. Beings are able to aid or hurt others because of internalized extraordinary power.

The basic characteristic of any god, demon, or ghost is the powers which he/she controls and represents--the fact that he/she is, in essence, power. The only noun in Hindi which comes close to including all possible powerful beings is deva, which is defined to in-

clude both demons and "good" deities, but not the most evil beings--
ghosts and other spirits of the dead. *deva* can be contrasted to
devatā, which definitely refers to only good or goodish supernatural
beings. Fortunately, there is an adjectival phrase which refers to
all gods, ghosts, demons, etc.--*shakti-sanpann*, "power-filled."
Those beings filled with power are the supernatural beings; they make
up the village pantheon.

Since the one common characteristic of all Karimpur deities,
both good and bad, is *shakti*, power, the concepts implied by *shakti*
are important. Probably the most widely known connotation is that
of the goddesses, of the Goddess Shakti. In this sense, *shakti* implies the female energy of the universe, the energizing principle of
the universe without which there would be no motion. But *shakti* does
not mean just female power or the representative of female power, but
power in general. *shakti* carries the concepts of strength, energy,
and vigor; but the strength is based on spiritual force, not physical force.[2] Each item of the universe has its share of *shakti*, of
power. As Marriott and Inden note, "Every genus of living beings
shares from the moment of its generation its defining qualities
(*guna*), powers (*shakti*) and actions (*karma*)" (1972:7). Thus every
being of the universe embodies its share of *shakti*, power, a share
originating "from a single all powerful, perfect, undifferentiated
substance (commonly called '*brahman*' by Hindus)" (Marriott and Inden
1972:8). However, some beings have more power than others--those
beings with more power (*shakti*) are the powerful beings (supernatural
beings) for those beings with lesser powers. Moreover, because every
being in the universe embodies some power (by definition), everything
in the universe is potentially a powerful being.

Some beings considered power-filled in Karimpur are the normally recognized deities such as Shiva, Krishna, Parvati, Ram, Lakshmi,
Ganesh, etc. But there are others. Khan Bahadur, the village guardian deity, began life as a mere Muslim raja but, because he once aided the village, is believed to continue to do so. The wheat seeds
which are planted on *nāg pānchme* (Snake's Fifth) are allowed to grow
for two weeks, are worshiped, and are then discarded--but they must
be worshiped to ensure the year's crops. The yogi, because of his
asceticism, has extraordinary powers. There is also the woman who
died in childbirth and comes back to create havoc among those still
on earth. These are all *shakti-sanpann*, are all power-filled.

Those beings with internalized, extraordinary powers include
all that exists in the universe. However, an analytical distinction
can be made between most of the deities of this world and those of

the other worlds. Unmarked (or less marked) deities may be differentiated from marked (or more marked) deities; unmarked deities are
those which under all conditions are recognized as powerful beings
(thus including the yogi on earth), whereas marked deities are those
which are recognized as powerful beings only under some conditions
in defined circumstances. This distinction is closely related to
the kinds of power which a given being is believed to represent.

Examination of a few Karimpur deities should clarify this
point. Krishna is at any time in any place a power-filled being with
active or potentially active power. Khan Bahadur is also an unmarked
(or less marked) powerful being--a specific earthly condition is not
necessary for his power to be invoked or activated, but his power is
seldom invoked except for specific conditions. However, the wheat
seeds planted on *nāg panchmī* (Snake's Fifth) and worshiped on *rakshā
bandan* (Tying on Protection) are marked powerful beings; like all
beings they have their given power (*shakti*), but they cannot be recognized as really powerful except in this particular situation or
other situations involving ritual activity. Likewise, the boy and
girl in the marked situation of bride and groom are recognized for
the period of the marriage ceremonies as god and goddess. In Karimpur they are usually considered to be Ram and Sita--so much so, that
their feet are touched by their elders, including at times elders
from higher-ranking castes (an acknowledgment of superiority comparable to eating leftover food).[3] The plow, worshiped before the sugarcane is sown, is another marked powerful being, as are the bullocks,
also worshiped, which draw it. Husbands are marked powerful beings
at *karvā chauth* (Pitcher Fourth), when women worship them, and the
snake is during the summer monsoons. These marked deities are all
power-filled, but their power is recognized only in given situations.
Unmarked deities, however, are always powerful and are always treated
with care. In relation to the kinds of powers embodied by a given
powerful being, this distinction will be discussed at length in Chapter VIII.

Gods, ghosts, and demons have powers of varying kinds, whose
primary characteristic is their possible control over human conditions. Thus the wheat seed is power-filled because, if it does not
grow, men will starve. The plow is power-filled for, if it does not
turn the earth correctly, there will be no sugarcane. A bride and
groom are power-filled because they represent fertility and prosperity, the future growth of the family. A snake is power-filled because it can kill. All that exists in the universe contains some
power and can be part of a Hindu "pantheon." It is this potential

"allness" which we must recognize in attempting to discuss a Hindu pantheon, particularly in setting limits to it. Thus, in discussing a Hindu pantheon, we must take into account the marked (more marked) and unmarked (less marked) supernatural beings; we must recognize the inclusive nature of the Hindu pantheon and avoid setting arbitrary limits to it; we must recognize that there is no native (Hindu) conception of a bounded domain of "religion" or the "spiritual."

One may ask, "But how does one know who/what is a supernatural being?" The individual believes, he acts, he is rewarded or not rewarded for his action; he then believes or does not believe. Certainly there are power-filled beings that most individuals in a given village or region believe in; on the other hand, there are many which most individuals do not believe in. Some have powers over only certain families or lineages; others, like Khan Bahadur, over only one village. Deities and demons of varying kinds exist if people believe that they exist, if people believe that a given being is filled with power enabling him to act positively or negatively in regard to man's life.

It is impossible, then, to define the pantheon for a given area, village, or family without interviewing every last man, woman, and child, constantly hoping that they have not forgotten someone, that some minor deity who can aid or hurt them in some relatively unimportant aspect of their lives has not been temporarily mislaid. Moreover, I do not consider this a worthwhile task. It is possible, however, to make statements about the potential characteristics of that pantheon, about the relationships believed to exist among its members, and about the ways in which those members will be treated by men on earth.

In the following pages, I use "supernatural beings" as meaning beings who are in fact powerful. "Pantheon" is meant to include all of these power-filled beings. Given these implications, the task of understanding the nature of a Hindu village pantheon becomes one of understanding the differential distribution of embodied powers.

Conclusion

This perception of the Hindu idea of "supernatural" provides insight into the "religiosity" of the Hindu villager. If everything in his world is in some circumstances a power-filled being, then we can honestly say that "Hinduism is a way of life." This stance is especially plausible if we accept Spiro's definition of religion as "an institution consisting of culturally patterned interaction with culturally postulated superhuman beings" (1966:96) where superhuman

beings are "any beings believed to possess power greater than man"
(1966:97). Clearly, in the Hindu case, power-filled beings ("super-
humans," in Spiro's terms) are also other men, wheat seeds, the plow,
etc. What is important is that everything can be considered to have
shakti, and, whenever something is considered to have *shakti*, interaction with it on the basis of that *shakti* is religious behavior.
To Spiro, a religious belief system consists of beliefs about the
value and manners of interaction with supernatural beings, that is,
the proper forms for treating superhuman power. The definitive characteristic of Karimpur supernatural beings is that they are power-
filled. But humans and other earthly things are also power-filled:
the pantheon of the village of Karimpur is potentially enormous and
without boundaries. Thus interaction with supernatural beings can
be and is frequent and does indeed affect all aspects of life.

Obviously, we cannot take a "bits and pieces" collection of
all that exists in the universe in order to understand the workings
of a Hindu pantheon. But we can attempt to understand the powers
held by various beings and the principles which generate all the categories of these power-filled beings. Thus this monograph is concerned with understanding the powers of Karimpur gods, ghosts, and
demons, particularly as they are relevant to men, and with finding
principles which will allow us to create order within apparent chaos.
I am seeking the principles which generate religious behavior in Karimpur, principles which do not get us lost in "god" collecting. Given
the premise that "supernatural beings are powerful beings," we can
attempt to comprehend the roles underlying the ascription of power,
the behavior of power-filled beings, and thereby ritual behavior, by
examining the ways in which power is used, explained, and dealt with
by the people of Karimpur. Our task, in part, is to determine what
the people of Karimpur see as necessary divine powers over the world
and men's lives. This poses three related questions. What specific
aspects of their lives do the people of Karimpur believe can and
should be controlled by divine power? How do they perceive the ways
in which these powers are distributed among their deities? How do
powerful beings function in controlling the relevant aspects of life?
Ultimately, we must also examine the correlations (if any) between
ritual form and the roles of the deities involved. But first, let
us examine more thoroughly the actions of divine beings in Karimpur.

NOTES

1.   This problem is reminiscent of Gombrich's discussion of the nature of the Buddha (Gombrich 1971, chap. III).   But whereas the Buddha is said not to be a supernatural being, he is treated as one, that is, the "Buddha is still felt to be potent" (142).   Likewise, many Karimpur supernatural beings are treated as if they are potent and called *deva* but recognized as being somehow different from other *deva*.

2.   The Hindi term closest in meaning to *shakti* is *bal*, but *bal* implies a physical strength in contrast to *shakti*, which implies a spiritual power, although that spiritual power can be manifested physically.   Thus the village wrestler is said to have *bal* but not necessarily *shakti*, and the gods have *shakti* but not necessarily *bal*. Professor A. Bharati substantiates this interpretation with an added invective against the Hindu/Sanskrit Pandits in New Delhi who have had the audacity to call electrical power stations *shakti-griha*, "powerhouses," but spiritual powerhouses!   The term should in fact be used in the sense of "house of the goddess," not "house of electrical power" (personal communication, April 1973).

3.   There are limits, however, to this physical acknowledgment of powerful status.   My "mother," a proper Brahman lady, refused to touch the feet of a Thakur bride and groom, although she did give them money.   She could call them god and goddess, but her rank was so high that her touching their feet was out of the question.

Chapter IV: MYTHOLOGICAL JUSTIFICATION FOR RITUAL ACTIVITY

A STRUCTURAL ANALYSIS OF *kathā*

Introduction

As mentioned previously, one of the major forms of verbal traditions
in Karimpur is the *kathā*--the religious stories connected with some
religious observances. These stories are told as part of an act of
worship and are also an essential element of that act of worship.
They are the formal *raison d'être* of the ritual as well as an important segment of it. This chapter focuses on this class of explanations of worship in an attempt to begin to discover what makes the
performance of rituals necessary and to begin to understand the relationships existing between men and deities.

These questions have never been adequately considered in the
literature. Harper states "Gods are superior to men and thus must
be worshipped by men; in return, gods bestow benefits on men" (1964:
151). He never explicates the exact nature of this superiority and
never accounts for his "and thus must be worshipped." Moreover, Harper never tells us what the relationship between men and the gods is
which mandates, as he declares, that men should be and are given benefits by the gods. Clearly there is a transaction of some sort--men
worship, gods give. Yet aside from the fact of god's superiority,
the literature offers little relevant to this transaction and its
underlying principles. Babb (1970b) has explained in detail the importance of the physical transaction, the transfer of food, that occurs in the *pūjā* itself. The fact of a transaction between unequals
is symbolically demonstrated in the rite: men eat the leftovers
(*prasād*) of the gods. The idiom based on food which is used in these
rites, the affirming of superiority by taking the higher beings'
leftovers, is well known and typically Hindu. The fact of the gods'
superiority is thus confirmed. Yet Babb, like Harper, does not specify the nature of the ultimate transaction, the fact that worship
returns benefits. To give meaning to the ritual idiom, it is necessary to examine the conceptual system to discern the related "belief"
transaction--in this case, to discover the exact nature of the opposition: worship-benefit.

The myths associated with worship provide one path to understanding the conceptual system underlying the ritual transaction.
These myths are in themselves a form of exegesis of the act of worship, and in Karimpur they are the primary forms of conscious interpretation of ritual. When asked why and whom they are worshiping,
most informants respond, "I'll tell the *katha* of this ceremony."
Most informants also find it difficult or impossible to offer ratio-
nales apart from these standard forms of explanation. Since these
are the readily accessible and common forms of explanation for ritual,
I am concentrating on them in the hope that, through analysis of
them, I shall be able to understand and present elements of the rationale for ritual activity. By examining these public, legitimate
explanations of worship, even in their standardized forms, I believe
that it is possible to begin answering in depth the "why" of ritual
activity in the villages of North India.

This chapter is divided into three sections. In the first, I
have described in detail the role of the *katha* in the ritual activity
of Karimpur and have attempted to justify an analysis of the *katha*
that treats them as a class with a common structure, rather than as
individual myths. In the second section, I present five *katha* which
are a representative sample of the total corpus (thirty-two) of *katha*
obtained in Karimpur. The third section provides an analysis of the
persistent and recurring internal structure of *katha*, especially in
these five, as a category of myths. These myths are primarily concerned with the "why" of worship and, within their structure, the nature of the worship-belief transaction between men and gods is re-
vealed. This transaction is based on the exchanges of devotion for
mercy and service for boons: man gives devotion to the gods; in return, the gods give mercy; man provides services for the gods; in
return, the gods provide boons for men. Another aspect of the *katha*
shows the necessity of devotion and service. Some *katha* also are
concerned with the nature of the opposite transaction--a lack of devotion evokes anger; a lack of service evokes physical disaster. By
portraying the transaction between men and gods that is opposite to
that represented by worship, the myths reemphasize the superiority of
the gods and the necessity of worship. The *katha*, then, conceptual-
ize the food idiom found in the rite of worship itself: as the ritual idiom of food transactions physically represents the relationship
between men and the gods, so does the myth provide meaning for these
ritual transactions.

The Role of katha *in the Ritual Cycle*

I have stated that all *katha* are a necessary element of at least some rites of worship. In Karimpur, *katha* occur as a part of a *vrat*. In its widest connotation, a *vrat* is a religious act often involving penance (Platts 1968:1186); in the *Mahabharata*, it was a religious vow or practice, a meritorious act of devotion or austerity (Monier-Williams 1956:1042). *vrat* in Karimpur refers to the acts of devotion associated with particular days of the week, of the month, or of the year. *katha* is one of the elements of the totality of *vrat*: a *katha* should be heard or read on every occasion of a *vrat*, although it is sometimes omitted if no one knows an appropriate one. The obvious purpose of the *katha* in these ceremonies is to elaborate on the character of and the reasons for worshiping a particular deity.

The rite of worship known as a *vrat* and the place of a *katha* in this rite are fundamental to the assumptions underlying our analysis. Let us look briefly at the rules given for a *vrat*, to examine its constituent elements.

The Rules for Doing the *vrat* of Sunday

For the fulfillment of all mind's desires, Sunday's *vrat* is excellent. The rules of this *vrat* are this way: in the morning after being free of daily routines, put on clean clothes. Getting into a peaceful mind, begin the *vrat*. Do not eat food more than once. It is proper to eat your meal as well as fruit within the light of the sun, but if the sun is hidden without [your] eating, then on the second day after sunrise eat after first offering water to the sun. At the end of the *vrat*, one should hear the *katha*. On the day of the *vrat*, never take oily or salty foods. By doing this *vrat*, one gains respect and status; enemies are destroyed; and except for eye trouble, all other pains are removed.[1]

There are many variations on the specific rules for a *vrat*, but three elements are common to all *vrat*: fasting; *puja* (worship); and the reading of a *katha*. The overall implication in *vrat* is a vow of worship given to the deity concerned. To do a *vrat*, *vrat karna*,[2] can mean "to fast," although fasting per se is normally associated with other types of religious observances. In Karimpur, *vrat karna* includes the idea of *upas karna*, to do a fast, *upas* having only the meaning of abstinence from food, contrary to the broader implications of *vrat*, where there is a vow to fast, to do a *puja*, and to read or hear a *katha*. So, as a part of the doing of a *vrat*, a religious observance, whether the *vrat* of *shiv teras* (Phagun 1:13)

once a year, or the *vrat* of Sunday once a week, the reading or hearing of the *kathā* is necessary.

In the context of the weekly cycle, the place of the *kathā*
is clearly demonstrated in pamphlet after pamphlet of rules, as illustrated above. That is, in order to have a *vrat* we must have a
upās, fast, *kathā*, myth, and *pūjā*, worship, which themselves have a
deeper structure that we must attempt to delineate. The particular
vrat is dependent on the rules concerning the *upās*, *kathā*, and *pūjā*.
Therefore the *upās*, fasting, gives various options for duration,
foods not to be eaten, etc. The *pūjā*, worship, is composed of the
deity worshiped, the offerings to be made, etc., as well as the more
general configuration of a *pūjā* itself (see Babb 1970b for a discussion of the ritual act known as *pūjā*). But the important point is
that the *kathā*, if we disregard the specific semantics of the situation, has a particular function and structure within the totality of
the *vrat*. Given this function, there is an implied similarity of
structure to be found in every instance of those things called *kathā*.

Moreover, the *kathā* are myths. I use "myth" here in the
sense used by Leach, "A myth is a story about past or present events
the truth of which is asserted as a dogma" (quoted in Robinson 1968:
123). Ideally, myths themselves have a coherent, describable internal structure. They are also linguistic units (if Levi-Strauss is
correct and myths are one type of linguistic unit). Linguistic units
have, when they are categorized as the same kind of unit, an underlying consistency of structure. In attempting to elucidate the structure of this category of myths called *kathā*, we must assume a common
deep structure for given linguistic units.

Rather than attempting to present the structure of *a* myth in
all its variant forms, I have determined the structure of a native
category of myths. These myths all exist in the same position--in
this case, as a necessary element of rites of worship. If the position of this series of myths within these rites (*vrat*) can be pre-
cisely defined, then it is likely that their structure will, at one
level, reflect some aspects of the rationale for worship and perhaps
allow us to perceive this rationale. Furthermore, the overall explication of worship does not detract from a particular aspect. In
fact, I hope that, rather than detracting from the specific *raison
d'être* of any given rite of worship, this analysis will add to that
raison d'être.

In the rest of this chapter, I shall attempt analysis of the
persistent and recurring internal structure of *kathā* as a category
of myths in an attempt to answer the question "Why do you worship?"

The kathā

In the following pages, I shall give a selected set of five *kathā* found in Karimpur. Pertinent facts about those not presented will be mentioned when necessary. Some of the *kathā* here are found in the vernacular, regional great-tradition bazaar pamphlets; others are known in Karimpur only through oral traditions. Numbers 1, 2, 3, and 4 are translations from the *saptvār vrat kathā* printed in Delhi by Anand Prakashan and read in Karimpur. Number 5 was told by a middle-aged Water Carrier to a teen-age Muslim boy (tenth class), who wrote it for me.

This representative selection was made from eleven *kathā* in the pamphlet mentioned above, six longer *kathā* found singly in bazaar pamphlets--for example, *satyā narayan vrat kathā* ("The *vrat kathā* of the True Narayan")--and several taken from *vrat, parv aur tyohar* ("*vrat*, Worship, and Festivals"), an inexpensive book printed in Kanpur, U.P., that presents the *kathā* of the annual *vrat* rather than those of the weekly cycle. Last, there are ten *kathā* told by villagers at the time of the corresponding *vrat*.

The translations here have been kept purposely literal to facilitate later explanations where the Hindi phraseology becomes important. Although smoother translations might make easier reading, the semantics and relations of various terms and ideas would become obscured. In this connection, a further comment is necessary: many sentences have been separated when designating mythical elements. Hindi prose style, particularly the unsophisticated kind, is rambling and has long sentences containing a variety of ideas and, in analytical terms, many mythical elements.

I am presenting this assortment of *kathā* to indicate the variety of issues involved and at the same time the overall similarities which I hope will begin to appear as the *kathā* are read.

Number 1

The *kathā* of the *vrat* of Monday[3]

1) There was a very rich man in whose house was wealth, etc., and no kind of lack.
2) But he had one sorrow: he had no son. He lived with this worry day and night and
3) for his desire of a son, he did Shivji *vrat* and *pūjā* every Monday, and in the evening, going to Shiv temple, lit a lamp by Shivji.
4) One time Parvatiji, seeing his feeling of devotion,
5) said to Shivji, "This Sahukar is your great devotee and always does your *vrat* and *pūjā* with great trust.

6) You have to make his mind's desire full."

7) Shivji said "Parvati, this world's field of rules is such that such seeds as a farmer sows in the field, those fruits he cuts, and in this world such acts as are done, that fruit is tolerated."

8) Parvati said with persistence, "Maharaj, when your devotee is such a one and he has this kind of sorrow, then you must without doubt make them go far because you are always generous to your devotees. You make their sorrows go far. If you will not do so, then why will men do your service, *vrat* and *pūjā*?"

9) Seeing Parvati's obstinance, Shivji Maharaj said "Oh Parvatiji, he has no son. From this care, he is exceedingly unhappy. In his fortune [*bhāgy*] a son is not to be.

10) So I am giving him the gain of a son, but the son will live only to twelve years. This is enough, I am not doing anything more."

11) The Sahukar heard all of this talk.

12) From it he was not a little happy and not a little troubled.

13) He first in the same way did Shivji Maharaj's fast and *pūjā*. After the passage of some time, the Sahukar's wife was pregnant and in the tenth month, from her belly a very beautiful son was gained and in the Sahukar's house there was much happiness

14) but the Sahukar, knowing that he would live only to twelve years of age, was not very happy and did not tell anyone of the secret.

15) When eleven years had passed, then the boy's mother spoke of his marriage preparations to his father,

16) but the Sahukar said "I will not do his marriage now. And I will send him to Kashi[4] for study."

17) Then the Sahukar called his brother-in-law or the boy's mother's brother and, giving him much wealth,

18) said "You take this boy to Kashiji for study and on the way going to any place, do sacrifice[5] and give food to Brahmans."

19) Both the mother's brother and the boy did in all places all kinds of sacrifice and gave food to Brahmans.

20) On the road, a city came. It was the time of this city's daughter's marriage and a second king's son who had been brought in *bārāt*[6] for the marriage, he had one eye malformed. This matter caused his father much fear that seeing this groom, the girl's mother and father would give birth to objections.

21) Therefore when he saw the very handsome son of the Seth he
then had the idea that why not, at the time of the ceremony,
have this boy do the work of the bridegroom.

22) Having this thought, the king spoke to the boy and his uncle,
and they also were willing, and the Sahukar's boy was bathed
and dressed in groom's clothes and put on a horse and very
beautifully all the ceremonial work was done.

23) The groom's father thought that if the marriage acts are also
done with this boy, what is the harm?

24) So thinking, he said to the boy and the boy's uncle, "If in
addition you will do the work of the fire and the *kanyādān*,[7]
then your kindness will be great and I will give much wealth
for this change."

25) They accepted this also and the marriage work was done in a
very good manner. But at this time, the boy beginning to go,
he wrote on the end of the Rajkumari's sari that "Your marriage was with me, but they will send you with this Rajkumar
and he is malformed in one eye. I am going to Kashi for
study."

26) When the Rajkumari found on her sari such writing, then she
refused to go with the Rajkumar and said that "He is not my
husband. I was not married to him, that one went to Kashiji
to study."

27) The Rajkumari's mother and father did not send her and the
bārāt went away.

28) Meanwhile, the Seth's son and his uncle arrived in Kashiji.
Going there they did the sacrifice and began the boy's study,
when the boy's age became twelve years.

29) Then one day in arranging the sacrifice, and the boy said to
his uncle, "Uncle, my condition is a little bad today."

30) The uncle said, "Go inside and sleep."

31) The boy going inside, went to sleep, and a little later, his
breath came out.

32) When his uncle going inside saw that he was dead, then was
very sad and he thought that "If I now should begin to scream
and wail, then the sacrifice actions will remain incomplete."

33) Therefore he quickly finished the work of the sacrifice and
after the going to the Brahmans, he started to scream and
wail.

34) At this time, accidentally, Shivji Maharaj and Parvati were
going from there. Then they heard the sound of very loud
crying and shouting.

35) Shiva said "Parvatiji, his age was this much, so it is ended."

36) Parvatiji said, "Maharaj, having *kripā*,[8] give this boy more life. If not his mother and father will die from palpitation." Parvati again and again persisting in this way,

37) and so Shivji gave to him the *vardān*[9] of life and from the *kripā* of Shivji the boy lived. Shiva and Parvati went to Kailash.

38) Then the boy and his uncle did more sacrifices and left in the direction of their house. On the road, they came to the city where the marriage had occurred. Coming there,

39) they did a very good sacrifice then the boy's father-in-law recognized them and

40) going to his house, complete with much respect and with the services of many servants, did the *vida*[10] of the girl and son-in-law.

41) When they came near their city, the uncle said, "I going first to your house, will make known all the news."

42) At this time, the boy's mother and father were sitting on the roof of their house and they took this vow that "If our son in good health comes to the house, then with much happiness, we will go down.

43) If not, falling from the roof, we will take our lives."

44) During all of this, the boy's uncle, going, gave the news that "Your son has come" but they did not believe.

45) Then the uncle said an oath that "Your son has come bringing much wealth and with his wife."

46) So the Seth with much happiness made him welcome and lived very happily.

47) In this way, anyone who does Monday's fast, and reads this story or hears it, all of his sorrows being made far, all of his

48) desires will be fulfilled.

Number 2

The *kathā* of Tuesday[11]

1) One Brahman Dampati had no son, for this reason the husband and wife were very sad.

2) In order to do Hanumanji's *pūjā*, this Brahman went to the forest.

3) Along with *pūjā*, he made known to Mahavir his desire for a son.

4) At the house, his wife did Tuesday's *vrat* for the gain of a son. On Tuesday at the end of the fast, making food and after offering to Hanuman, she herself began to eat.

5) One time a fast came for which the Brahman woman could not prepare food and then could not offer to Hanuman. Making the promise in her mind that "When on the next Tuesday, giving the offering to Hanuman, I will eat grain and water," she slept.

6) She remained hungry and thirsty for six days. On Tuesday she fainted.

7) Then Hanuman seeing her great love [*lagan*] and faith [*nishTā*] became very happy.

8) Giving his *darshan* [vision], he made her conscious and said, "I am very pleased with you. I am giving to you one handsome boy who will do all of your service." Giving his *darshan* in the form of a boy, Hanuman vanished.

9) Getting a handsome boy, the Brahman woman was very happy. The Brahman woman named the boy Mangal.

10) Some time later at sunset, the Brahman man returned from the forest. Seeing the boy happily playing in the house, the Brahman asked his wife, "Who is this boy?"

11) The wife replied that "Being happy from the Mangalwar *vrat*, Hanumanji gave *darshan* and gave me this son."

12) Knowing the wife's story full of deception, he thought that "This bad person, in order to hide bad habits, made up this story."

13) One day this husband went to the well for water. His wife said, "Take Mangal with you."

14) He went with Mangal and dumping Mangal in the well he obtained water and returned.

15) Then the wife asked, "Where is Mangal?"

16) Some time later, Mangal, smiling, returned to the house.

17) Seeing him the husband was very astonished.

18) At night Hanuman said to the husband in a dream, "I gave this boy. You understood a fault of your wife."

19) Knowing this the husband was happy.

20) Then the husband and wife, keeping Tuesday's *vrat*,

21) began to spend their life in happiness.

22) Any man who reads or listens to the story of Tuesday's *vrat* and keeps the *vrat* by the rules,

23) to him from the kindness of Hanumanji all troubles being removed,

24) to him all happy gains are.

70

The *kathā* of the *vrat* of Wednesday

1) One time there was a man who went to his in-laws' house to have done his *vida*[12] with wife. After staying there some days,

2) he spoke to his mother and father-in-law about *vida*, but everyone said that "Today is Wednesday. On this day, you cannot go."

3) This man listened to nothing and firmly persisting,

4) doing his wife's *vida*, on Wednesday went to his village.

5) On the way, his wife was thirsty so she said to her husband that "I am very thirsty."

6) So taking the waterpot and climbing from the chariot, the man went to bring water.

7) Bringing it, the man came near his wife and seeing her, he was very astonished that a man with a face just like his and in such clothes [as his] was sitting with his wife in the chariot.

8) He said angrily, "Who are you? You who are sitting near my wife?"

9) The second man said that "This is my wife. I am just now having done *vida* bringing her from my in-laws'."

10) Both men started fighting together,

11) Then the king's police coming, grabbed the waterpot-man and asked the woman "Who is your true husband?"

12) Then the wife was quiet because both were as one. Which one was her true husband?

13) The man said, praying to Ishvar, "Oh Parmeshvar, what is this *līlā*[13] that true is made false?"

14) Then a voice from the sky came and said "Stupid, today is Wednesday. You should not go. You don't heed anything. All this *līlā* is that of Budhdev Bhagvan."[14]

15) This man prayed to Budhdev and asked forgiveness for his error, and

16) Budhdev disappeared.

17) Taking his wife, he came to the house and from then

18) both husband and wife with all rules began to do Budhvar's fast.

19) The man who hears or reads this *kathā*, on Wednesday there will be no trouble in his making a trip and to him all kinds of happy gains are.

The *kathā* of Thursday[15]

1) In some village a Sahukar lived. In his house there was no lack of grain, belongings, or wealth

2) but his wife was very miserly. She never gave anything to beggars and took the whole day to do housework.

3) One time on Thursday, a Sadhu Mahatma came to her door and asked for reward.

4) At this time the woman was cow-dunging the courtyard; for this reason she said to the Sadhu Maharaj, "Maharaj, now I am cow-dunging, I cannot give you anything. Come again in another leisure time."

5) With empty hands the Sadhu Maharaj left.

6) After some days the sadhu came there and in the same way begged. The Sahukarni this time was feeding the boy and she said, "Maharaj, what can I do; there is no leisure; therefore I cannot give to you."

7) The Mahatma came a third time; then she avoided him a third time in this way;

8) but the Mahatma said "If you should have some leisure, would you give to me?"

9) The Sahukarni said "Yes, Maharaj, if you will do in that way, your kindness [*kripā*] will be great."

10) The Sadhu Mahatma said, "O.K., I will tell one thing: on Thursday, you get up and, sweeping the whole house, put the refuse in one corner. Don't clean the oven. Then bathing, tell all the people of this house that on this day all should shave. Making *rasoi*,[16] put it behind the stove, never in front. At night after darkness, light a lamp. On Thursday never wear yellow clothes, nor give yellow things for offerings. If you will do like this, then you will not have any work in your house."

11) The Sahukarni did like this. On Thursday she got up, and sweeping the house, put the refuse in a corner. The men shaved after making offerings. She did this way every Thursday.

12) After a little while, there was no grain for food in this house.

13) In a few days, the Mahatma came again and begged,

14) but the Sethani said, "Maharaj, there is no grain for food in this house, what can I give you?"

15) Then Maharaj said, "When everything was in your house, then you gave nothing; now you have only leisure time and still you give nothing. What do you want? Tell that."

16) Then with folded hands the Sethani petitioned "Maharaj, now tell such a thing that my former wealth will come again; now I promise that exactly as you will say, like that I will do."

17) Then the Mahatma said, "Early morning rising, finish bathing and with cow's dung, clean your house. The men of the house not shaving should shave on Wednesday or Friday. To the hungry give grain and water; in the very evening light a lamp and if you will do like this, then with the kindness [kripā] of Bhagwan Brihaspatiji, all your heart's desire will become filled."

18) The Sethani did in this way and

19) in her house there was such wealth as had been formerly.

20) In this way from the kindness [kripā] of Bhagwan Brihaspatiji

21) there is every kind of happiness as long as life lasts.

Number 5

The *kathā* of Hardaul

1) Near Jhansi in the kingdom bearing the name Aurchhe a raja ruled. His name was Nar Sinh. He had two sons, the first Jujhar Sinh, the second Hardaul. There was a girl Kujjawati. Jujhar's wife was very beautiful.

2) Between Hardaul and this "fairy"[17] there was a very strong love. Hardaul considered her like his mother. And the "fairy" thought of him as a son.

3) Jujhar was hated in his kingdom.

4) When a man saw between the two of them such a love, he said to the king "Your wife sleeps with Hardaul."

5) When the king heard, he closed the court and, going to the queen's palace, said "You shameless woman, you are sleeping with your younger brother-in-law."

6) The queen replied "No, lord husband."

7) The king answered "You speak lies."

8) Again the queen replied "No, lord husband."

9) The king then said "O.K., now go and make poisoned food and feed it to Hardaul. If you will not do this, then first killing him before you, I'll then kill you."

10) The queen being helpless made poisoned food and coming to Hardaul, began to say "*devar sāhab*,[18] your brother *sāhab* had poisoned food made for you charged us with sleeping together."

11) Hardaul said, "Oh Bhagvan.[19] But bring the food. It is my older brother's order. I will eat."

12) The queen brought the platter of poisoned food and laid it down.

13) Eating the poisoned food, Hardaul said, "My dear god, you are my proof, and oh sky, stars, sun, and moon, you are my proof."[20]

14) Then Hardaul said, "Oh *bhābhī*,[21] it is my time."

15) Astonished the queen began to cry. Then the gods caused a rain of flowers over Hardaul and the city people, hearing this news, were sad.

16) But this wicked king was unsatisfied. And he said, "Throw out this body."

17) The assassin threw out the body and lighting it, burned it to ashes.

18) Elsewhere his sister heard the news and became tearful and rebuked Jujhar. "Why did you do like this?"

19) But the cruel king Jujhar said, "Go to Datiya.[22] Here you are nothing. Your brother Hardaul was slain."

20) Poor Kujjawati, what could she do? At last she went away.

21) Some time later, Kujjawati's daughter's wedding was about to occur.

22) So with her friends urging, she asked for *bhāT*[23] from Jujhar.

23) But the king shook the barber[24] and said, "I am not Kujjawati's brother. Ask Hardaul for *bhāT*."

24) When Kujjawati heard this tale, she coming to Hardaul's *than*[25] from Datiya began to cry and said, "Who will give *bhāT*? You are in heaven."

25) When there was much crying and shouting, Hardaul *dev*[26] said, "Sister, go to your own house. I will clothe you with *bhāT*." The queen of Datiya went away.

26) Then in a dream, Hardaul said to a Seth, "The one from Datiya is my sister. See that she is clothed. In a tank in the western direction is a treasure. From there take whatever you need."

27) The Seth went off taking the treasure and bought a very expensive *bhāT*. At the time of *bhāT* giving, the Seth began to pile up the *bhāT*, but Kujjawati, not seeing her brother, began to cry. The Seth tried to make her understand, but she still cried.

28) Perplexed, Hardaul gave *darshan*[27] to his sister Kujjawati.

29) Then the Seth gave the *bhāT*.

30) On the second day, the *bārāt*[28] arrived.

31) When the time for eating the food arrived, the boy became angry and said, "As long as Hardaul does not give *darshan*, I will not eat."

32) Hardaul showed *darshan* and giving five rupees, disappeared.

33) Coming from there to the throne of the Shah of Delhi, Hardaul said, "Have made my *than*[29] in every village."

34) The Shah had Hardaul's *than* made in the villages--those of today also.

35) For Hardaul the tailor brings a shirt and the carpenter a cot. With these his life is comfortable.

36) And he is happy.

Structural Analysis of the kathā

If, in analyzing these myths, we follow Levi-Strauss's theory about the structural analysis of myths, we must be concerned with the bundles of relations. The constituent units of a myth are themselves relations, bundles of which point out the underlying structure of the myth (Levi-Strauss 1963a:207). If I am correct and this series of myths called *kathā* have a common underlying structure, then the bundles of relations are formed individually in each *kathā* and are shared throughout the series. It is also possible that the meaningful bundles of relations will become clearer if we look at the series as a whole. For this reason, the first four *kathā* belong to the weekly series, the "seven days' *vrat kathā*," whereas, to illustrate how the structure carries over into other kinds of *kathā*, the last is taken from the yearly cycle of *vrat kathā*.

In table 5, the vertical columns represent the "bundles" of the relations of the myths told above; each bundle consists of several relations which exhibit a common feature. The plots of the myths may be discerned by disregarding the columns and reading horizontally from left to right.

Table 5 and the first part of the analysis below are based on the narrative (syntagmatic) message of the *kathā*. The paradigmatic "structural" message will be discussed later in this chapter.

The entries in column I show a fact of happiness and good fortune. Column II relates acts which are contrary to "proper conduct" or conceivably to *dharma*, an ambiguous collection of rules of "right conduct" varying from region to region, caste to caste, and so on. For example, killing a snake need not be wrong in all parts of India, but it is certainly rarely done in Karimpur.[30] However, the miserly wife who refuses to feed the sadhu acts contrary to rules of right conduct common throughout Hindu India. In the sense that breaking rules of "right conduct" or *dharma* is a sin, all acts in column II are "sins" (*pāp*). All the relations of column III are a deity's acts of revenge and/or anger because of the rule broken in column II.

The units in column IV include only acts or states of unhappiness or sorrow. The entries in column V are acts of devotion or worship by the lower being for the deity. These are also acts of merit (*punya*). Column VI represents the deity's being happy, giving his *darshan* ("vision"), or having a feeling of mercy toward his devotee. The entries in column VII can be categorized "happiness"-- they represent some kind of gain: a son, the return of one's wealth, the life of one's parents, salvation, removal of sins, etc.

Ignoring for a moment columns I, II, and III (which do not occur in all *kathā*) and looking at columns IV, V, VI, and VII, we perceive that the fundamental narrative opposition is between sorrow (column IV) and happiness (column VII). The problem posed by these myths is thus seen to be, "How does a person with an overwhelming sorrow obtain happiness?"

That this question is the basic one posed in most *kathā* should not be surprising, given the closing sentence of each of the weekly *kathā*, one version of which is "and doing the *vrat* and reading the *kathā*, all his mind's desires were fulfilled." The oppositions and transformations represented in columns V and VI answer this question. The answer is, however, somewhat complex and dependent on the implications of several Hindi phrases. Before completely explicating these mediating factors in the narrative structure of the *kathā*, I shall digress briefly to consider the implications of the Hindi phrases important to this mediation.

Examining the acts of column V more closely, we must focus on several concepts: *bhakta* (devotee), *bhakti* (devotion); *shraddhā* (faith); and *vrat* and *pūjā*, rites of worship that are acts of faith. For the devotee, the most commonly used word is *bhakta*, which has in both Sanskrit and Hindi the connotations of loyalty, faithfulness, worshiper, the one who does the service of the god. The feeling of a devotee is known as *bhakti*, devotion. This idea of devotion represents a level of very personal feeling between the devotee and deity. The god Krishna's calling of his devotees with his flute, his calling of man to join with god, represents the concern of the deity. Likewise, the cowherd girls' love for Krishna, their joy in his presence, and their sadness at his departure express the feeling of man for the god. A song very common in Karimpur gives the most prevalent expression of *bhakti* in the village:

Table 5

Plot and Structure in the *kathā*

	Happiness	Man's Action	God's Anger	Sorrow	Man's Action	God's Action	Happiness
	I	II	III	IV	V	VI	VII
#1				sorrow, no son (1-2)	pūjā (3)	P. sees, Shiva feels *kṛpā* (4-9)	gains son for 12 years (10)
				father knows son will live only 12 years (11-12)	pūjā (13)		son born (13)
				only 12 years (14)	sends boy to Kashi(15-18)		
					son does sacrifice(19)		marriage (20-24)
				separation from wife (25-27)	sacrifice in Kashi (28)		
				illness of boy (29-30)			
				death of boy (31)	sacrifice (32-33)		
				sorrow at death (33-34)		Shiva has *kṛpā*, gives boon (35-37)	life of boy (37)
					worship (38)		
					worship (39)		meets bride(40)
				parents vow to die (42-43)			happiness (44-46)
					worship (47)		happiness (48)

#2

	no son (1)	pūjā (2-5) fast (6)	Han. happy (7); gives *darshan* (8)	a son is gained (9)
hus. returns, wife tells story (10-11)				
he calls her a liar (12)				
kills son (13-14)	where is son? (15)			son returns (16)
	hus. astonished (17)		Han. in a dream (18)	hus. happy (19)
		vrat (20)		happy (21)
		vrat (22)	Han. happy (23)	gains (24)

#3

vida (1)				
wants on Wed. (2-3)				
does *vida* (4)	thirsty (5-6)			
	finds man like him (7)			
angry (8)	2d says is hus. (9)			
	fight (10)			
	who is hus.? (11-12)	prays Ishvar (13)		
god angry (14)		pray forgive- ness (15)	Budhdev leaves (16)	home (17)
		do fast (18)		happiness (19)

Table 5--*Continued*

	Happiness	Man's Action	God's Anger	Sorrow	Man's Action	God's Action	Happiness
	I	II	III	IV	V	VI	VII
#4	wealthy Sahukar (1)	wife miserly (2)					
	sadhu comes (3)	won't give (4)					
		empty hands (5)					
		again won't give (6)					
		again won't give (7)	give leisure (8)				
	wife (9)		sadhu tells wrong rules (10)				
		wife does wrong (11)		no grain (12)			
		sadhu begs (13)		wife unhappy (14)			
			sadhu angry (15)		wife prays (16)	sadhu tells rules (17)	
					wife follows rules (18)		wealth (19)
						sadhu has mercy (20)	happiness (21)
#5	Raja Nar Sinh (1)	Jujhar hated (3)			proper love (2)		

man lies (4)

Jujhar angry (5)

proper behavior (6)

lies (7)

proper behavior (8)

kill Hardaul (9)

queen does nec. (10)

Hardaul prays (11)

queen brings food (12)

Hardaul prays and eats (13)

Hardaul's time (14)

sorry in city (15)

throw out body (16)

burns body (17)

sorrow of sister (18)

sends sister away (19)

sister goes away (20)

daughter's wedding (21)

ask *bhāṭ* (22)

brother won't give *bhāṭ* (23)

who will give? (24)

Hardaul will give (25)

Hardaul gives *bhāṭ* (26)

sister--where is Hardaul? (27)

Hardaul gives *darshan* (28)

bhāṭ (29)

bārāt comes (30)

angry boy (31)

Hardaul gives *darshan* (32)

one *than* per village (33)

made in every village (34)

gifts for Hardaul (35)

Hardaul happy (36)

What work do I have in this world, my beloved is Shri
  Krishna.
You are the Ganga, you are the Yamuna, you are the edge
  of the Saryu.
What work do I have in this world, my beloved is Shri
  Krishna.
You are the moon, you are the sun, you are the stars of
  the sky.
What work do I have in this world; my beloved is Shri
  Krishna.
You are mother, you are brother, you are all my helpers.
What work do I have in this world; my beloved is Shri
  Krishna.31

Song #2

The devotee not only loves his god but has trust in him--trust and a
faith that the deity will respond to the devotee's devotion by aiding
him in times of crisis, trouble, etc.

Parvati's comment to Shiva in *katha* #1 illustrates these
points. "Seeing his feeling of devotion [*bhaktibhav*], [Parvati] said
to Shivji, 'This Sahukar is your great devotee [*bhakta*] and always
does your *vrat* and *puja* with great trust [*shraddha*]'" (5). Later
she adds, "'When your devotee [*bhakta*] is such a one . . . you must
without doubt make them [their sorrows] go far because you are always
generous to your devotees'" (8). In *katha* #2 these points are reiterated. Hanuman is made happy by the old woman's six-day fast,
through which he recognizes her love (*lagan*) and faith (*nishTa*) (7).
Apparently that fast was a prerequisite for his recognizing her devotion. In these and other cases, acts of worship of the deity as
well as a feeling of devotion are necessary for the deity to recognize a devotee. A line from another story emphasizes this idea:
"Do the *vrat* of sixteen Mondays with devotion [*bhakti*]. Shivji will
remove your sorrow."32

Thus the individual becomes a devotee by regularly courting
the grace of the deity through worship and supposedly inner feelings
of faith and allegiance. As the myths demonstrate, there is a necessity for return action by the deity. In a version of an episode of
the *Mahabharata* told in Karimpur, Krishna says to his consort "You
don't know that today a very large calamity fell on my devotee
[*bhakta*]. [She] is in much trouble. My devotee stands on one foot."
At this time, the devotee (Dropadi) has called out to Krishna to save
her from nakedness in the court of her in-laws. Krishna responds by
covering her with an endless sari. At the time he made the statement
quoted, he was in the midst of a dice game with his consort Rukmini
and was required to explain his inattention. When the devotee calls
for help, the deity feels concern and ideally goes to his/her aid.

The deity acts in such instances from a feeling of compassion

(*kripā*). The idea of compassion (or mercy) is vital in the relationship of gods and men in Karimpur. Let us look at its usage. In
kathā #1, there is the phrase "from the *kripā* of Shivji, the boy
lived" (37). Parvati had urged Shiva to this action saying "Maharaj,
having *kripā*, give this boy more life" (36). But the boy did not
obtain the boon (*vardān*) of life without his and his uncle's inces-
sant *pūjās* and sacrifices throughout their trip to the holy city of
Benares (*kāshī*). The boon[33] itself and the state of *kripā* depend on
the devotee's prior action, for example, "If you will do like this
[*vrat* and rules for *vrat*] all your desires *from the* kripā *of Brihaspati Bhagvan* will be fulfilled" (emphasis added).[34] Or in another
instance, "From doing such a *vrat* . . . from the *kripā* of Shri Hari,
no kind of trouble or sadness was in the house."[35] Numerous examples
of this sort can be cited, all dwelling on the relationship between
mercy (*kripā*) on the deity's part and devotion (*bhakti*) on the devotee's part. A common phrase in village parlance when something good
or good-unexpected has occurred is "from Bhagvan's *kripā* [*bhagvān kī
kripā se*] I am happy." The one dictionary of Hindi semantics states
that *kripā* refers to someone's kind disposition.[36]

Closely connected to *kripā* in meaning is the frequently used
term *dayā*, "pity" (or, again, "compassion"). It too describes the
emotion of the deity when he gives a boon after some kind of devotion
is shown. "So having the desire for a son, she did *vrat*. From the
pity [*dayā*] of Shivji, a boy was born from her belly."[37]

There is, then, a reciprocal arrangement between the gods and
men. Man is a *bhakta*, devotee, and gives the gods devotion and service in the form of *vrat*, *pūjā*, fasts, songs, stories, etc. The gods
must in turn complete the transaction by giving a boon (*vardān*) because of their *kripā*. Their *kripā* is a feeling of kindness and is
manifested in the giving of a boon, based on their concern for someone who has given them devotion and made them happy. It is, in other
words, a transaction of the patron-client variety, as are many transactions in a North Indian village. Unlike the secular patron-client
transaction, where the client's services are given to the patron in
return for food, in the "sacred" transaction services are given in
return for sons, prosperity, release from sins, or, perhaps, salvation.

This attitude toward the deity seems in other respects to
parallel that of the hereditary patron-client relationship of *jajmān-
kamīn*. The client (*kamīn* or *kām karne vālā*) has a duty to serve his
patron, in return for which he receives foodstuffs and other goods,
a house plot, firewood, cow dung, fodder for the cattle, etc. (Wiser

1958 documents this extensively for Karimpur.) Moreover, the client feels able to count on his patron for aid at times of crisis and for special gifts and goods on the occasion of births, deaths, marriages, illness, or whatever. In this respect, the contract is very similar to that between the god and devotee when the devotee says, "'I am in your shelter [sharan].' To the mother [Santoshi Mata] pity [dayā] came." Eventually the boon is gained.[38] The hereditary client feels himself protected and to some extent sheltered by his patron, in very physical manner (food, housing, etc.), as the devotee feels himself protected by and in the shelter of the god.[39] (I shall return to this idea of shelter and the kind of protection obtained by the devotee in later chapters.) It should surprise none of us that the pattern of transactions and reciprocity that exists in this world should be repeated in a different form in relations between men of this world (majhlī lok, middle world) and those of the other worlds (svarg, heaven, and pātāl lok, underworld).

From the preceding discussion, we know that a person gains by having devotion for the gods. The feeling of trust is reciprocated by that of kindness; the act of service is reciprocated by boons of various sorts. Certainly these two messages, from trust comes kindness, from service comes boons, are important to the structure of the these myths. The question with which we were originally concerned, "How does a person with an overpowering sorrow obtain happiness?" is in part answered by the relationships existing between men and the gods. And the relationship between man and the gods is the structural message of the kathā. We are given the opposition of columns IV and VII, sorrow and happiness. This opposition is mediated by columns V and VI. In this mediation, the dual opposition of feeling and action and the transformation of the feeling and action of column V to the feeling and action of column VI are critical. There is, in fact, an opposition-mediation at two levels--that of feeling and that of action.[40]

Columns V and VI represent mediation through the oppositions, service-boon and devotion-mercy. All the actions of column V are acts of worship-recognition of the deity (vrat, pūjā, havan) plus a feeling of faith, trust, devotion, or such statements as "I came into your shelter." Column VI, on the other hand, includes only acts of recognition of devotion-kindness and the giving of a boon. Faith is rewarded with kindness; service is rewarded with "goods." The two fundamentally antithetical states of sorrow-happiness found in columns IV and VII are then mediated by the transformation of service-devotion to boons-mercy: only the gods and their actions in response

to service and devotion can create happiness for man. Thus the opposition between man and gods is also mediated by service-devotion and
boons-mercy. I shall return to this point in a moment.

The episode in *kathā* #1 where Parvati urges Shiva to reward
his devotee can be used to sum up this segment of analysis. "Parvati
said with persistence, 'Maharaj, when your devotee is such a one and
he has this kind of sorrow, then you must without doubt make them
[sorrows] go far because you are always generous to your devotees.
You make their sorrows go far. If you will not do so, then why will
men do your service, *vrat* and *pūjā*?'" (8).

In the other myths, those in which the structural elements
represented in columns I, II, and III occur, yet another "unresolva-
ble" is mediated. In the totality of the myth, the myth moves from
happiness to happiness. The question thus presented is, "Why does a
person who has happiness have to obtain happiness?" Its resolution
involves a second opposition and two sets of mediators. Note that
there is an opposition between columns I and IV, between happiness
and sorrow; likewise, there is the opposition discussed above, between sorrow and happiness (columns IV and VII). As the relations
of columns V and VI mediate between the relations of columns IV and
VII, so do those of II and III mediate between those of I and IV.

In these *kathā*, the initial state is happiness, but a "wrong"
act is performed. This misbehavior results in sorrow. The pattern
discussed above is repeated, but in reverse: happiness results in
sorrow, rather than sorrow in happiness. Quite logically, the mediated factors are also opposite to those represented in columns V and
VI; that is, misbehavior is opposed to actions of worship, nonrecog-
nition of the deity is opposed to faith. Anger is opposed to *kripā*,
and revenge, to boons.

Again there are two levels of mediation--that of action and
that of feeling. The "main character" in sinning (*a*) does not worship the gods and (*b*) does not feel trust or faith for them. And
the gods (*a*) take revenge because of the misbehavior and (*b*) are angry
with the unbeliever.

Once the state of sorrow is reached, happiness is reattained
through the process already discussed. The answer to the question
posed by these *kathā* is that a person who is happy has to seek happiness because he acts sinfully. He regains his happiness by honoring
the gods who, with a feeling of mercy, restore happiness. A statement from the fourth *kathā* emphasizes the point: "Then with folded
hands the Sethani petitioned, 'Maharaj, now tell such a thing that
my former wealth will come again; now I promise that exactly as you
will say, like that I will do'" (16).

The paradigmatic structural message of these myths is the opposition of man to gods. Mediation of both happiness-sorrow and sorrow-happiness requires action by the gods. Men can act, but the true fruit of their actions is dependent on the acts of those higher.[41] Faith-service (*bhakti-seva*) on the part of the worshiper is reciprocated by the deity by mercy-boons (*kripā-vardān*). These two sets of words define the relationship and union of man and the gods, as do their opposites, disrespect-wrong acts by men and anger-revenge by the gods. The paradigmatic structural message of these myths is that the relationship between man and god is built on the transformations of faith to mercy and of service to boons, and vice versa. Because the gods are powerful beings and men recognize this power, man and god are united by these two transformations. The same set of transformations that leads men from sorrow to happiness also designates his relationship to powerful beings. Or, in other words, the narrative (syntagmatic) message of these myths mirrors the structural (paradigmatic) message, and the same sets of terms provide for both transformations.

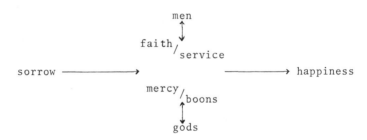

These myths are revealing in still another way. As Geertz has noted (1966), symbols are both models "of" reality and models "for" reality. I suggest that the *katha* are mythical "symbols" representing both these aspects. They are models "of" reality when considered paradigmatically--men are told that they and the gods exist and are related through the transactions in faith-service and mercy-boons. At the same time, the *katha* present a model "for" reality in that they give a model for action--if you are unhappy, worship the gods and you will be happy.

The *katha* presented here emphasize the distinction between man and the gods. However, one *katha* of the weekly series all but obliterates this distinction yet simultaneously provides man with a way of dealing with the fact of the gods. In this *katha*--Thursday's-- a god is "sinful" and proper action is taken by a more powerful god to hold the erring one in line. Indra is very proud and refuses to rise in respect for Brihaspati, the guru of the gods, at his entrance into the court. Brihaspati is very angry at this dishonor and refuses to forgive Indra. Meanwhile, the demon king's army defeats Indra's. Only after Brihaspati has returned his protection do Indra's troubles end. Man, then, is not unlike the gods, even though his happiness is to a large extent dependent on them. The gods too err; they too must be punished; they too have sorrows and must, like men, act correctly.

This story again emphasizes the importance of right action (*dharma*) in life. Both men and the gods must act correctly; if they do so, their "mind's desires" can be fulfilled. The phrase "mind's desires" (*manokāmanaye*) is obviously ambiguous, yet at the same time it defines happiness. Interestingly, the ambiguity allows happiness to be of any variety *so long as* the rules of right action are followed. Desire (*kāma*) is allowed, but desire must never go against *dharma*. Wealth, too, is allowed, as long as it is used correctly (as *kathā* #4 so carefully states).

If we look at the total structure of these myths called *kathā*, one more opposition is developed and resolved--that between sin (*pāp*) in column II and merit (*punya*) in column V. More classical (great-traditional) Hinduism dwells on the effects of sin or merit on one's future lives. In the *kathā*, one sees clearly that even in this present life, sinful acts lead to sorrow; meritorious acts, to happiness.

Table 6 illustrates the dichotomies that we can see developed and mediated if we look at the structure of *kathā* as a whole.

Table 6

Main Structural Oppositions and Resolutions in the *kathā*

Columns						
I	II	III	IV	V	VI	VII
happiness			sorrow			happiness
	disrespect	anger		faith	mercy	
	wrong acts	revenge		service	boons	
	men	gods		men	gods	
	sin			merit		
	sinner			devotee		

On a broader scale, we may also say that the *kathā* allow men
to seek happiness in this life, although their position in life has
been previously determined by *karma*. Happiness can be attained in
this life regardless of one's initial state--devotion to the gods
and faith in their superior action are the path to happiness. On the
other hand, if one does have a good initial *karma*, one can still lose,
even in this life--the gods do have the power to punish men whenever
they misbehave.

If I may speculate for a moment: it is possible that the
kathā are attempting to resolve a paradox in Hindu religious thought
that has its roots in history. In Vedic times, the ritual of sacrifice guaranteed the proper working of the universe. The sacrifice
was a rite concerned with causality, a rite of causality, and the
gods had to act accordingly. The gods were as responsible to men as
men were to the gods. With the growth of the *bhakti* movements, man
began to love god and god in turn to love man. Yet this love was
based on noncausality: the anguish of extreme *bhakti* poetry represents men's recognition that they had no guarantee of a god's actions
toward them.[42] The idea of a lack of causality represented by these
bhakti movements was a radical departure from earlier Hindu thought--
and a departure which was short-lived even in *bhakti* movements.
Though the relationship between man and the gods based on love and
noncausality remained an important ideological element in *bhakti* belief, causality was subtly reinvoked through a redefinition of *kripā*.
However, *kripā*, while maintaining an ideological connotation of noncausality, is nevertheless associated with causality. As the *kathā*
continually state, it is not mandatory for the gods to have *kripā*,
but they should have it. Without a background belief in causality,
the message of the *kathā* is lost. The tension between action and
result--man's devotion and the gods' mercy, underlaid by the ideology
that there should not be a causal relation between action and result-
is always being played upon in these *kathā*. In the world of the
Hindu peasant, action without reward--love for god merely to love
god--is without meaning and support. The *kathā* use the terminology
of the *bhakti* movements while postulating an entirely different con-
cept--that, as Harper says, "in return, gods bestow benefits on men"
(1964:151).

There is still another peculiar ambiguity about man's relationship to the gods. The gods are powerful. In fact, they are
power, they attain their status only by having power over men and
each other. The very essence of the sacred as it can be comprehended
by men is power. And the gods have the power both to punish men when

they sin and to reward them when they act correctly. The gods therefore should be feared, yet the whole concept of devotion (*bhakti*,
faith and trust in the gods) emphasizes the love of god for man and
the love of men for god. Do you then fear a god whom you love? The
ultimate question in the *katha* may be exactly this. The answer appears to be that you do and you do not. If you properly love a god,
have complete faith in him, and act righteously (a way of honoring
the gods?), you need never fear him. As the third *katha* shows, men
may not travel on Wednesdays unless they previously worship Budhdev.
On the other hand, if you do not have devotion for the gods and act
wrongly, you must fear them. As all men know only too well, despite
various attempts to think and act otherwise, a society does not remain viable through love alone. Therefore, the gods must be able to
censure men; why else would men (at least some men) act correctly?
The question of whether to fear or love the gods is the last message
of the *katha*: only through man's own behavior is it answered.

Conclusion

Analysis of the *katha* answers part of the question, "Why worship?"
These myths, used as an exegesis of the *vrat* cycle, proclaim man's
dependence on god and the necessity of periodic ritual activity in
order to prevent disaster in this life, to obtain one's mind's desires, and to add to one's merit for the next life.

The *katha* provide meaning for the ritual transactions between
men and the gods by underlining the transactions between them--the
exchanges of devotion for mercy, service for boons. The ability of
the gods to provide boons asserts their superiority over men. Their
ability to punish men who have acted wrongly reaffirms this superiority and also provides incentives for "right action."

However, there are various kinds of acts of worship. *vrat*,
and thereby *katha*, are only one kind of ritual activity. There are
also different types of powerful beings, as the literature often
points out (see Harper 1959; Babb 1970a; Dumont 1959). Some of these
are openly feared and no one ever feels devotion for them. The deities in the *katha* are able both to censure men and to reward them.
Other deities have varying kinds of control over men's lives.

The *katha* are a special class of explanation for a particular
style of ritual activity. Conceivably, the explanations for other
facets of ritual activity and the corresponding relations between
men and the gods may vary. The following chapters elaborate on the
perceptions of the Karimpur villager about the powers that deities
have over men and the cultural explanations of ritual activity that
may correspond to these powers.

NOTES

1. Translated from *saptvār vrat kathā*, Anand Prakashan.

2. K. C. Bahl, in his work on Hindi verbs, considers *vrat karnā* to be "abstention from self-indulgence" (n.d.:160). Moreover, if it has the secondary meaning of fasting, it is with the implied purpose of atonement. In dictionaries, *vrat* is defined first as "an act of religion" (*dharmik kritya*) and only later as "with the thought of merit to do a fast" (*punya ke vichār se upās karnā*) (Prasad et al. n.d.:1326).

3. Monday, *somvār*, is the day of Shiva worship.

4. The holy pilgrimage site, Benares.

5. *havan* (see Chap. II).

6. The marriage procession for a bridegroom.

7. The giving of a girl in marriage--literally, "girl-gift." Among Vaishnavites, it is the central act of the wedding that symbolizes ritual consummation.

8. Compassion or mercy.

9. Boon.

10. The ceremony of the girl's leaving her father's house.

11. Tuesday is the day of Hanuman worship and is called *mangalvār*.

12. That is, to take her home with him (a ceremonious leave-taking).

13. Game of illusion or sport of the gods.

14. Budhdev is "the god of Wednesday."

15. Thursday is the day for the *vrat* of Brihaspati, the guru of the gods. The sadhu who is the main character in the story is Brihaspati in disguise.

16. "Cooked food."

17. This *kathā*, as related by a member of the Water Carrier caste, was written for me by a sixteen-year-old Muslim boy, with his own additions. One is the word "fairy," picked up in his high school English class.

18. *devar* is "younger-brother-in-law" in the village's dialect of Hindi.

19. *bhagvān* is an inclusive village term for "god."

20. Again, this sentence was written by my overzealous helper in English.

21. *bhābhī* is "older-sister-in-law." I should note here that sexual relations between a *devar* and his *bhābhī* are sometimes condoned in North India.

22. Apparently, her husband's kingdom.

23. The *bhāṭ* is a "trousseau" that her mother's brother gives a bride. It includes clothes for her family, and is obligatory according to his means.

24. The barber is often the mediator in transactions between two affinally related families.

25. "Place"--of burning a body or of worshiping a particular deity.

26. God, one with godly qualities.

27. *darshan* is the view of a person, supernatural being, etc. "Vision" is, perhaps, a Western correspondence.

28. See note 6 above. The bridegroom is brought to the bride's house with great honor, accompanied by male friends and relatives. All of his wishes and commands are to be filled by the bride's family--and above all, he must eat.

29. Here, a ritual place belonging to Hardaul where he can be worshiped.

30. Apparently the killing of snakes is much more condoned in Bengal than in U.P., where a snake can psychologically possess a person--so that killing the snake means killing the person bitten by it.

31. See Appendix I for the original Hindi.

32. From the *katha* of the *vrat* of sixteen Mondays (*solah somvar vrat katha*) in *saptvar vrat katha*, Anand Prakashan.

33. In Sanskrit, *dan* means "a compensation."

34. From the *katha* of Thursday in *saptvar vrat katha*, Anand Prakashan.

35. From the *katha* of Sunday, ibid.

36. K. C. Bahl states "*anugrah, kripa* and *meharbani* all refer to expression of one's feeling of gratitude by verbally acknowledging someone's act of kindness. . . . *kripa* is a reference to someone's kind disposition exhibited in the act" (n.d.:72).

37. From the *katha* of sixteen Mondays' *vrat* in *saptvar vrat katha*, Anand Prakashan.

38. In *shukrvar vrat katha*, the story of Santoshi Mata, Anand Prakashan. Santoshi is a benevolent goddess, believed to be the daughter of Ganesha. Women, particularly, worship her for the benefit of their husbands and children. Although Santoshi should be a goddess of the Shivite variety (in this case malevolent), because of her connection with Ganesha, she is anything but nasty. Interestingly, Lakshmi is worshiped on Fridays in South India, for the same kinds of prosperity (H. Daniel Smith, personal communication).

39. It is fascinating to contemplate the changes in religious attitudes of the Hindu villager as the secular situation changes. In Karimpur, many patron-client ties have already been cut or limited from those of the 1920s (see Wiser 1958 for a baseline). Do both religious beliefs and secular beliefs have to form a coherent whole (Geertz 1957)--and, if so, will religious attitudes in Karimpur change to accommodate a new pattern of secular beliefs and actions?

40. An argument could be made for subdividing these two columns into four. However, I feel that the emotion and acts represented are so closely bound together in Indian thought that it would be an error to separate them.

41. An idea which recurs in the secular world. The reprisals visited by high-caste *jajmans* on low-caste *kamins* who refuse to follow their traditional occupations--their *dharma*--and thereby sin are reminiscent of the dealings between gods and man.

42. I wish to thank A. K. Ramanujan for his helpful comments on these issues. I hope that I have done justice to his insight and I take full responsibility for this discussion.

Chapter V: DIVINE POWERS

The relationships between men and various deities, relationships
which underlie ritual action, can best be perceived in the kinds of
roles which men believe their gods capable of performing. The Hindu
peasant conceptualizes his deities as much by the kinds of roles
which they can play as by their individual characteristics and specific roles. The roles and expected actions of powerful beings vary
greatly, and the actions which different kinds of divinities are expected to perform are based on their perceived powers. In the last
chapter, I explored the nature of the links between men and the gods
that support the ritual activity of *vrat* and *pūjā* and, in the process,
delimited some of the roles which deities can perform in Karimpur.
Here, I shall examine another realm of data to explore further the
Karimpur villager's beliefs about his gods and try to determine the
nature of divinity. I shall analyze the phrases forming the semantic
set defined by "deliverance" to differentiate another aspect of powerful beings' intervention in the world of men--the ways in which the
gods aid men.

It is plausible to suggest that one of man's most universal
concerns is with "deliverance"--being set free from something. In
Hinduism, deliverance means being freed from the cruelties of fortune
in this life or being freed entirely from the cycle of birth and
death, of attaining release (*moksha*). In Karimpur religious thought,
forms of "deliverance" are dominant concerns, if not the end factor
around which all else revolves, since most general appeals for positive divine action are stated in terms of deliverance, of appeals for
safety.

The Meaning of Deliverance in Karimpur

Here I shall examine four terms dealing with deliverance to determine
the elements constituting the Karimpur resident's idea of divine aid.
It is necessary to delineate that from which a devotee is delivered,
by what action he is delivered, and what goal he attains on being
delivered. We can then culturally define the implications of the
use of a specific term for deliverance and further understand the nature of man-god relationships in Karimpur.

91

The definitions developed here are consciously extensional
definitions, that is, definitions based on connotation and context.
I am concerned not with the literal denotation of these terms but
with their correct cultural usage. My definitions are specifically
cultural definitions based on contextual usage. The semantic load
carried by these terms dealing with divine aid to men is fundamental
to understanding the Hindu belief system of Karimpur; furthermore,
analysis of these terms in context leads us immediately to another
relevant set of religious ideas.

These phrases are found in the songs and stories heard in
Karimpur. The total corpus of songs and stories was examined for
every instance of these four phrases dealing with deliverance. Then
a contextual analysis of the use of each term was made. These terms
are generally found in myths (*katha* or *kissa*) or in religious songs
about the feats and actions of the gods. *bhajan*, *kirtan*, and *gana*
provide the most examples of these terms. The *bhajans* and *kirtans*
sing the praises of the gods and call on them to show their skills.
Moreover, *bhajan* and *kirtan* are songs with strong devotional over-
tones, deriving from the *bhakti* tradition. The goddesses seldom appear as characters in these songs. Favorite male deities, particularly Krishna and Rama, provide the characters and settings for them.
These two deities, especially Krishna, represent most clearly the
devotional character of Karimpur religion. As will be shown, the
devotional tones of Karimpur religion (discussed in Chapter IV) reappear as critical for understanding "deliverance."

bhajans, *kirtans*, and *ganas* can be sung on any occasion, although they are most often sung in connection with major rituals,
such as those for Krishna's Birthday, Holi, or Divali. For these
events, the women of a joint household or compound will have a songfest to praise the gods by singing to and about them. And the men
gather in groups on verandahs and add their songs of praise to the
night sounds of the village. The following song (*gana*) suggests
some of the feelings associated with these songfests.

> Without your existence, Prabhu,[1] the root of blessings [is
>   absent].
> Leaves also do not wave, buds do not blossom.
> Rama's name is not taken [remembered] for the love of God. [2]
> Those people who go in this way are as a field of radishes.
> Prabhu, songs to god are the root of life,
> And live in this world as a lotus lives in water. [3]

Song #3

In Karimpur, there are four major concepts dealing with "deliverance."[4] Two are closely related and for many purposes can be
considered the same--*par karna*, "to take across," and *par lagana*,

"to ferry across."[5] The other two are *tārnā*, "to save," and *bachānā*, "to rescue." All come under the general category "deliverance" in that they refer to the types of "setting free" that the gods can perform rather than to the specific actions taken by the gods in setting free their worshipers. That is, they do not define the particular actions by which the deity sets his devotee free but, rather, the fact of "setting free."

To comprehend "deliverance" in Karimpur, we must understand the situations in which deities set free their devotees--the actions by which the devotees are set free (how does the deity "rescue" his devotee?); that from which the devotees are being set free (e.g., misfortune, existence, etc.); and, in conjunction, what the devotee attains as a result of being set free.

We must be able to define the rules for using the sentences presented below. The linguistic context for each is the same; they are paradigmatically related. When each has been analyzed, its broader contextual "fitness" should become clear.

> *bhagvān ham ko pār karnā*   God, take me across.[6]
> *bhagvān ham ko pār lagānā*   God, ferry me across.
> *bhagvān ham ko tārnā*   God, save me.
> *bhagvān ham ko bachānā*   God, rescue me.

In each case we need to know what specific divine actions are indicated by each phrase, in what life crisis a devotee will use each, and from what he is asking to be delivered. By answering these questions and in the process discovering the multitude of implications contained in them, we should be able to determine the actions which they represent and the control over men's lives thus designated.

The most inclusive of these phrases is *pār karnā*, "to take across." *pār lagānā*, "to ferry across," is closely related, although there are important differences between them because of the implications of their respective verbal roots. But first, let me treat them as one to elucidate that from which a devotee is asking to be set free.

The common element *pār*, "the other side," is important in determining from what a devotee is delivered--in this case, what is crossed. *pār* glosses as "the other side," "the far shore," or, in some cases, "the utmost reach" or "limit" of anything. In religious contexts, this word is usually associated with rivers, oceans, and/or boatmen. There are two "other sides" indicated by *pār* in religious contexts. First, *pār* is often the other side of existence or being (*bhav*), and, in keeping with the nautical flavor, the "ocean of existence" is a common phrase. Existence suggests life, being in this world, being part of the cycle of birth and death. It can be considered antonymous to "release," *moksha*. Thus to reach the far side of existence means to have achieved release from existence, i.e., *moksha*. In the following example, existence is to be crossed.

> At the edge of the Ganga, Bhagvan called a boat.
> The boatman brought a boat there.
> "I have to go a long way."
> Bhagvan called for a boat at the edge of the Ganga.
> "Boatman, what is your fee, tell me quickly."
> The boat entered a *whirlpool*,
> Call victory Ganga Mother.
> "Bhagvan, do not give me a fee--
> I am *taking* [you] *across* the Ganga,
> You *take* [me] *across existence*."[7]
>
> Song #4

Here God is asked to take man to the farthest side, to take him from existence, from being--as opposed to the boatman's taking God across the river.

Second, God is asked to take man across whirlpools, *bhanvar*-- the crises of existence, the suffering of some instant. In these cases, the devotee and/or his boat are in the middle of a whirlpool or the boat is shaking and sinking, etc. For example:

> Bhagvan, a servant came begging at your door;
> Prabhu, give your sight to the beggar.
> My boat is in the middle of a *whirlpool*.
> Prabhu, without you who is the boatman?
> I am standing at the door. I will pray.
> Prabhu, *ferry me across*.
> I do not want grain or riches. The house left [behind]
>   is no concern.
> From the world this heart is troubled.
> This servant comes into shelter.
> Bhagvan, a servant came begging for your sight [*darshan*].
>
> Song #5

Or, in an even more poignant example, we have this lament of Radha for Krishna:

> Krishna did not take care, how will I get along?
> Manmohan[8] said he would come yesterday, but he has not
>   returned.
> [So] Radha thought and rising daily, tears flowed.
> [Her] eyes full like a pot, how will I get along?
> No rest at day, no sleep at night, always tortured by
>   separation.
> [I am] thirsty for [you], [my] eyes greedy for *darshan*.
> How could you forget, Savariya,[9] how will I get along?
> Krishna did not take care, how will I get along?
> Without you Shyam[10] and no other who will give hope,
> To whom can I tell my sorrows, whom can I make understand
>   my mind?
> Without you, I am mad.
> Now show [your] dark face, [your] enchanting body.
> *Ferry* Chintanani's[11] boat from the middle of the *whirlpool*.
> How did you forget, Savariya, how will I get along?
> Krishna did not take care, how will I get along?
>
> Song #6

Thus it is possible to use *pār karnā*, "to take across," and *pār
lagānā*, "to ferry across," when asking to be set free from existence
or to be set free from whirlpools--from momentary, this-worldly troubles.

In order to understand how a devotee is set free, we must return to the full phrase under consideration and discover the implications of the verbs *karnā* and *lagānā* when attached to *pār*, "crossing."
pār karnā, "to take across," implies two kinds of help for the devotee. First, it can be used in situations where abstract, inspira-
tional help in crossing is desired. The deity is asked to take the
devotee across by giving him the strength and knowledge to find his
own way across. The following song illustrates this idea:

Oh my Bhagvan, tell me where to search for you.
In the whole world I searched and I never found you.
Take me and my unworthy boat *across existence*, Oh Prabhu.
Because you hear a sad voice, come and *rescue me*.
You came, I heard, and rescued Prahlad: This is a true story
    or fake, tell me.
You did that to Ganka and Ajamil and Gautam Silmani.
Tell me the path, Prabhu, the stairs by which you can be
    reached.
Prabhu, now open all the windows of knowledge.

Song #7

Note the lines, "Tell me where to search for you," "open all the windows of knowledge"--in this way, "take me across existence." Prabhu
is not asked to pick up the oars and row the boat (the devotee)
across but to teach his devotee to row his own boat. Conceivably,
an actor could himself do the crossing (if no object is presented or
implied); that is, "I crossed to the far shore" (*main ne pār kiya*)
is a correct sentence. This possibility becomes critical when we
consider *pār lagānā*.[12]

On the other hand, *pār karnā* can also be used to denote physical aid in helping the devotee to cross:

My boat of life is in the middle, Kanhaiya.[13] *Take [me]
    across.*
Loaded with sins, the boat sinks, without you there is no
    boatman.
Enough. You are my boatman, Kanhaiya, *take [me] across.*
The poet Winod with folded hands praying, fulfill my hopes
    Prabhu.
Now take me up, Kanhaiya, *take [me] across.*

Song #8

Here Krishna is the devotee's boatman in the physical, tangible sense.
pār lagānā emphasizes this physical sense of "boatman" and,
contrary to the spiritual strength requested when *pār karnā* is used,
it implies only "pick me up and take me." Furthermore, *lagānā* is
causative, it suggests "to cause" whatever the noun implies--in this
case, to cause crossing, to cause to ferry across. An agent is both

implied and necessary--the object doing the crossing is acted on by
the subject noun: the subject does not cross but causes something
to cross, as a boatman causes a passenger to cross a river. Thus
lagānā indicates a physical act by the agent (a divine being), giving
tangible aid to the "passenger" (devotee). The following song gives
an example of this usage:

> You are a cheater, taking birth as Shri Krishna.
> You graze everyone's cattle, you graze everyone's cows.
> Why are my cows lost in the forest?
> You fill everyone's pots,
> Why throw my pots in the water of the Jamuna?
> Prabhu, you *ferry* everyone's boat *across*;
> Why is my boat stuck in the middle of a *whirlpool*?
> You are a cheater, taking birth as Shri Krishna.

> Song #9

Note that the deity has acted in a concrete way in the lines preceding "you ferry everyone's boat across." The line also illustrates
the tangible aspect of "to ferry across," because of the implication
that the deity is the boatman, and shows the causative nature of
lagānā. This message is reiterated in the song below:

> Awake, awake, India's saint.
> Awake, awake, India's saint.
> I will shout Gandhi baba's fame:
> He gave the boat *to ferry* everyone *across*,
> He gave the boat *to ferry* everyone *across*.

> Song #10

An even clearer example is the following, in which the deity is asked
to pick up the oars and row the boat:

> *Ferry* my boat *across*, Kanhaiya. *Ferry* my boat *across*.
> My lifeboat is sinking, without you there is no boatman.
> In the middle of the *ocean of existence*, Kanhaiya,
> The boat of a sinner shaking in a *whirlpool*, spinning.
> You are the boatman, Kanhaiya.
> I came in your shelter, Prabhu, I will do your prayer with
>   folded hands.
> You grab the oars, Kanhaiya;
> Without you there is no one, give to the poet "Winod" your
>   help.
> Praying all the time, Kanhaiya.

> Song #11

The same theme runs through another song:

> Rocking, rocking, shaking is my boat.
> You *ferry* [it] *across*, then I know [you are] a boatman.
> In four directions, a circle of sinners,
> Darkness was spread in the world.
> Kanhaiya [was] coming to *rescue* prestige.
> You *ferry* [it] *across*, then I know [you are] a boatman.
> Rocking, rocking, shaking is my boat.
> You *ferry* [it] *across*, then I know [you are] a boatman.
> Devotees called you with *bhajan*.
> I will also call you with this intention.
> Come and lift me who is falling, Kanhaiya.
> You *ferry* [it] *across*, then I know [you are] a boatman.

Rocking, rocking, shaking is my boat.
You *ferry* [it] *across*, then I know [you are] a boatman.

Song #12

One other grammatical difference between *pār lagānā*, "to
ferry across," and *pār karnā*, "to take across," is important. Because the verbal root *lagānā*, "to ferry across," also implies "finally to arrive at the far shore," to ask to be ferried across means to
ask for the final goal of the shore of existence or of the whirlpool
here and now. (And not surprisingly, *lagānā* is rarely used with
"existence" but is frequently used with "whirlpools.") However, when
asking for "deliverance" with the verb *karnā*, the devotee asks for
general aid, and reaching the far shore is only a final aim; he asks
for help without necessarily having the far shore as his immediate
objective. In other words, *pār lagānā*, "to ferry across," suggests
immediate (perfected) aid, whereas *pār karnā* suggests continuous
(imperfective) aid.

This difference in the implications of these verbs becomes
critical in determining what the devotees attain on being delivered.
The deity is a boatman in a spiritual and/or physical sense; he takes
his devotee from existence or from whirlpools. Yet what the devotee
attains by being delivered is more complicated. Clearly, in the
first case, what is attained is nonexistence, with some qualifica-
tions--if the devotee asks for deliverance from existence using *pār
lagānā*, he asks for immediate removal and the far shore is his first
and primary aim. If the devotee uses *pār karnā*, he is asking for
continuous aid in reaching nonexistence, which may be a desire for
the future. In this circumstance, the deity, if he does "take across,"
is committed to freeing his devotee from the whirlpools on the way
as well as from existence at the end. Furthermore, there is an assumption that the devotee will be shown the right path of conduct
and that his sins will be forgiven or ignored. The devotee is, then,
in the shelter of the deity and, if he acts correctly, can remain
there--the deity will be his boatman, will guide him through existence and ultimately to its far shore.

When he requests deliverance from whirlpools, the devotee is
obviously asking for deliverance from this-worldly troubles. Here
the devotee reiterates his devotion, his prayers, and his right conduct, claims his right to the deity's shelter, and proclaims the deity's obligation to be his boatman in this time of trouble. If *pār
lagānā*, "to ferry across," is used in conjunction with whirlpools,
only immediate relief from that particular trouble is demanded, although the deity must give relief by taking the devotee into his

shelter. *pār karnā*, "to take across," when used with "whirlpool," suggests a large whirlpool, because the actual attainment of the far shore is not necessarily implied. In fact, although "God take me from a whirlpool" (*bhagvān ham ko bhanvar se pār karnā*) is possible and correct, "God take me from existence" (*bhagvān ham ko bhav se pār karnā*) is more common, because "to take from existence" incorporates the idea of "to take from whirlpools." On the other hand, "to ferry from existence" (*bhav se pār lagānā*) does not include the idea of "to ferry from whirlpools" (*bhanvar se pār lagānā*), because the completed action, the actual arrival at the far shore--the ultimate shore, nonexistence--is emphasized, and therefore additional relief from intermediate troubles is not demanded.

Grammatically, then, there are two distinctions made between these phrases: causative/"optional causation"[14] (*pār lagānā/pār karnā*) and immediate/continuous (*pār lagānā/pār karnā*). These distinctions are reflected conceptually in "deliverance" as follows: *pār karnā*, "to take across," implies deliverance (1) from existence or from whirlpools or both (and from one's sins) so that one may (2) attain the shelter of the deity, with the deity's acting as boatman, be free from everyday troubles, acquire knowledge of the right way, and ultimately to attain nonexistence; (3) by having the deity give spiritual and/or physical aid to the devotee. *pār lagānā*, "to ferry across," suggests deliverance (1) from existence *or* from whirlpools, but not both, (2) to attain either freedom from this-worldly troubles or nonexistence, with the deity's recognizing his obligations as boatman, thereby giving his shelter (3) by rowing the boat and giving physical aid to the devotee.

A different configuration of culturally relevant ideas is associated with *tārnā*, "to save," and *bachānā*, "to rescue." Although the kind of aid (physical or spiritual), the kinds of troubles involved, and the ultimate goals of "deliverance" belong to the same set of ideas involved in the first two terms, their distribution among the latter two varies.

tārnā, "to save," often occurs in reference to specific divinities' actions in dealing with those in this world who are facing adverse circumstances. In Sanskrit, *tārana* can mean "to cause" or "enable to cross," "to liberate," "to help over a difficulty." In Hindi dictionaries, *tārnā* is given the meaning *pār karnā* or "to keep afloat." However, when its usage in Karimpur is investigated, a more limited meaning is found. In brief, "to save" refers to a deity's interceding for a devotee in a time of crisis, such as Dropadi's impending shame in the court of her in-laws. There are no direct references to existence or permanent escape. The deity is asked to deliver the devotee from this-worldly troubles, that is, the whirl-pools of existence (although whirlpools as such are rarely found in conjunction with *tārnā*). In asking to be saved, the devotee contin-uously refers to those mythological actions of deities whereby a dev-otee has been delivered from some near disaster. For example:

> Oh come flute player, play the flute one time.
> Shyam, you *saved* Radha,
> Oh come flute player, play *rās*[15] one time.
> Shyam, you *saved* Narsi,
> Oh come flute player, give *bhāt*[16] one time.
> Shyam, you *saved* Dropadi,
> Oh come flute player, make a big sari one time.
> Shyam, you *saved* all of us,
> Oh come flute player, show yourself one time.

> Song #13

Or

> Bhagvan, when will you *save* me?
> Bhagvan, you *saved* Dropadi, giving the excuse of a sari;
> When will you *save* me?
> Bhagvan, you *saved* Mira, giving the pretense of a cup;
> When will you *save* me?
> Bhagvan, you *saved* Shivji, giving the excuse of a *Thamru*;[17]
> When will you *save* me?
> Bhagvan, you *saved* Arjun, giving the pretense of an arrow;
> When will you *save* me?

> Song #14

The references in these examples are to mythological events known to the villagers. Radha is Krishna's chosen milkmaid and is called to him as god and lover by his flute. The dance, *rās*, between Krishna and the *gopīs* symbolized their love and concern for one another. When Dropadi, the wife of the Pandavas, has her sari ripped from her in the court of her in-laws, the Kauravas, Krishna "saves" her from the shame of nakedness by providing her with an endless sari. The reference to Mira is to Mirabai, the poet-saint of Maharashtra who proclaims herself married to Krishna. Not liking life on earth, where she is condemned for her love of the god, she drinks a cup of poison and is given salvation by Krishna. Shiva plays his drum (in this song, it is given to him by Krishna) and thereby sets the beat for his dance of creation. Arjun, the Pandava hero instructed by Krishna in the *Bhagavad Gītā*, destroys his and the world's enemies with an arrow given him by Krishna.

These songs also indicate the manner in which the devotee is delivered--by an endless sari, an arrow, a cup of poison, etc. In all cases, the devotion of the individual is a prerequisite for de-liverance. The phrase "to save" implies more than just the physical gift of a sari, cup, or whatever--other examples suggest the god's acknowledgment of devotion through "saving" sinners, as the following illustrate:

[For] your regard, Kanhaiya, I became a yogin,
Ashes were rubbed on my whole body.
    I waited, you didn't come--
    On your path, my eyes rested.
[For] your regard, Kanhaiya, I became a yogin,
Ashes were rubbed on my whole body.
    In my heart it came that I wrote a letter to Shyam;
    Love was great, but paper there was none.
    Then from my eyes there was water like a river,
    But in the pen nothing came.
[For] your regard, Kanhaiya, I became a yogin,
Ashes were rubbed on my whole body.
    You gave love to a hunchback, do as your heart says.
    You left me alone, no mercy came.
    Returning to give time is not enough;
    In my mind I waited and waited--
    In my heart there is much burning.
[For] your regard, Kanhaiya, I became a yogin,
Ashes were rubbed on my whole body.
    You *saved* sinners[18] base and despicable--
    I am a sinner but not more than they.
    So why are you angry, I don't understand;
    In my service perhaps there is a lack?
[For] your regard, Kanhaiya, I became a yogin,
Ashes were rubbed on my whole body.

Song #15

And

Give me this power, all-merciful,
This is the only thing in [my] mind
Service to others, benefit of others, makes my life a success.

I am poor, sad, without strength, without shape.
Bhagvan, how to protect those who are dear--
Those stuck on the wrong path, they were *saved*, all *will be
    saved*
From every deception, pride, jealousy, boasting, disunity,
    injustice, keep aloof.

In this nation and group [I] took birth, for it I should
    sacrifice.
Give me this power, all-merciful;
This is the only thing in [my] mind,
Service to others, benefit of others, makes my life a success.

Song #16

If a deity "saves" sinners, he gives them permanent refuge and acknowledges their right to his shelter in this world--but not their
ultimate escape from this world. He keeps them afloat on the ocean
of existence and out of whirlpools. This act of saving sinners is
more than the mere physical aid in alleviating disaster that is one
aspect of "to save." Only those who have proved themselves by devotion can be saved.

    The last deliverance concept, *bachānā*, "to rescue," suggests
immediate relief from trouble. In some way, trouble is averted or
eliminated. In some situations where "to save" is used, "to rescue"
can also be used. However, in "to rescue" there is no suggestion of
forgiveness of a person's bad qualities, and the person afflicted is

not given refuge or shelter. Some physical aid, such as the destruction of an enemy or the removal of troubles, is indicated constantly,
as seen here:

> Without Bhagvan my boat is stuck halfway,
>> You did not come.
> Nath, you *rescued* everyone,
> How did you *save* Gautan Sila?
> You also *saved* sad Dropadi;
> Nath, today you *rescued* her name from dishonor.
> When the elephant and crocodile fought in the water,
>> The elephant lost.
> You came without shoes; the elephant was *rescued* from the
>> crocodile.
> When Prahlad took Nath's name; then Harnakush wanted other-
>> wise;
> Killing Harnakush in the form of Narsinh, you went and
>> *rescued*.

Song #17

The difficulty is alleviated; god can rescue Dropadi's name from dishonor; he can kill Harnakush and "rescue" Prahlad, but he cannot give
shelter to a sinner who has become his devotee by "rescuing" the
sinner. The act of "rescue" begins and ends with the giving of the
sari, the killing of Harnakush, etc. "To rescue," *bachānā*, is a
very transitory action by the deity, whereas "to save," *tārnā*, suggests a permanent commitment of the deity to his devotee and of the
devotee to the deity. All that the devotee obtains when he is "rescued" is relief from a particular trouble.

Thus "to save," *tārnā*, means deliverance (1) from this-worldly
troubles and one's sins, (2) to attain acknowledgment of devotion and
the shelter of the deity, (3) by having the deity provide physical
relief and by having him show himself as a sign of his (the deity's)
obligation. On the other hand, "to rescue," *bachānā*, implies deliverance (1) from impending disasters, (2) to attain life or honor,
(3) by having one's enemies destroyed, one's troubles removed. In
both cases, the implication is not deliverance from existence; rather,
some extreme misfortune is alleviated. "To save," *tārnā*, has the
same implications as one aspect of "to take across" (*pār karnā*) and
"to ferry across," (*pār lagānā*), that is, of escaping from the whirlpools of this life. But it differs in that it cannot suggest "deliverance" from existence.

The Distinctive Features of Divine Aid

I have tried to show the cultural configuration of "deliverance" in
Karimpur. It was necessary to analyze the situations in which devotees are delivered--from what, by what action, for what goal. We
have found that devotees are delivered from two things, existence and

whirlpools. If a devotee wishes deliverance from whirlpools, he may use any of four phrases. If a devotee wishes to be delivered spiritually, that is, to be given the knowledge to find his own way out of the whirlpool of existence, he can say only "God, take me across." When physical aid is desired, the devotee may use any of the phrases, taking into account the limits set by that from which he is asking to be delivered. If a devotee wishes to attain acknowledgment of his devotion in the form of an enduring contract with the deity and freedom from his sins, he can use any phrase except "God, rescue me." When the deity is asked for his shelter, for alleviation of sins, for his prowess as a boatman, *pār karnā*, *pār lagānā*, or *tārnā* may be used. These rules may be stated in the forms used in table 7.

Table 7

The Meaning of Divine Aid

A Devotee Can Use: / Given:	Whirlpools	Physical Aid	Shelter	Existence	Spiritual Aid
To take across	+	+	+	+	+
To ferry across	+	+	+	+	−
To save	+	+	−	−	−
To rescue	+	+	−	−	−

Notes:

   + means that the term for deliverance can be used in the situation.

   − means that the term for deliverance cannot be used in the situation.

A Transcendental or Pragmatic Complex?

In the process of answering questions about the meaning of "deliverance" in Karimpur, we can also deal with classifications of the forms of religion cross-culturally. In particular, I am concerned with the distinction made by Mandelbaum between the pragmatic and the transcendental complexes of Indian religion. (He also regards this distinction as a replacement for the unwieldy great-tradition/little-tradition distinction so prevalent in the literature [Mandelbaum 1964:10].)

Underlying Mandelbaum's (and others') argument is the assumption that all religions must ultimately answer certain universal questions, provide certain kinds of support for believers. It is possible to consider any particular local Hindu pantheon in terms of the universal roles played by its various gods, goddesses, ghosts, etc. These universal roles have been classified by Mandelbaum (1964, 1966) into two groups, those with transcendental functions and those with pragmatic functions. The transcendental group is concerned with man's long-term welfare, system maintenance, and ultimate goals. The pragmatic group is concerned with personal or local exigencies, individual welfare, and proximate means (Mandelbaum 1964:10). Leach makes a similar distinction:

> One of the major functions of religion is to provide man with reassurance in the face of threatened danger. In active life he needs to be assured that life will go on, that sickness and threatened dangers will not succeed. But in old age man needs to be reconciled with his inevitable fate; the fearfulness of death must be eliminated. It is perfectly logical that these two concerns of religious activity--the maintenance of life and reconciliation with death--should be separated out (Leach 1963: 101).

Certainly maintaining life and avoiding sickness and threatened dangers are remarkably reminiscent of individual welfare, etc. And reconciliation with death is man's ultimate goal, if not his long-term welfare. The issue is how the Karimpur villagers perceive the functions of deities--functions belonging, in Mandelbaum's terms, to both the transcendental and pragmatic religious complexes. And finally, can we say that one can distinguish between these two categories in the Karimpur belief system?

As I originally defined "deliverance," it could belong to either the transcendental or the pragmatic category. The roles defined by Karimpur conceptions of deliverance illuminate the rather arbitrary distinction between transcendental and pragmatic complexes of religion. In some ways I believe this distinction to be useful; however, it must not be overemphasized. In Karimpur, the broadest role is *pār karnā*, "to take across." This role contains critical elements of what Mandelbaum classifies as those functions belonging to the transcendental *and* pragmatic religious complexes. Even contextually, it is often difficult to tell whether a devotee asks for the "ultimate goal" or "individual welfare." I grant that two of the phrases dealing with deliverance are specifically concerned with pragmatic functions--not astonishing, since the villager is primarily concerned with his life in this world, his riches, his sons, his health, etc. Yet the fact that a major role of the village deities reduces both "complexes" into an almost indistinguishable "oneness" is certainly suggestive. It is worth remembering that a similar reduction occurred in the myth discussed in Chapter IV. The recurrent phrase "mind's desires" was all-inclusive, and at various times references would be made to salvation, sons, grain, a wife, or any other desire.

Mandelbaum's classification is based on assumptions about the psychological needs of man, cross-culturally. I am not concerned here with man's needs per se but rather with the way in which the symbols (in this case, language symbols) of the religious system are ordered. It so happens that these symbols are role symbols and therefore there is an overlap with Mandelbaum's argument. The result is, nevertheless, that, whatever value could be obtained from a cross-cultural (and evolutionary) classification of religious roles, the North Indian villager does not perceive such distinctions.

Conclusion

In Karimpur, positive action by powerful beings is broadly described in terms of deliverance, of answering appeals for safety. These terms can be distinguished by other culturally based ideas, a set of culturally determined distinctive features. These two sets of interlocking concepts do not, however, present the full implications of divine power. In particular, they do not allow us to comprehend the actual act of aid, nor do they define negative actions by powerful beings. In the next chapter, these two problems will be considered in detail, in order to develop a model of the types of possible actions of the powerful beings of Karimpur.

NOTES

1. One name for god.

2. I.e., easily broken.

3. I.e., are not worldly.

4. There are other terms closely connected in meaning to these four. As far as I have been able to determine, these other terms are rarely used in Karimpur, and analysis of their semantics suggests no significant changes for the following analysis of the structure of roles of Karimpur deities.

5. *pār karnā* and *pār lagānā* are conjunct verbs or, for my purposes, composite lexemes. In Hindi, those verbs formed with a verb plus a noun or an adjective are conjunct verbs (as above); those formed of two verbs are compound verbs. All these forms are treated as one meaningful unit when occurring together.

6. Several Hindi scholars have noted that these usages are not those found in present-day urban Hindi. Karimpur is in a Hindi-language area with a village dialect that can be described only as part Braj and part Kanauji (based on the discussion of these two dialects in Kellogg 1972). Using phonetic and grammatical variation indicated by this source and my own familiarity with the speech of Karimpur, I have to admit a great mixture in recognized dialect forms. Braj seems to be dominant--although for my purposes the issue of

which is dominant is not particularly relevant. In Karimpur, 100 miles from Mathura, the influence of that center of religious culture seems great. Many of the North Indian poet-saints are known by name, and Braj versions of the epics are popular with those in the village who are literate.

7. The Hindi text for each song of this section is found in Appendix I.

8. Manmohan is another name for Krishna.

9. Savariya is another name for Krishna.

10. Shyam is another name for Krishna.

11. Chintanani is the singer.

12. According to K. C. Bahl, the differences between these two verbs are found in other contexts and support my interpretations. I am grateful to Mr. Bahl for aiding me in arriving at these conclusions and for telling me the results of his work with these verbs (personal communication).

13. Kanhaiya is yet another name for Krishna.

14. In Standard Hindi, *pār karnā* is normally noncausative; the causative form is *pār karānā*. This distinction does not hold in the Karimpur dialect, where both forms are apparently reduced to one, at least in religious situations.

15. The circular dance performed by Krishna and the cowherd girls. Krishna saved Radha, his chosen sweetheart and later his consort, by calling her with his flute.

16. *bhāt* is the rice at the marriage ceremony where the bride's father gives a feast to the bridegroom's party.

17. *Thamru* is the two-headed drum played by Shiva to mark the rhythm of his cosmic dance.

18. Literally, *pāpō*.

Chapter VI: THE CLASSES OF KARIMPUR POWERFUL BEINGS

Previous studies have dealt in part with the interrelationships of
gods, demons, and ghosts in a particular locale. The most important
of these studies have been primarily concerned with the characteristics and identities of the deities discussed. No doubt the character
of a given deity is fundamental to his perceivable actions. However,
there are many possible deities in a given locale, and even within
such a locale, specific individuals' pantheons may vary drastically.

Any analysis based primarily on the character of powerful
beings will tend toward total confusion as the complexities of all
of the gods, goddesses, ghosts, demons, etc., of that area are delineated. It is possible, however, to begin to comprehend the organization of a specific "pantheon" by analyzing other attributes of the
roles connected to various powerful beings, particularly as these
roles are expressed in verbal comments about the actions of powerful
beings. If we learn the principles underlying the perceivable roles
of powerful beings, we can then more fully comprehend the importance
of the character of a deity and his relations with other deities.

We cannot completely determine a model of the roles of powerful beings in Karimpur merely by looking at the cultural conception
of "deliverance." The concepts of deliverance connote various kinds
of aid (spiritual and/or physical) but do not specify the particular
action by which these varities of aid are given to the devotee. Men,
in addition to crying "save me," are apt to ask for particular kinds
of aid. It is these kinds of aid as much as the overall categories
of deliverance that are fundamental to the perceived roles of various
deities in Karimpur.

The specific acts of deliverance allotted to various powerful
beings influence and are influenced by men's view of the ordering of
relationships among the deities themselves. Powerful beings do not
exist alone, each in a vacuum. They are believed to be related to
one another in various ways. We must know the paradigmatic ordering
of these powerful beings' roles with regard to men if we are to understand their roles with regard to each other. In the next two chapters, I shall delve more deeply into the organization of the perceived

107

roles of deities in Karimpur and relate this model of the roles of powerful beings to native classifications of powerful beings and to their relations to each other.

I have sought the principles that generate the symbolic forms (particular deities) belonging to the domain of the "Hindu pantheon" of Karimpur. I hope that these principles, based on the roles that powerful beings can and do act out in Karimpur religious thought, will aid us in understanding the diverse facts constituting the empirical corpus of religious behavior in Karimpur.

The Cultural Meaning of Positive Action

If we look at powerful beings' other kinds of role expectations in Karimpur, we find another realm of actions. These actions represent related aspects of the act of deliverance--"from what" and "how" does a deity deliver his devotee? The actions are the results of the acts of deliverance in a more concrete manner. Furthermore, they expand the implications of the rules in table 7, and this elaboration becomes important when we deal with the patterns of role filling among powerful beings. Only by defining more accurately the roles of deities as perceived in what men feel them able to do can we hope to perceive accurately the organization of roles of a Hindu pantheon.

The acts of deities fall into three groups, correlated with the kind of deliverance. By looking closely at what is implied by "deliverance," we can understand the specific acts of the deities-- the results of deliverance. Relating the results of the actions of deities to the major criterion defining deliverance given earlier, we find the following correlation: If a devotee attains total release, the deity gives him *moksha*. If the devotee merely receives relief from whirlpools, the deity may destroy enemies or give various kinds of physical aid. If a devotee attains shelter, the deity may remove the devotee's sins and may fulfill his mind's desires.

Let us examine each of these in detail. The attainment of release by the god's giving of *moksha* is the ultimate desire of the Hindu devotee. It is the only desire not concerned with life in this world. *moksha*--release, salvation, or nonexistence--means "to be liberated from the captivity of the life of birth and death."[1] To attain *moksha* means that one no longer exists; birth and death and the self as an individual personality are exchanged for union with that which is unknowable, *brahmān*. The far shore of existence, that reached when existence (*bhav*) is crossed, is *moksha*, release from existence, nonexistence. And the gods can give *moksha*--in a religious tale, Bhagvan Shri Hari says "and at the end of time, I give the gift of *moksha*." It is important to note, however, that although the phrase "to give release" (*moksha denā*) does occur, it occurs rarely. The village devotee is much more concerned with life in this world (an often mentioned fact; see Kolenda 1964). And the frequent occurrence of "to take across" would seem to substantiate this fact: "to take across" existence does imply ultimately achieving nonexistence; however, an equally real concern is with getting across and not with the final goal.

All other acts of deities are concerned with "getting across," with the journey through existence. These acts fall into two groups, those involving rescuing the devotee from immediately disastrous situations and those involving giving him shelter.

The first group comprises those acts defined by "to rescue" (*bachānā*), that is, physically aiding the worshiper to escape the whirlpools of existence. Here the deity must keep the devotee from being destroyed either by giving him physical aid or by destroying his enemies. The essential act is to attain minimal welfare for the devotee, that is, to keep him alive and out of troubles of his own or others' causing. These acts are included in the phrase "to remove conditions of distress" (*dashā kā kashT dūr karnā*), which may be removing illness (*pīRāyen dūr hotī hai*), or taking obstacles far (*shattuon kā kshaya*), etc. Any one of these can be limited to more and more specific actions--for example, "freedom from illness" can be "freedom from smallpox," "freedom from typhoid," etc. Since some deities are believed able to offer only very specific kinds of aid (for example, to be able to cure only smallpox), it will later be necessary to define the expected actions of powerful beings more specifically. Now, however, my concern is with the overall categories and their implications for the structuring of man-god relationships. Moreover, acts of rescue, the removing of conditions of distress, cannot be fully understood until we have examined those acts implied by shelter--a critical contrast exists in the difference between shelter and rescue.

The word "shelter" in North Indian religious belief is another semantically loaded lexeme. Before discussing the kinds of acts implied by the giving of shelter, I must examine some other concepts essential to understanding these actions.

As noted in Chapter IV, the *kathā*, ritual myths, deal, among other things, with two transformations--from sinner to devotee, and from unhappy devotee to happy devotee. When we are dealing with those acts of deities implied by "shelter," we are primarily concerned with the first transformation, that is, with the meaning of being a devotee in relation to the idea of having attained shelter.

Shelter of a god means the protection of the god. We find
that the dictionary meaning of shelter, *sharan*, is "place of safety"
(*basav kī jagah*). To say, "I came into your shelter" (*sharan tumhārī
ham aī paRe hai*) means, more fully, "I came into the place of safety
made by you." There is also an implication of extreme humility and
humbleness, of "I place myself completely in your hands." In a typical use of "shelter," *sharan*, we find:

> You are mother, you are father.
> You are brother, you are friend.
> You are companion, you are helper.
> There is no one except for you,
> You are boat, you are boatman.
> You are brother, you are friend.
> Those buds which burst, that flower is I;
> I am the dust of your feet;
> I came into your shelter.
> You are mother, you are father.
> Give your glance of mercy,
> Fill me with great power.
> I came into your shelter,
> You are friend, you are brother.
>
> Song #18

The prerequisite for receiving shelter is that the individual be a
devotee, that he honor and trust the deity involved. Once in the deity's shelter, the devotee can expect the deity to act in those ways
most necessary for his happiness and welfare, as described by the
many roles ascribed in the above song and/or the roles of that deity.

In the religious tales told earlier, the implication is that
those who read this tale, who do the fast, and who worship the deity
will be in the shelter of the deity. The last line of each *kathā*
lists the benefits derived from performing the acts prescribed for
that particular day or ceremony. However, as the first transformation of the *kathā*, that from sinner to devotee, shows, the deity must
initially remove the faults or sins of his (new) devotee. Coming
into shelter definitely requires this removal of sins:

> Oh Prabhu, giver of pleasure, give me knowledge.
> Quickly, take my faults far from me.
> Bring me into shelter, I will be a truth speaker.
> I will be a Brahmachari, a defender of *dharm*,
> A hero and a keeper of fasts.
>
> Song #19

Thus in the devotee's attainment of the shelter of a given god, we
find incorporated the idea that the concerned deity has removed the
devotee's sins.

The same song indicates one particular action implied by the
second transformation of the *kathā*, that of unhappy devotee to happy
devotee. This suggests the second major aspect of shelter. The song
says, "giver of pleasure, give me knowledge." Devotion, and there-

fore shelter, also indicates influence with the deity who will reward
the devotee with the removal of his sorrows and the attainment of
happiness. "Shelter" implies both the removal of sins and the possible attainment of happiness. To repeat, the phrase which often
ends a *kathā* goes, "and removing all his sorrows, his mind's desires
were filled."

The removal of sorrows is distinctly opposed to the removal
of conditions of distress. The latter is the specific action correlated with rescue, as seen above. There is an important difference
between "to remove all sorrows" (*sab dukh dūr karnā*) and "to remove
conditions of distress" (*dash kī kashT dūr karnā*).[2] This difference
is based on the implications of *dukh* ("sorrow") versus *kashT* ("distress"). *kashT*, distress, implies that the physical well-being of
the individual is endangered; *dukh*, sorrow, tends to emphasize the
individual's mental well-being. Moreover, in *kashT*, distress, there
is an emphasis on an external inflicting agent; whereas *dukh*, sorrow,
tends to emphasize some lack or wrong action on the part of the one
who is sorrowful. Finally, *kashT*, distress, is brief, immediate,
now; *dukh*, sorrow, can be long-lasting, extending over a period of
time, timeless.

Sorrows, *dukh*, are generally due to one's actions and related
to one's fortune (*bhāgy*). Distress, *kashT*, is due primarily to the
actions of others, especially enemies, in this life, and are not in
one's fortune. Sorrows, *dukh*, are eliminated by the actions of deities concerned with rescuing an individual.[3]

The concept of fortune, *bhāgy*, is vital for understanding
these acts. *bhāgy* (fortune) is included in the broader concept of
karma (fate), the results of past acts and a pervasive condition
based on past acts. *karma*, fate, is allocated to individuals in the
form of *bhāgy*, the visible known fortunes and misfortunes of an individual's life. One's *bhāgy* is capricious; while never going against
karma, *bhāgy* may leave *karma* less than fully disclosed. It is the
gods who, because of one's proper conduct (following the rules of
dharma, which include service to the gods), can reward one by removing one's sins (in this life) and seeing that one attains one's full
share of fortune, one's full share of *bhāgy*. In other words, if it
is not against one's *karma*, one's fate, one's sorrows are removed
and one's mind's desires fulfilled. Only in cases of extreme devotion
are the gods able to alter one's fate (*karma*) and fortune (*bhāgy*),
an act which, because fortune is written on the basis of acts in former lives, amounts to removal of sins committed in former lives.
One's true *bhāgy* is known only when one follows all the rules of

right conduct. Deities, in fulfilling one's mind's desires and in removing one's sorrows, are fulfilling one's fortune, one's *bhāgy*. (See Wadley 1967 for a fuller explication of *bhāgy* and *karma*.)

The removal of sorrows (*dukh*) and the removal of conditions of distress (*kashT*) are thus very different. Distress, *kashT*, is associated with outside influence and intervention and brief physical danger; it is opposed to sorrow, *dukh*, which is associated with one's own fortunes and sins and is mental, not physical, anguish. Acting to remove sorrows is a greater action than that of removing distress. The deity removing sorrow must be shown that the devotee is serious, that he will become a keeper of fasts and a follower of *dharma*; in most cases, the plaintiff must have asked and sought the deity's shelter before that deity will remove his sorrows. But, like those actions implied by rescuing, by the removal of distress, the removal of sorrows can be made even more specific, that is, the gods can give sons, wealth, knowledge, sovereignty, etc. Again, some gods cannot perform all of these actions; some can give only sons, others can give only wealth. However, the fact that they are able to deal with sorrow, that they are able to remove sins and effect the disclosure of one's fortune, is for the time being the important fact. These very specific acts will be relevant when we look at the scope of power for specific powerful beings.

The results of divine actions then fall into three groups, related to the factors underlying the meaning of deliverance in Karimpur:

Group A	"salvation"	(1) to give release
Group B	"shelter"	(1) to remove sins
		(2) to fulfill one's mind's desires
Group C	"rescue"	(1) to make conditions of distress distant
		(2) to destroy enemies

This set of actions forms an interlocking set with the acts of powerful beings characterized by "deliverance." If we define these two sets in terms of each other, we obtain the paradigmatic set seen in table 8.

As should be clear, it is possible to comprehend the roles of deities in Karimpur in terms of a set of culturally relevant ideas. The broadest role of the gods, the "deliverance" of a worshiper, must be explained on the basis of the specific results of actions of Karimpur deities. These actions and their results are, in turn, bound to the culturally defined initial state of the worshiper, whether it be existence, sorrow, or trouble. If we comprehend the actions and results of actions of powerful beings in culturally conceptualized

113

Table 8

Correlation of Results of Action with Types of Deliverance

Deliverance \ Results of Actions	A "salvation"	B "shelter"	C "rescue"
To take across	+	+	+
To ferry across	+	+	+
To save	−	+	+
To rescue	−	−	+

Notes:
+ means that the type of "deliverance" is correlated with the given "result of action."
− means that the type of "deliverance" is *not*
correlated with the given "result of action."

terms, we may be able to achieve further insight--which we are not
likely to do in an etic analysis.

Malevolent Power in Karimpur: The Structural Implications

The actions of malevolent powerful beings in Karimpur represent role
behavior which is, with some limitations, the inverse of benevolent
roles. Malevolent powerful beings are able to cause illness, cannot
remove it; they can *be* enemies, cannot remove them. Their behavior
can be best understood in terms of our discussion of the implications
of "deliverance" in the Karimpur religious system.

In table 8, I considered only positive roles; powerful beings'
actions were described in what may be called a neutral to positive
direction. However, each of these actions could logically be re-
versed--for example, instead of removing illness, the deity could
give it. Instead of giving wealth, the deity could remove it. If
this chart is revised to incorporate negative divine action, the following symbolic adjustments are necessary. The sign "0" will indicate that a particular deity cannot participate in decisions on that
matter, whether as named or the reverse; "+" will mean that the deity
can act as the action is described; and "-" will mean that he can act
in its reverse. Not all divine actions are good, not all aid the
individual on his journey through existence. Some do indeed make his
journey more troublesome--we must acknowledge that these negative
acts, as well as positive acts, are a definitive factor if we are to
comprehend the nature of divine action in North India.

A few other comments must be made to clarify the implications
of table 9. These, again, involve the possible actions which deities
may perform. First, "0" marks neutrality: no action of the defined
sort is possible by that kind of god. Second, "-" signifies oppo-
siteness of the stated category, so that the opposite of "to give
nonexistence" is "to take away nonexistence," and the opposite of
"to remove sins" is "to give sins." And "to fulfill one's mind's
desires" becomes "to take away one's mind's desires." I stated earlier that logically each of the above actions could be reversed.
However, logic and culture do not always form a 1:1 relationship.
The reader may note that no negative actions are attributed to any
kind of deity for actions classified under categories A and B. Within North Indian village Hinduism (and probably Hinduism in general),
none are possible: the state of nonexistence cannot be taken away
and existence reimposed; the gods may remove sins as a boon, but they
cannot give sins;[4] desires cannot be taken away, only filled. On the
other hand, opposites of category C are possible; a deity can cause
distress and can create (or be) an enemy. The culturally defined
"logic" must be recognized. It overrides etic logic.

Third, it is necessary to recognize that I have indicated
only possible actions; any deity need not act, whether positively or
negatively. When divine beings act negatively, the victim obviously
wishes that they would not act. Likewise, men also wish that those
who can act positively would do so.

Table 9 indicates the broad outlines of action by powerful beings in Karimpur. It is based on the roles of deities as perceived by
a member of this culture; all more specific roles can be categorized
as the type of A, B, or C. In the table, the general type of powerful
being (vertical column) is defined by the roles which he can fulfill
(horizontal column). Thus a deity of class 1 can give salvation, aid
as defined by "shelter," and physical aid as defined by "rescue."
And a deity of class 4 cannot give salvation or shelter, but can rescue individuals or cause them physical distress. A class 6 powerful
being only can harm; he cannot even, by himself, undo his harm.

The implications of this model of the possible roles of Karimpur divine beings can best be seen by examining the named powerful beings of Karimpur and their characteristics. In this regard, native
classifications of deities are important. These classifications coincide in part with the structural roles defined in table 9. Since
there is a partial folk taxonomy of deities in Karimpur, let me make
a brief excursion into this area to add to our understanding of divine
beings, in the process elaborating on the implications of table 9.

Table 9

The Structure of Roles of Karimpur Powerful Beings
A Model for Divine Action

Class of Powerful Being	Possible Action	A "salvation"	B "shelter"	C "rescue"
1		+	+	+
2		+	+	+ (−)
3		0	+	+ (−)
4		0	0	+ (−)
5		0	0	− (+)
6		0	0	−

Notes:

+ means can act positively in this category.

0 means cannot act in this category.

− means can act negatively in this category.

( ) means unlikely but possible action.

Karimpur Categories of Powerful Beings

In understanding Karimpur categories of powerful beings, we must examine the way in which power is differentiated. At a sophisticated level of systemization, we find *brahmān*, the undifferentiated world-soul of philosophical Hinduism. *brahmān*, the Unknowable, although the ultimate source of all being and power, has only the potential of power. Only embodied beings have actual power; deriving from the single, all-powerful *brahmān*, living beings are representatives of the total power of the universe. *brahmān*, the ultimate source of all force and being, is represented in all that is manifested (*prakaṭ hogayī*) in the universe; each of these manifested beings embodies its particular share of the power of the universe. Those beings with more powers than other beings are the deities of the lesser beings. The kinds of powers embodied by various deities and the manner in which this power is believed to be derived from the ultimate source of power and being, *brahmān*, are important aspects of the ordering of deities' roles as perceived by men. I shall examine the correlations between the roles which deities play (as presented in table 9) and Karimpur categories of powerful beings.

Karimpur Terms for Deities

In Karimpur, the most inclusive category of deities, as opposed to
the Unknowable, *brahmān*, are the *deva*. The class *deva* includes both
benevolent and malevolent gods and goddesses; only the most evil powerful beings are not *deva*. This dictionary definition corresponds
to the Karimpur usage of *deva*: "*daitya* [demon]; *danav* [demon];
bhīmkāy manushya [dreadful or fierce men]; *svarg me vicaraN karnevālā
divya shakti-sanpann amara prāNī* [animate immortals filled with divine power who 'stroll' in heaven], *devatā* [gods]."[5] Included in
the category *deva*, then, are the malevolent demons, as well as the
normally good, benevolent deities, the *devatā*. The most malevolent
spirits, the *bhūt*, *jinn*, and *churalin* (all ghosts), are usually considered to be outside the class of *deva*.

　　As the predominant deities of Karimpur belong to the classification *devatā*, let us examine it further. The *devatā* category is
immediately split into two groups, male and female *devatā*, with corresponding lexical terms, *bhagvān* and *devī*. At one level of meaning,
bhagvān means male *devatā*: this maleness is opposed to the term designating female *devatā*, *devī*. At another level of meaning, to be
discussed later, *bhagvān* includes the female *devī*. Both *bhagvān* and
devī can be used in an unmarked sense to imply a general type of deity and in a marked sense to refer to specific gods/goddesses of that
type. To comprehend how these two words, *bhagvān* and *devī*, function
in Karimpur belief systems, let us look more closely at the uses of
each in the oral traditions of Karimpur, investigating both the kinds
of roles implied by each term and the differentiation of powers indicated by these roles.

The Roles of bhagvān

bhagvān[6] is the most common term for collective male *devatā* and is
often used in everyday conversation. A customary response to a question to which the answer is unknown is "*bhagvān* knows" (*bhagvān jāntā
hai*). Besides verifying grammatically the fact that *bhagvān* is male,
this phrase also tells us that he is capable of knowing or perceiving
the workings of the universe. However, no activity beyond being pas-
sively aware is indicated. Another habitual phrase shows potential
activity; in times of stress or danger, the shout goes up "Oh *bhagvān*"
(*he bhagvān*). Contextually, this call by a pious individual requires
some subsequent action by *bhagvān*. Other contexts where *bhagvān* is
used indicate the nature of this potential activity: *bhagvān* is perceived to have one explicit function, one particular area of control
over men's lives. This control (role or power) is that of *pār karnā*,

"to take across" (existence) (see Chapter V). The potential action
of *bhagvān* is this single, all-encompassing, positive action. *bhagvān*
is to aid men to cross from existence or to cross the dangerous situations in existence. The importance of the appeals and songs is
that *bhagvān* must aid his devotee to obtain relief from existence
and the troubles of existence. This aid in crossing existence also
encompasses the roles defined by class 1 deities in table 9. It implies salvation, shelter, and rescue, as presented in table 9.

If man is a devotee, *bhagvān* should aid him in crossing existence. However, if a person is not a devotee, he must not abuse the
power of petition and prayer:

> In whom is not the name of *bhagvān*
> He must not sing songs.
>
> Song #20

Songs are rarely secular in Karimpur; most are sung to honor some
form of divinity. Singing is therefore worship; you must not sing
if you do not believe. You must not abuse the shelter and aid of
bhagvān. On the other hand, this song and the next reiterate one of
the messages of the *kathā*: if you are a devotee, you will be recog-
nized--in this case, by *bhagvān* and all the deities whom he represents.

If you are a believer, a devotee, *bhagvān* can be relied on
not to refuse to aid you if you have given your devotion.

> Even if the whole world is disapproving,
> Bhagvan should not be against you.
> Even if a most beautiful girl,
> [She] should not roam in the lanes.
> Even if a boy is much loved,
> [He] should not be given undo affection.
> Even if a brother's worst enemy,
> [He] should not be removed from the heart.
> Even if the whole world is disapproving,
> Bhagvan should not be against you.
>
> Song #21

bhagvān, then, connotes no negative action. *bhagvān* indicates constant, auspicious, unmarked relationships between man and god, if
that man is a devotee. *bhagvān* represents an auspicious relationship
because he can never, as the song just quoted indicates, be against
you. It is a constant relationship because *bhagvān* gives shelter in
taking man across existence. It is an unmarked relationship because
bhagvān is normally used as a lexeme only when action is broad and
unspecific as *pār·karnā* is indicated. It is a relationship based on
hierarchical exchange because the gods and men have a commitment to
each other, as the *kathā* discussed in Chapter IV suggest.

bhagvān has this one role, to take men through life. Nevertheless, *bhagvān* is still characterless: he is, he knows, he acts,

but he has no personality, no features, no characteristics. He is
not a ruler, a lover, or an ascetic. No image can be made of him:
he is not dark or light; he wears neither a crown nor a peacock
feather. Nor does he participate in particular events. He acts only
in the most unspecific manner possible--he helps one to cross existence, but how he goes about giving this aid is not indicated. He
is only diffusely anthropomorphized. In the sense that "crossing
existence" includes all potential positive powers of a deity, he
does represent all powers incorporated into a single divinity, and
for exercising this one all-inclusive power he can be approached.
In this sense, *bhagvān* is the Karimpur equivalent of our idea of
"God"--a supreme being who holds the whole world in his hands. But
unlike our God, *bhagvān* delegates his powers. He does not take specific actions, lesser beings do so for him.

The fact that *bhagvān* is rarely approached in real, stressful
situations is significant. *bhagvān* represents the potential power
to aid men in this-world crises. As such, he is called upon. However, when a crisis is explictly defined, men go to a god (or goddess)
who has control over that kind of crisis. In references to these
more specifically defined deities, we again find *bhagvān* being used,
but in a marked sense.

In many instances, *bhagvān* is attached to the particular name
of a specific god with known features, such as Krishna Bhagvan, Ram
Bhagvan, Shankar Bhagvan.[7] For example,

> My Krishna Kanhaiya Bhagvan
> Let the boat go from the shore.
> Look at my hero who plays the flute.
> The time has come now,
> Now you must fulfill the commitment,
> Now if you will not, who will, my flute player?
> Oh Shyam,[8] my beautiful.
> Oh Shyam, my beautiful. Mira is calling you.

Song #22

In cases where *bhagvān* is used in such a way that a personality and
specific kinds of actions are attributed to him, it is not the diffuse impersonal *bhagvān* to whom the person is singing or about whom
he is telling a tale. The particular deity, named or not, is the
reference. However, the underlying assumptions of the association
of the lexeme *bhagvān* with particular named deities is fundamental
to the village concept of divinity.

If we are to understand this aspect of divinity, we must take
two factors into account--the syntactic structure of Hindi and some
statements by the people of Karimpur. First, in the above example,
the names "Krishna" and "Shyam" act as adjectives on the primary form

bhagvān. Thus we could read these statements as "that *bhagvān* who is is Krishna" or "that *bhagvān* who has the character of Krishna." These implications are further clarified by statements such as, "He was so much a devotee in this life that he became a part of *bhagvān*."[9] That is, those concrete characters (male) who are *devatā* are all sections or parts of that widespread, umbrellalike, primarily undifferentiated being, *bhagvān*. Or, as another informant said, "*bhagvān* is one. His helpers are all separate. And *bhagvān* is the biggest *devatā*." These lesser beings, these parts of *bhagvān* such as Ram, Krishna, Vishnu, etc., each has its own particular personality attributes and its own realm of defined actions (own roles) in regard to men.[10]

In action, *bhagvān* is unmarked and superordinate to *bhagvān* particularized and used as a marked noun. If table 9 were expanded to include all possible kinds of troubles which the gods can remove or all the mind's desires that the gods can fulfill, *bhagvān* (unmarked) would be able to do all. Yet any part of *bhagvān* can deal only with certain defined troubles or certain defined desires. It is these secondary types of *bhagvān* who are the primary male deities under role classes 2 and 3 in table 9. Some of them are believed able to give salvation; others, with lesser powers, cannot. Most generally act positively toward a devotee.

I do not think that the question of why these intermediary gods exist need be considered at length here. Hindu philosophy requires their existence: because *brahmān* is Unknowable, divinity can be known only in "bits and pieces."[11] *bhagvān*, as the village's partial manifestation of *brahmān*, is both impersonal and remote. Krishna, Ram, and others are real. They can be imagined, dreamed about, and loved. Stories can be told of them, and their very humanlike (and therefore nonremote) characteristics can be stressed. And one can carefully choose, in times of stress, a god to call upon who one knows has control of the appropriate powers.

The different identity characteristics specify the various powers and concerns which these intermediary gods possess. Both their similarities and their differences are clearly recognized, as the following song illustrates.

> Whatever Ram says, whatever Krishna says,
> The meaning of both is the same.
> In Shri Ram's hands are bow and arrow,
> In Shri Krishna's hands a flute.
> Shri Ram's mother is Koshilya.
> Shri Krishna's mother is Jasoda.
> Whatever Ram says, whatever Krishna says,
> The meaning of both is the same.

Shri Ram's father is Dasharath.
Shri Krishna's father is Nand Baba.
    Whatever Ram says, whatever Krishna says,
      The meaning of both is the same.
Shri Ram killed Ravan,
Shri Krishna defeated Kans.
    Whatever Ram says, whatever Krishna says,
      The meaning of both is the same.

Song #23

These variations in character are then used by men to define whom
they must approach in given situations. In Karimpur, Krishna is the
god most often meant when a relationship of love between man and god
is recognized, as the popular song below demonstrates. In this episode, Krishna falls asleep in the forest and a *gopī* steals his flute,
hoping thereby to obtain his love.

I took Krishna's flute from the forest.
I took Shyam's flute from the forest.
    Get up Jasoda Mother:[12] open the door
    I have come to the house to return a flute.
    Hearing the voice, Mohan[13] rose quickly.
    Give to me, friend, my Mohan flute.
    Along with the flute, my silver bracelets go.
    Oh friend, give to me.
I took Shyam's flute from the forest.
    I said a little love will come.
    Oh, the opposite.
    Shyam thought a thief.
I took Shyam's flute from the forest.

Song #24

Ram, on the other hand, is the warrior-king, acceptably married, and
the role model for a bridegroom:

Pull the bow, bridegroom, Janki will do the marriage.
Today my bridegroom lifted the bow
And took it to grandfather and uncle
On [his] head a yellow crown,
Look at how beautiful a bridegroom Ram has become.

Song #25

Thus the total, all-encompassing power of *bhagvān* is differentiated
and specific powers are attributed to the correspondingly "semantically" correct intermediary gods, including, finally, the bridegroom
himself.

    bhagvān connotes constant, auspicious relationships with men.
Likewise, all the intermediaries represented by *bhagvān* or those
whose names are used with *bhagvān* do not have roles designated by
classes 4, 5, and 6 in table 9. On the other hand, all male deities
of classes 2 and 3 are representations of aspects of *bhagvān*.

    Other primarily well-behaved male deities with whom there is
no constant/frequent relationship but, rather, infrequent relationships, fulfill the roles of class 4 deities. They can rescue man but
cannot give him long-term aid. They are usually considered to be

devatā, since their relationship with man is a benevolent one. However, they would not have the appellation *bhagvān* attached to their names. In Karimpur, Zahir Pir, the god who controls snakes, is this type of deity. He generally aids men, however, he is called upon only when there is a crisis. No one would say that he "shelters" one, although he does represent an auspicious, infrequent relationship. Being a primarily good god, he is a *devatā*; lacking long-term commitments from men, he is not truly a kind of *bhagvān*.

The Roles of the Goddesses

The category *devī* is, in its internal structure, similar to that of *bhagvān*. There is an all-enveloping *devatā* "femaleness" (*devī*) which becomes more easily worshiped (or worshipable) when given specific characteristics--as was *bhagvān*. First, we find, as with *bhagvān*, the term *devī* being used in an undifferentiated sense, that is, *devī* with few human identifiable traits beyond "femaleness." Further, we find the use of *devī* in a marked manner, e.g., Lakshmi Devi, Sita Devi, etc. These sundry *devī* have special traits, because of their femaleness, that are essential individual characteristics and alter their role playing (as contrasted to *bhagvān*), as indicated in table 9.

    Although there are categories of purely malevolent female deities (*jinn* and *churalin*), the goddesses in the category *devī* are also potentially malevolent--and to a much greater extent than the male gods categorized as *bhagvān*. As Babb (1970a) and Beck (1969) have shown, there is an ever present awareness that female power may become uncontrolled. And when male authority (usually a consort) is absent, the malevolent use of female power is almost assured. Two important aspects of this potential for evil affect the types of roles played by Karimpur goddesses.

    First, the male deities can always dominate the female deities, both ultimately in actions over men and also within the pantheon itself. One may say that males can put down or contradict females of equal rank. Second, female deities are more ambivalent--less predictable--than male deities. Their potential for malevolent action makes them more suspect than male deities. In terms of the types of roles which female deities play as defined by the paradigm in table 9, *devī* is not comparable to *bhagvān* as a class 1 powerful being--her potential for negative action is always recognized. Likewise, *devī* can imply a class 4 powerful being; if one is dealing with a malevolently inclined *devī*, one does not ask her for shelter. Furthermore, other *devī* are almost totally malevolent and act positively

only to remedy their own actions: these goddesses are of class 5.
Sitala, the goddess of smallpox, is approached primarily after she
has spread the disease among men and is a class 5 deity. *bhagvān*,
on the other hand, is never used as a designating category for this
class of powerful being--for deities fulfilling these primarily malevolent roles. Thus, in comparison to male roles, the roles and
types of female deities are skewed downward. This skewing also results in "devotion," "shelter," and enduring relationships' being
concentrated in the hands of male deities, not female deities. An
example of this control of such relationships by males is seen in
the weekly cycle of *vrat*. The only weekly *vrat* for a female deity
is for Friday, and even this *vrat* is an aberrant case and is not
listed in the most commonly used pamphlets for *vrat*. On this day,
Shukr, Venus, is normally recognized. However, many women instead
do the *vrat* of Santoshi Mata, a benevolent goddess.

Likewise, there is a concentration of totally malevolent power in female powerful beings. The most dangerous ghosts, the *churalin*,
are always female (in fact, women who died in childbirth), and *bhūt*
are usually female spirits. As should be clear by now, the specific
character of a given deity is closely related to the class of roles
in which it can perform or is believed to perform. The details of
the relationship of character to role are complex and fascinating--
but beyond the scope of this paper. For our purposes, the critical
element is the fact that female deities are more likely than male
deities to be involved in malevolent action.

The Correlation of Categories of Deities with Classes of Powerful Beings

The roles of Karimpur's powerful beings, as presented in the paradigm
in table 9, are roles based on broad cultural categories. The possible variation in action represented by "shelter" and "rescue" is
infinite. Yet these broad classes of roles are closely paralleled
in Karimpur categories of powerful beings.

Relating the various categories of deities discussed in the
preceding sections to the classes of roles outlined in table 9, we
find correspondences. *deva* as a category can include powerful beings
of classes 1 through 5 but not class 6. *deva* are not totally evil
creatures; they are not the mortal beings who did wrong or continue
to do wrong as they wander the earth. They have at least the potential for good action. *devatā*, on the other hand, are primarily good
deities and have only the potential for bad action. *devatā* include
gods fulfilling the roles designated by classes 1 through 4. They
are to be feared most because of their curses, usually arising out

of anger. *devatā* represent an auspicious relationship between man and god, but not necessarily a constant relationship. Many of them act only periodically to aid men and do not demand continuing allegiance or give long-term shelter.

bhagvān implies deities' filling only role classes 1, 2, and 3. The giving of shelter is a primary implication of the idea of *bhagvān*, that being who is always there, and this implication carries over to the marked *bhagvān*, the parts of *bhagvān*. And *bhagvān* in both the unmarked and marked senses implies continuing relationships between deity and man. On the other hand, the goddesses, *devī*--with their female inclination to get out of control--while often implying enduring relationships can always go against one and would seldom be recognized as a class 1 powerful being. Some *devī* are also class 4 deities, goddesses whom one does not necessarily love. Furthermore, *devī*, while classified as *devatā*, can sometimes be class 5 powerful beings, goddesses who are really feared. The relationship of categories of deities to the roles which they play is summarized in table 10.

Table 10

Karimpur Categories of Divine Beings Correlated
with Classes of Powerful Beings

Categories of Divine Beings	Classes of Powers		
(deva, devatā, devī, bhagvan, jinn, bhūt)	salvation	shelter	rescue
1	+	+	+
2	+	+	+ (−)
3	0	+	+ (−)
4	0	0	+ (−)
5	0	0	− (+)
6	0	0	−

Notes:
        Solid lines represent the range of powers (as defined by the classes of powers) covered by the given deities.

        The broken line represents potential but less likely range of powers.

There is, then, a distinct relationship between the types of powers that a given powerful being has and his categorization as a kind of deity. Moreover, the ambiguity of the goddesses is also clearly illustrated. The goddesses are definitely *devatā*, but they do have that overriding inclination for evil which skews their actual roles toward possible malevolent action, while they retain their classification as *devatā*.

Conclusion

The classes of powerful beings, as developed from Karimpur conceptions of divine action, are closely related to Karimpur categories of deities. Although these two aspects of the roles of powerful beings do provide insight into the internal structure and workings of the Karimpur "pantheon," they do not allow us to comprehend relationships within the pantheon itself. Rather, they delineate the structure of the pantheon without regard to its internal interrelationships. As noted, a specific being is a "powerful being" when it embodies more power than another being. Some gods themselves sometimes represent more power than other gods. We shall consider the ramifications of this aspect of divinity in the following chapter.

NOTES

1. *jīv kā janm-maran ke bandhonse chhūTnā.*

2. "To make all sorrows far" and "to make all conditions of distress far."

3. I do not mean to imply that a given deity can perform only one of these roles (actions). Some can both provide shelter and physically rescue a devotee, as table 7 indicates.

4. In an earlier attempt to understand the role-playing possibilities of Hindu deities, I included the "giving of merit," only to realize much later that Hindu gods do not give merit. Merit accrues only through the actions of men (and gods) without the outside intervention of another individual. Merit (*punya*), though not given by the gods, is rewarded by them in both this life and the next. Complementing merit is sin (*pāp*). Man sins, powerful beings do not cause/force him to. The Satan/devil paradigm of Christianity, where man is urged/compelled to sin/hell, is lacking in Hindu belief systems. This is not to say, however, that disaster does not occur; it does, but it is not tied to a desire to cause man to sin. Recently I discussed this matter with a North Indian Hindu; he said that people who have acted in an apparently wrong way will say "a demon is sitting in me." The idea of one being's sitting in another being is, in North India, tied to the idea of possession. Essentially, it means that the being who possesses me acted thus: "I myself did not-- that being sinned, I did not." As I understand the texts and these ideas, the above comment substantiates the idea of no one being's causing another to sin.

5. Translated from Prasad et al. n.d.

6. Three other lexical items have meanings similar to or synonymous with *bhagvān*: *prabhu*, *nāth*, and *gusāī*. *prabhu* has the same
referential meaning but more limited connotations. *nāth* and *gusāī*
refer generally to male *devatā*, but their use is more readily extended into the everyday world, where they become terms of respectful
address meaning "master," "lord." The important factor in this-
worldly meaning is the concept of a master or lord who cares for one,
who provides shelter.

7. In some cases, *bhagvān* is used alone without the specificity
of a particular named deity, but in a marked manner: the actions
attributed to him are not characteristic of the diffuse, impersonal
deity delineated above. However, if we look closely at these examples, we find that in actuality *bhagvān* is clearly identifiable as
one of the well-known deities of the village.

8. Shyam is another name for Krishna, literally, "the dark one"
(black or blue).

9. This statement occurs in a story referring to Zahir Pir, a
god of snakes known in western U.P. and Punjab.

10. I am dealing with these specific deities as if none of them
were an *istha devatā*, one's chosen deity. Any individual may have
his own chosen deity (male or female) to whom he owes particular
allegiance and who he believes can solve all (or most of) his problems in this life. Any deity can become an *istha devatā* if the worshiper believes that the deity can function broadly and powerfully
enough.

11. There are other reasons why divinity must be known "in bits
and pieces." Power must always be embodied: *brahmān* is unembodied
and undifferentiated; in him power is not embodied (see Chapters VII
and VIII).

12. Jasoda is Krishna's substitute mother.

13. Mohan is another of Krishna's names.

Chapter VII: POWER RELATIONSHIPS AMONG KARIMPUR DEITIES

Several other facets of the behavior and character of divine beings
in Karimpur must be explored before we may add more features to the
model of the classes of powerful beings in table 9.   There is a hierarchy of deities to whom to appeal for aid and protection.   When the
lower-level deity cannot or will not help one (and one never knows
which), one appeals to a deity believed to embody more powers than
the first.   Finally, one can appeal to *bhagvān*, who can counteract
the actions of all other powerful beings and who is able, ultimately,
to control *devī* as well.   In fact, on one level of meaning, *bhagvān*
can be interpreted to include the goddesses--that is, they, as well
as most male *devatā*, are a part of *bhagvān*.   This kind of control of
one deity by another is closely tied to ideas of intermediaries and
the transfer of power.   This chapter is concerned with the relationships which exist among the deities of Karimpur as they are presented
in myth and ritual.   First, myths relating tales of deities seeking
control over each other and over men are examined.   Then the types
of bridges which allow for varying powers among deities (intermediaries) are investigated, including the intial attainment of defined
powers.   Finally, the use of power in a ritual which requires divine
control of lesser deities is explored.   Understanding these facets
of the fact that deities embody power is particularly important for
comprehending men's actions toward powerful beings of various sorts,
including other men.

Divine Control of Deities in Mythology

A deity of small and limited powers is, in many senses, as much under
the control of higher, more powerful beings as men believe they themselves are.   This can be seen through reference to table 9.   If, for
example, a given deity can remove conditions of distress and another
can cause them, then the former can undo the actions of the latter.
The "good" deity must, of course, be talked into giving this aid and
very often is not called upon until after the recalcitrant "bad"
spirit has been asked to change his behavior.   One requirement of
this system is that the top, most inclusive beings must be more pow-

erful in the long run than those malicious beings who cause particular kinds of troubles. The literature of both Karimpur and classical Hinduism is full of myths about situations in which malevolent,
often capricious, action by one deity is countered by the actions of
a more powerful one. I shall relate some of these as they are told
or read in Karimpur, briefly schematizing each at its conclusion.

The Myth of Sixteen Mondays' vrat
(solah somvār vrat kathā)[1]

Parvati becomes angry with a priest because he has said that she
will lose a dice game with Shiva. She curses him with leprosy.
The priest in turn is told by some sympathetic damsels to do
Shivaji's vrat for sixteen Mondays with great faith and devotion
and on the seventeenth Monday, Shivaji will cure him of leprosy.
He does the vrat for sixteen Mondays with true devotion and on
the seventeenth Monday he is cured through the mercy [kripā] of
Shivaji.

> Power hierarchy: Shiva
>
> Parvati
>
> Priest

The Myth of Thursday's vrat
(Brihaspati vrat kathā)[2]

Indra, the king of the devatā, is cursed by Brihaspati, the guru
of the gods, because Indra refuses to stand in respect when Brihaspati enters Indra's court. Brihaspati, as the guru of the
gods, is able to act against Indra, his inferior, in the same
way that he can act against men who have erred. When Brihaspati
removes his support from Indra's cause, Indra loses his war with
the demons [daitya]: he is able to defeat the demons only when
he retains the services of a powerful priest (not Brihaspati).
Indra then makes the error of killing a Brahman (his priest) and
regains Brihaspati's support in the process of cleansing himself
of this extreme sin.

> Power hierarchy: Brihaspati
>
> The new priest
>
> Indra   demons

The Myth of gobardhan

The following story, about gobardhan pūjā (Cow-Dung Wealth, or, sec-
ondarily, worship of the mountain Gobardhan, Kartik 2:1) also illustrates these themes. In the associated ritual, the first step is to
construct ritual figures out of cow dung, collected by the women ear-

lier in the day and deposited in a corner of the courtyard. The
women use the cow dung to make a rectangular, three-dimensional figure. The figure has a head and often feet, and around the boundaries
are a series of mountains (*pahar*). Within the rectangle, cow-dung
images of all the members of the family are placed, along with images
of all the family's animals (including the ubiquitous dogs), and other valued agricultural items, such as a plow, the village pond, etc.
(see figure 9). The *sīnk*, straws, used in Pitcher Fourth (*karvā
chauth*) eleven days previously are then stuck into the tops of the
mountains. The basic figure itself is variously identified as a cowherd or, more specifically, as Krishna. The mountains are there to
protect the family which they enclose, an obvious reference to the
Krishna legend related in the associated myth. At some time during
the day, one of the women will worship the figure and the mountains
for the family. Later, when the figure has been destroyed, the cow
dung will be fashioned into cakes which will be preserved until the
Holi bonfire three months later.

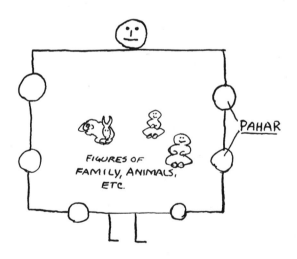

Fig. 9. Design for *gobardhan*

In ancient times, the *pūjā* of the gods [*devatā*] and the *pūjā*
of the swami of clouds [Indra] occurred. In the third age [*yug*]
when Bhagvan Shri Krishna became an avatar [of Vishnu], Shri
Krishna, seeing that in every house people were cooking and preparations were being made, asked, "Whose *pūjā* will take place today?" The people of Braj answered--"On this day, the king of
gods', Indra's, *pūjā* is held and for this reason all these preparations are being made." Hearing this, Shri Krishna said, "The
mountain king Gobardhan is bigger than Indra because grass and
weeds grow there [on the mountain] and from these all the cowherds and cows are maintained, therefore you people should not
do Indra's *pūjā* today, but should do instead Gobardhan's *pūjā*."

Minding Shri Krishna, the cowherders and cowherdesses did
the *pūjā* of Gobardhan mountain and did not do the *pūjā* of Indra.
Being enraged by this slight, Indra sent torrents of rain in
order to destroy all of Braj. When this happened, Shri Krishna
lifted Gobardhan mountain with his finger and held it as an um-
brella over Braj. And with his power of illusion [*maya*], Shri
Krishna made Gobardhan mountain so hot that those drops of rain
which fell on it became on fire [steamed?]. For seven days,
there was unceasing rain, yet Braj was not damaged and all the
water evaporated. Seeing this event, Indra learned that Bhagvan
Vishnu had become an avatar in the form of Shri Krishna and that
Shri Krishna had saved Braj with this power. Then Indra, feeling
extremely ashamed, came to Braj and falling at the feet of Shri
Krishna Bhagvan began to beg forgiveness for his offense. Seeing
Indra's humility, Shri Krishna gave him forgiveness.

Power hierarchy: Krishna

Gobardhan

Indra

The Myth of Jalandhar

Another myth, connected with another festival day, *deothan* (Gods'
Awakening, Kartik 2:11), represents similar themes. On this day,
the gods are awakened from their four-month sleep; and after this
date, marriages can again take place. Although village belief considers that all the gods have been sleeping, Vishnu in particular
has been sleeping. On this day he is worshiped, along with the new
sugarcane crop. Some people say that Vishnu has been recovering from
the battle described in the associated myth, given below.

There was a demon [*daitya*] named Jalandhar. He had a very
beautiful and faithful wife named Branda. Because of the power

[*prabhāv*] from the faithfulness [*pativrat dharma*, "conduct of husband worship"] of his wife, the demon conquered the whole world.[3] Meanwhile, the poor rishis and munis and gods were in trouble, so they all prayed to Vishnu Bhagvan to murder him. Vishnu decided to murder all the demons and spoil the faithfulness of Jalandhar's wife. He did it in this way: changing one dead body into the shape of Jalandhar, Vishnu threw it into the courtyard of the house of Branda's family. Thinking that it was the dead body of her husband, Branda started crying and wailing. At the same time, Lord Vishnu gave life to the body and in this way, Branda embraced another man and spoiled her faithfulness. Owing to her loss of faithfulness, Jalandhar's power [*shakti*] was weakened and Vishnu killed him in a big war.

When Branda learned that she was cheated by Lord Vishnu, she became annoyed and cursed him saying, "You gave me separation from my husband--in the same way, you will also tolerate the separation of your wife." And when Vishnu was in the [form of the] avatar, Rama, he had to tolerate the separation of his wife Sita.

> Power hierarchy: Vishnu
> Jalandhar (Branda)

The Myth of Tripura

Another myth is associated with *kārtik pūranmānshī* (the full moon day of Kartik, Kartik 2:15). On this day, people should bathe in the Ganges, 40 miles away, and worship the *tulsī* tree (generally associated with Vishnu).

There was a demon [*rāksha*] whose name was Tripura. He did formidable penance [*tapasyā*] in Allahadbad[4] continuously for one million years.[5] Because of this, all the gods [*devatā*] and Indra were scared. He was not even shaken by the heavenly nymphs [*apsaras*].[6] Then Lord Brahma arrived at his place to give him a boon and Tripura asked for one boon--that he should not die by the hand of any man or any god.

After receiving his boon, Tripura started misbehaving and caused discomfort for all people. Once he attacked the mountain of Kailash.[7] After this, Shiva killed him with the help of Lord Vishnu and Lord Brahma. Since then, this festival has been celebrated.

> Power hierarchy: Shiva, Vishnu, Brahma
> Tripura

One ordering feature of most Indian epics, such as the *Rāmāyana*, *Bhagavad Purānā*, and *Mahābhārata*, is that of finding the right

powerful good deity to destroy/defeat an extremely powerful bad deity.
I do not think that the point needs further elaboration. Ultimately,
the more powerful, good deities restore proper action.

In addition, gods and goddesses of all kinds fight and quib-
ble with one another. Most of these confrontations have to do with
who had the rights to certain actions/powers over men. As said earlier, men need the gods, but the gods also need men. The gods want
men to serve them, they want as many worshipers as possible, and they
constantly try to outdo one another, to claim more devotees, more
powers or commands over one another. Brihaspati's control of Indra
in "The Myth of Thursday's *vrat*" partially reflects this kind of situation, as does Krishna's superseding Indra in "The Myth of *gobardhan*."
The "Myth of Saturday's *vrat*" shows more pugnacity, as Shanicar
proves that of the nine heavenly bodies, he is the greatest (at least
on Saturday!).

The Myth of Saturday's *vrat*

Once upon a time, the nine heavenly bodies, Surya [sun], Chandra-
man [moon], Mangal [Mars], Budh [Mercury], Brihaspati [Jupiter],
Shukra [Venus], Shani [Saturn], Rahu, and Ketu got into a fight
among themselves on the issue, "Who is the greatest of us all?"
All of them called themselves great. When they could not decide
among themselves, and continued fighting one another, they went
to Indra and told him: "You are the king of all gods [*devatā*].
Therefore do justice to us by telling us who is the greatest
among the nine of us. Who is the greatest among the nine of us
planets?" King Indra got nervous on hearing their question and
said, "I do not have this ability to say who is great and who is
small. I cannot say anything on my own. But there is one way
out. At this time, King Vikramaditya rules the earth, he is the
remover of miseries. Therefore you should all go to him. He
alone will remove your difficulty." Hearing this advice, all the
planet-gods journeyed to the earth and presented themselves in
King Vikramaditya's court and put their question before the king.
On hearing them, the king was very puzzled and thought: whom can
I call great and whom small? Whosoever I call small will get
annoyed. But in order to settle their quarrel, the king thought
of a way out. He would have nine seats made of the nine metals--
gold, silver, bronze, brass, glass, tin, pewter, mica, and iron--
and would place all the seats in order, for instance, gold first
and iron last. After doing this, the king told all the planets,
"All of you please be seated on your own seats. Be it known that

whoever has his seat in front is the greatest and whoever has
his seat at the end is the smallest." Because the iron seat was
right at the end and it was the seat of Shani [Saturn], Shani
thought that the king had made him the smallest. Shani got very
angry at this and told the king, "You do not realize my prowess.
Surya stays in the sign of the zodiac for one month, Chandrama
for two days and a quarter, Mangal for one month and a half,
Brihaspati for thirteen months, Budh and Shukra for one month,
Rahu and Ketu both going in opposite directions for only eigh-
teen months. But I remain in the sign of the zodiac for three
years [?]. I have caused grave troubles even to the great gods.
Listen, O King, when Rama was passing through *sarhe-sati* he was
exiled and when it came on Ravana, Rama and Laksman attacked
Lanka with their army and destroyed Ravana's kin. O King, therefore you take heed." After this, the king said that he would suf-
fer whatever was written in his fortune [*bhāgy*]. After this, the
other planets left happily, but Shani left in great anger. After
some time, when the *sarhe-sati* came on the king, Shanidev came
to his capital disguised as a horse dealer with many beautiful
horses. When the king heard the news of the dealer's coming, he
ordered his stable manager to purchase good horses. The stable
manager, on seeing such a good breed of horses, and their prices,
was impressed and immediately reported to the king. The king,
on seeing the horses, chose a good horse and mounted it for a
ride. No sooner had the king mounted the horse than the horse
ran with great speed to a jungle, where after leaving the king,
the horse disappeared. . . . [Many troubles and adventures later]
the king announces: "Shani is the greatest of all the planets.
I considered him small and therefore I had to undergo suffering."
For this reason, in the entire city, Shanidev was worshiped and
his tales told and people enjoyed all sorts of happiness.

Fortunately for the gods and goddesses, there are many facets
of life which they can control, so that they can alleviate their dif-
ficulties by splitting up their realms of power. It is then up to
man to indicate what he believes to be important, as the following
story illustrates.

The Myth of Vishnu and Lakshmi

Vishnu said that he was bigger. Lakshmi said that she was. They
had a fight. Both came into the world where a ritual was taking
place. A Pandit was saying *kathā* [ritual stories]. Vishnu became like a Pandit and sat at the *kathā*. There Lakshmi made her-

self a beggar. She also came to the *kathā*. One man said to the beggar, "Please bring some water." So Lakshmi gave him a golden waterpot. She gave much wealth to all. Later, Lakshmi sat in a big house made for her. So she is bigger. So we always say Sita before Ram; Radha before Krishna.

In all of these myths, that deities embody various types of power and that some have greater or lesser powers than others are continuously reiterated. However, that deities represent different levels and types of powers is not the only message found in the mythology of Karimpur. Many, if not all, of the Karimpur deities are connected through various means to other higher- or lower-level divinities. These links become particularly important in rituals and are investigated in the next section.

The Roles of Intermediaries

One manner by which ordered relationships are created among various deities is through mythologically supported "intermediaries," that is, deities who are considered to be related to but lesser than a superior and often more remote divine being. In this sense, all embodied deities are intermediaries for Brahman. *bhagvān* and *devī*, the village representations in anthropomorphized form of Brahman, are the highest-level good intermediaries. As the divinities closest to Brahman, they are the deities with the broadest power. Yet they too are relatively undifferentiated, their traits and characters are only loosely defined, and their actions are correspondingly vague (see Chapter VI). Beneath both *bhagvān* and *devī* there are other intermediaries between them and men. These intermediaries represent, in turn, aspects of the power of *bhagvān* and *devī*. In addition, intermediaries ranked next to *bhagvān* and *devī* may have yet other levels of intermediaries under them, between them and man.

As intermediaries between *bhagvān* or *devī*, etc., and man are elaborated, the roles that a given lower intermediary can fulfill become limited (unless, of course, some individual considers that deity to be an *istha devatā*). The most common pattern seems to be that, if A has B and C below him, then B and C will have roles defining for them different realms of power over men--competition is not between B and C, but between A and B or A and C. Likewise, if deity A controls powers x and y, he can also ultimately control those deities specifically concerned with powers x and y. Thus *bhagvān* can ideally counteract the actions of all other powerful beings.

There are, however, several other factors related to the concept of intermediary that must be clarified. One is the manner in

which power is obtained.   There appear to be two basic ways, both related to the concepts of rebirth and right duty.   The first way is
by "being," that is, all living beings (including man), by definition,
have their share of power.   All beings embody a certain portion of
the power of the universe.   However, not all beings (deities and men
alike) have the same portions of power; at birth one's share of power
depends on one's actions in one's previous lives (that is, one's
karma).[8]   A being (whether god or man) is born into a particular family, group, *jāti*, chosen for him on the basis of his previous actions.
Or, one is born into a group with a recognized position in society
that is appropriate to his actions in his previous life.   A being's
actions in previous lives are weighed against the "code for conduct"
(*dharma*) defined for his group in that previous life and his individual embodied moral code for conduct (*svadharma*).[9]   Thus all beings
begin life with certain defined powers, powers which are embodied by
the very fact of their existence.

These powers can, however, be changed.   A given individual
in his present life can add to or subtract from his innate powers by
actions affecting his bodily substance--actions which are appropriate
or not appropriate to his various codes for conduct.   Thus a chaste
and virtuous woman obtains power in this life, as "The Myth of Jalandhar" shows.   In this myth, Branda not only adds to her powers
as defined by birth by being faithful to Jalandhar but is able to
transfer this power to her husband.   A similar transfer is seen in
the following story:

The Myth of *rakshā bandan*[10]

One time there was a continuous twelve-year war between the gods
[*devatā*] and the demons [*daitya*].   The gods were losing badly
and Indra said to the Guru of the Gods, Brihaspati, "Oh Lord!
This is such a bad situation that I can neither go nor stay here.
There is no way except for losing my life.   So please tell me
what would be good for me."   At this time, Indrani said to her
husband, "Don't be afraid.   I am a faithful [*pativrat*] wife.   I
will tell you one way by which you can win and protect yourself."
After saying this much, Indrani bound the *rakhī* on the wrist of
her husband on the last day of Savan.   After she bound the *rakhī*,
Indra again went to war and defeated all of the demons.[11]

One can also obtain power by being exceptionally pious and
celibate in this life (like Tripura in "The Myth of Tripura" or Ravana in the *Rāmāyana*).   One also obtains power by ascetic practices
which alter one's normal bodily substance--Shiva is noted for the

power which he obtains through ascetic practices. Another way in
which one alters one's power is through the learning of sacred words,
mantras, etc., which are passed on from guru to disciple and which
provide one with access to unusual power.[12] One can also change one's
coded substance and thereby one's power (which is part of one's substance) through removing or rejecting various bodily particles and
through performing various rituals.

Thus power is distributed among the beings of the Hindu world,
primarily through the dual conceptions of *dharma*, correct action, and
karma, the fruits of one's action. One gets good power when, as one
informant put it, one does good work. If one does not do good work,
one becomes an evil spirit or lesser being (perhaps going from Brahman to Sweeper) in the next life. Only those earthly mortals who
are very, very good become *devatā*, immortals. Examples of both ex-
isted in Karimpur. One Shepherd woman was continually afflicted by
the evil spirit of her dead husband, who had been "a bad man." And
the dead grandfather of one Brahman lineage was worshiped yearly at
his *than* ("place"), because he had been so "good" in his earthly
life that he was now a *devatā* and gave protection to his descendants.

Power Distribution in Karimpur Mythology

While obtaining power in these ways, a given deity is also connected
mythologically to recognized divine beings. Thus a "genealogy" is
created for powerful beings of all sorts based on the kinds of powers
with which they are blessed by belief. This genealogy relates them
to the appropriate higher-level deity who has wider control of these
powers.

Considering some examples of such a genealogy plus the corresponding distribution of power should clarify this point. The
highest deity with the most inclusive powers in Karimpur is *bhagvān*.
Two of his most recognized intermediaries are Shankar Bhagvan (Shiva)
and Vishnu Bhagvan. The manners in which their powers are delegated
and the corresponding "genealogical" links vary because of their defined characteristics--that is, Shiva often has offspring whereas
Vishnu has avatars. Nevertheless, a series of hierarchical relationships are used to justify the lesser's powers: these include father-
son (or daughter), guru-chela ("disciple"), avatar, etc.

Examining the deities associated with Shiva, we find first
the bridge of father-son existing between Shiva and Ganesha. Ganesha
in turn is connected to a lesser intermediary who is his daughter,
Santoshi Mata. Another intermediary for Shiva, Guru Gorakhnath, is
connected by the bridge of guru-disciple (as Gorakhnath and the Nath

yogis stole secrets from their guru, Shiva). And related to Gorakhnath is Zahir Pir, primarily his offspring via his powers of giving
fertility but also his disciple. Related to Zahir Pir and under his
control are the *nāgas* (snakes), headed by Basuk Dev--a relationship
which is carefully supported mythologically. Thus a series of mediating factors relate the deities to each other in a hierarchical
fashion.[13]

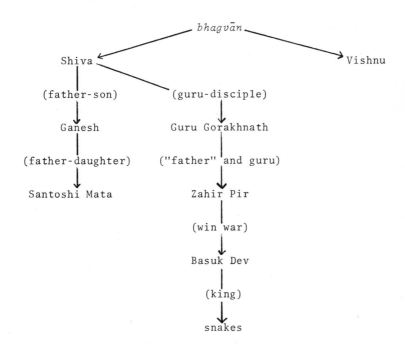

These genealogical bridges are paralleled by an appropriate
distribution of power, again based on the characteristics of each
deity. The basic power of the universe is distributed between Shiva
and Vishnu (Brahma is relatively unimportant to our analysis); Shiva
is concerned primarily with destruction and creation, and Vishnu with
protection, specifically with the correct following of *dharma*. Shiva
as the ultimate ascetic is the model for many gurus; he is also the
primary god of fertility, and he controls snakes and does various
other good deeds. His role as an ascetic, including the power of
fertility, is repeated in Guru Gorakhnath, who also controls snakes.
Gorakhnath's ability to control snakes is found again in Zahir Pir,
but with the loss of fertility and of the wider powers of a guru.
Likewise, Ganesh "inherits" the power to remove obstacles, and his
daughter Santoshi Mata represents the power to remove those hindering
one's family.

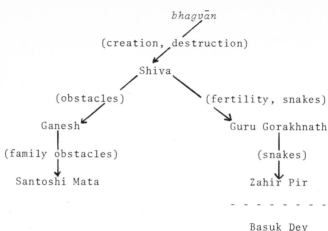

Basuk Dev

These delegated powers are in some senses more potent than the original ones. A deity with only a few powers is, if ritual patterns are correct, more recognized and in some senses more powerful than a higher-level intermediary with many powers. There is a saying from the Punjab which is appropriate here: "What is greater, Ram or Gugga?"[14] The reply--"Be who may be the greater, shall I get myself bitten by a snake?" The higher-level, more powerful deity is acknowledged, but men first approach, and believe that they should approach, the deity specifically concerned with their present trouble.

In a similar fashion, Vishnu and his intermediaries also represent the distribution of powers, although with some variations. Vishnu is concerned with maintaining correct moral action (*dharma*), and not specifically with fertility and destruction. Given these characteristics, he continually reappears on earth in the form of various avatars to destroy malevolent beings who are perpetuating disorder in the world. His avatars, although destroying different demons and having different characters, do not represent the same kind of intermediaries as Shiva's, who clearly represent a separation and differentiation of the powers of Shiva. Although Shiva and his various connections are worshiped and recognized in Karimpur and the surrounding area, Vishnu and his avatars, particularly Rama and Krishna, are the primary recipients of devotion (*bhakti*): of the approximately 600 devotional hymns which I collected (*bhajan*, *kīrtan*, and *gānā*), fewer than 50 are directed toward or concerned with devotion to Shiva and his intermediaries. Rather, Rama and Krishna dominate them.

Let us look just briefly at one of Vishnu's avatars (Krishna)

and the kinds of lower-level beings with which he is connected. I
am particularly concerned with his connections to *kālināga*, the black
snake, which he subdues during his boyhood in Brajmandal (the area
of Braj--Mathura and its environments, approximately 60 miles from
Karimpur itself). *kālināga* is particularly important in the Krishna
cult because of his ritual position in Karimpur. Once a year, on
Krishna's Birthday (Krishna *janamāstamī* or more popularly *kanhaiyā
āten*, Krishna's Eighth--Bhadon 1:8), the women of Karimpur make elaborate colored drawings on the walls of their homes (usually inside
an inner room) that they will worship at the conclusion of their
fast after the moon has risen (Krishna himself was born at midnight).
All these ritual drawings include Krishna himself (drawn in blue--
the color implied by his name); *kālināga*, on whose head(s) Krishna
is dancing (a huge intertwined black snake, often with two heads);
and the five Pandavas (Arjuna and his brothers) with whom Krishna is
connected in the *Mahābhārata* and later in the *Bhagavad Purāna* and
vernacular versions of the Krishna story. Other auspicious symbols
may be present, but the necessary ones are Krishna and *kālināga*, his
traditional enemy (see figure 10).

A version of the Krishna story collected in Karimpur by the
Wisers in 1925-30 from Mangu Lal, a fifty-year-old Farmer widower,
contains this segment concerning *kālināga*.[15]

The Play of Krishna and *kālināga*

One morning, Shri Krishna went with the cowherds and cows to
take the cattle grazing. Leaving the cows to graze, Krishna began to play ball with the cowherds. One time Shri Krishna hit
the ball so hard that it fell in the black river.[16] Shri Krishna
said to the cowherd, "Brother, the ball fell in the Kali river:
you stay here, I myself will go into the depths for the ball."
When he arrived in the river, *kālināga* was sleeping. His wife
was awake and the wife said to Shri Krishna, "Oh, boy, why did
you come here? Go away from here, if our snake wakes up he will
destroy you. Oh, boy, please go away. Your mother will cry and
cry if you are killed, because of this return to your home."
Hearing this much, Shri Krishna said, "Oh Snake Woman, wake your
snake, I have command over your snake." Upon hearing this, the
snake wife became angry and waking her sleeping husband said,
"You are happily sleeping, see who is standing on your head."
Seeing Shri Krishna, the snake became very angry and trying to
kill Shri Krishna, hissed enough to make his body turn black,
and showing all his heads, ran toward Shri Krishna to bite him.

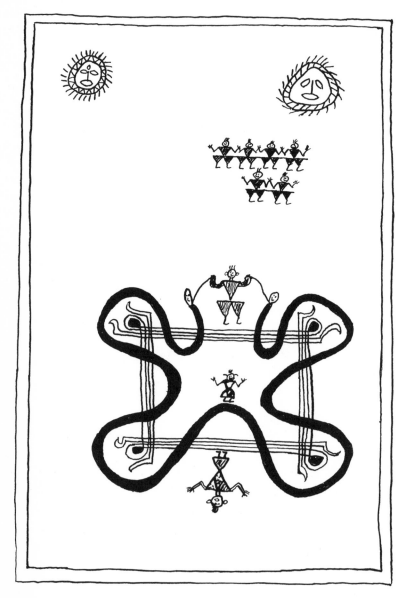

Fig. 10.   The design for *kanhaiyā āten*

Yet however many heads he showed Shri Krishna's feet increased
by the same amount. With his feet, Shri Krishna pressed on all
the heads and taking the snake in his hand, he tied him [liter-
ally, "bridled him"]. Then with her hands together, the snake's
wife said, "Oh king, let my snake go; do not kill him, oh let
him go." Then Shri Krishna answered, "I am not going to kill
your snake; I will take him to Gokul and will show him to the
companions and will feed him milk."

At this time, a cowherd ran to Nand and Jasoda and gave the
news that [Shri Krishna] had gone himself into the black river
after a ball and had still not come out. Hearing this, Jasoda
Mother and Nand Father and all the villagers were very troubled
and all ran and gathered at the river. When they did not find
Shri Krishna there, his mother and father began to cry and ask,
"Where did our dark son go?" Then one *gopī* told the mother, "Oh
mother, do not cry. When Shri Krishna went in, then the river
Jamuna stopped running. Krishna was in the form of *jurj* so why
do this [cry]?" Having said this Shri Krishna came out of the
Jamuna holding in his foot a halberd and on his head a crown and
in one hand a goad, and in one hand *kālināga*. Bringing him and
putting him before Jasoda and Nand Baba and the *gopīs*, he said,
"See, how I brought the king of the snakes. Everyone should do
darshan to this snake." Seeing the snake, everyone became very
happy and Shri Krishna said to everyone, "Go home; I will bring
the snake to Gokul and will show him to all of the companions
and will feed him milk." Seeing the king, the people were very
pleased and bringing milk and yogurt fed the snake and everyone
with folded hands said to Shri Krishna, "Oh son, let this snake
go. Don't cause much trouble." At the people's words, he let
the snake go back where he came from. Then Jasoda said to Shri
Krishna, "Oh son, the food is ready. Let's go and eat." The
play [*līlā*] is finished.

The ritual drawings and the fact that the snake drawn on
them is worshiped make it clear that snakes are closely connected
with Krishna in Karimpur. In an interesting shift from the *kālināga*
episode in the *Bhagavad Purāṇā*, *kālināga* is not banned from the Jamuna in the Karimpur version; rather, he is fed milk by the people
of Gokul, and Krishna is told not to cause him trouble. In both the
Bhagavad Purāṇā and the *Sukh Sāgar*, a Hindi-cum-*Braj*[17] version of the
Krishna story, *kālināga* is sent into seclusion. In Karimpur, he is
not; rather like other snakes, he is worshiped and respected (at least
for his malevolence). Nevertheless, *kālināga* has given his alle-

giance to Krishna and is repeatedly shown as subjugated by Krishna once each year in the ritual drawings.

The genealogical links for Vishnu and snakes can, then, be represented in this way:[19]

Vishnu
⟍(avatar)
Krishna
⟍(dancing on his head)
kālināga
⟍
snakes?

When the domain of power is narrowed, the deity's control of that one power becomes firmer. The deity with that limited control is the first appealed to. Only if there is no success with this spirit is the higher-level, more inclusive deity with wider powers appealed to. For example, when one has a real defined trouble, one does not call upon *bhagvān* himself--one appeals to an appropriate deity, a part of *bhagvān*, specifically concerned with that kind of trouble. Yet despite the intermediaries, *bhagvān* is always available for ultimate recourse, and any worship of his parts implies worship of him also. Therefore, one loses nothing by honoring the more approachable deities and probably gains within oneself, because they are more easily believed in.

Divine Control of Deities in Ritual

These various powers are regularly recognized in myth and a given deity's control, or possible control, of another is frequently acknowledged in ritual. One example of this phenomenon is when both Shiva's and Vishnu's genealogies are used in a ritual of snake possession which occurs in Karimpur during the rainy season (July-September) when snakes are prevalent. To see the use of one deity's powers against another's, let us examine this rite in some detail.

This ritual, called *Dank*, is performed either for snakebite--the snake, in biting his victim, possesses him--or for an oracle of the snake king (Basuk Dev). Both the snake (for the victim) and Basuk Dev (for the oracle) are considered dangerous, therefore mantras (magical ritual sayings) of various kinds are used by the exorcist, a ritual specialist, to control the possessing spirit.[20]

The first problem in *Dank* is to cause the possessing spirit to acknowledge his presence. This step is taken by appealing to the spirit in a series of songs called *kārikh* ("to pull"). The first *kārikh* sung are songs in praise of the snake king himself. Their aim is to make direct appeals to him, with the hope that he will come

and possess his oracle without further force. If these songs do not
entice him, that is, if possession of the oracle does not occur,
songs in praise of Zahir Pir, the god who controls snakes, are sung
(see the Shiva genealogy on page 138). These songs are repeated until possession does take place. There is no problem in obtaining
possession of the oracle. However, snakebite victims often remain
"unpossessed" in that the snake will not admit that it is possessing
its victim. If this situation develops, the oracle is called; he
becomes possessed by the snake king, Basuk Dev, and describes a cure
for his own underling, the snake who bit the victim.

Once Basuk Dev has come and possessed his oracle (in Karimpur
terminology, when he is riding on the oracle, who is thought of as a
horse), the exorcist must maintain control of this malevolent spirit
in the people's midst. He begins with a series of mantra termed
bāchā ("sayings"). These remind Basuk Dev that he is in the presence
of more powerful deities, in this case Vishnu/Krishna. Note the apparent confusion here--Basuk Dev is associated with *kālināga* (but
after all, they are both snakes!).

> *bāchā*: Oh God, as Bavan you deceived Bali;
> Becoming Krishna [you] destroyed Kans;
> Har Nar Kush was killed.[21]
> Being Ram, Ravan was ridden.
> The black [snake] was subjugated.
> Mathura was full of light.

The exorcist then checks to make sure that the king has heard his
words and that both the possessing spirit and his "horse" are happy.
In another set of ritual sayings, called *pūchonī* ("questioning"),
the exorcist says:

> *pūchonī*: Extending my hand, catching your arm.
> I'll repeat to you the words of the guru.[22]
> To you the guru's words, the warrior's[23] words, the
> strong words.
> If you hide your *jāt*, you will become a leper.
>
> King, who are you?

The oracle answers this question, "black" (i.e., *kālī*), returning us
to the question of what kind of separation is seen between *kālināga*
and Basuk Dev and their appropriate superiors. In the *pūchonī*,
"questioning," the snake is reminded of the superiority of Guru
Gorakhnath and Zahir Pir, as he was reminded of Zahir Pir in the
songs (*kārikh*) which began the rite.

The ritual goes on, with the snake king's being questioned
about various illnesses, thefts, etc., about which he can give advice. After he proclaims that he is tired, the exorcist recites
uThonī ("lifting") to make the oracle rise (and the snake king leave).
The "lifting" again uses the superior powers of another deity to
force the snake's obedience, in this case Hanuman:

> *uThonī*: A bangle of conch shells,
>   A garland of pearls.
>   Feet like a lotus,
>   Lanka was destroyed.
>   The ditch of Lanka was as wide as the sea.
>   Get up snake,
>   Hanuman the Great's decree.[24]

Since I know of no direct mythological connections between either
Ram or Hanuman and snakes, I must assume that the superiority indicated here is one of general power--that is, if they could cross the
ditch to Lanka, they can do anything, including the control of snakes.

  Dank sometimes concludes with the *uThonī*, but often the
snake king must be forced to leave with more powerful ritual sayings
called *khūn* ("blood," or, more likely, "murder"). *khūn* will be repeated until the possessing spirit has departed. There are a variety
of *khūn*, and their efficacy is dependent in part on the deities referred to in them. All of the *khūn* end with two lines:

> If life is in the edge of nails or cells of hair,
> Arise, awake, be conscious.

In about half the occurrences of *khūn*, these two lines are followed
by a third:

> Shri Guru Param Hans. Ram says.

Thus we again find deities considered more powerful than the snake
king called upon to make the latter recalcitrant, lesser, more malevolent spirit obey. Often the spirit invoked has popular mythological
links with the lesser deity. Thus the myths and rituals reinforce
one another, while continuously playing upon the theme of divine control of other divinities.

The Differentiation of Powerful Beings

Knowing the power relationships among the deities of Karimpur is fundamental to understanding the implications of table 9 as well as to
comprehending men's actions toward powerful beings of various sorts.
Intermediaries, "genealogically" related to their higher-level deity,
represent aspects of that deity--who should be able to maintain powers equal to or greater than those of the lesser being. The roles
of a given divine being do not exist in a vacuum but always in relation to those of other deities. Most important, these roles are related both by hierarchy and by exclusion or inclusion.

  The classes of powerful beings defined by their actions, as
outlined in table 9, can be further understood if we look at the part
which they play in clarifying the behavior of intermediaries. Using
the set of intermediaries for whom a Shiva "genealogy" was constructed earlier, we find the correlations between deities and classes
represented in table 11.

Table 11

Classes of Powerful Beings Correlated with the Shiva "Genealogy"

Shiva "Genealogy"	Deity Classes	Salvation	Shelter	Rescue
bhagvān	1	+	+	+
Shankar Bhagvan	2	+	+	+ (-)
Ganesh Santoshi Mata Guru Gorakhnath	3	0	+	+
Zahir Pir	4	0	0	+ (-)
Basuk Dev	5	0	0	- (+)
bhūt*	6	0	0	-

*Although not listed earlier, *bhūt*, ghosts, are often considered to be under Shiva's control.

In this genealogy, as in Vishnu's, we move from the least differentiated beings (with the broadest powers) in the first deity class to the most differentiated beings (the most marked beings with the most defined powers) in the last deity class. The more differentiated, more marked beings are most likely to be found acting in the world of men or to have derived mythologically from the world of men. Related to the amount of specification (differentiation) of deities is the idea of powers as embodied. *bhagvān*, only vaguely anthropomorphized, represents largely unembodied powers--and the least differentiated powers. At the opposite end of the deity classes are the *bhūts*, ghosts, and other beings of this sort (*churalin*, *jinn*). These beings can be understood as subtly embodied powers--they have no bodies; in fact, they are constantly seeking a body in which to reside (thereby possessing a living being). They are the spirits of the dead who have, because of their untimely deaths, lost their living bodies. As such, they search for an appropriate bodily substance in which to reside. Men can sometimes "see" ghosts as they loiter under trees or on village lanes. Men acknowledge that a ghost will take on various forms in order to entice human beings to approach so that the spirit can enter that person's body. After possessing a human being, such spirits must be provided with a new home, meeting with their approval, before they can be coerced to leave their victims' bodies. Spirits of this class only cause harm in the universe by "riding" on their victims--Karimpur terminology for possession by malevolent beings.[25]

The other deity classes all have "bodies" of various sorts, bodies which are actually visible to earthly beings--bodies which can be manifested (*lakshit ho gaya*). These "bodies" may be created by men in the form of images or may be men themselves. The fact that "bodies" must be created for these deities is particularly important--interaction with deities requires the exchange of substance, and substance cannot be exchanged with unembodied powerful beings. (Even the Vedic sacrifice requires a fire to carry the offerings of human beings, via the medium of *agni*, to the gods.) The fact that some divine beings are embodied (powers) and others are not (or less so) is a fundamental factor in ritual action in Karimpur. The implications of this reality are explored in the following chapter.

NOTES

1. This version is significantly condensed.

2. This version is condensed.

3. The idea that a husband can use the power his wife has accrued through her faithfulness is common in Karimpur and Hindu mythology. Being chaste is valued because of the benefits for one's husband.

4. In Hindu mythology, this city is generally named *prayāg*.

5. And because of the penances--literally "heating" or "powering"--he became very powerful. By distilling essences of the body through heat, power is obtained.

6. I assume that they were sent to tempt him and spoil the celibacy which was necessary to his *tapasyā*.

7. The abode of Shiva.

8. One's *karma* is not only used for defining one's position as a living being but also is incorporated into one's being.

9. For further uses of these terms and their relations to caste, see Marriott and Inden 1972.

10. *rakshā bandan* (Tying on Protection) is a festival celebrated in Karimpur on Savan 2:15 (July-August), when daughters are home visiting their parents. On this day, sisters tie *rakhīs* on the wrists of their brothers, and *kamīns* (clients) tie *rakhīs* on the wrists of their *jajmāns* (patrons), particularly Brahman priests on the wrists of their patrons.

11. Nowadays, wives do not bind *rakhīs* on their husbands but on their brothers (thus giving them some of their stored-up power?). However, the women do worship their husbands on another festival day, Pitcher Fourth (*karvā chauth*, Kartik 1:4).

12. The words themselves have power; they too are "beings." Yet the person using them also seems to change his embodied power when he obtains control of them. In Karimpur, one cannot merely learn the mantras for particular occasions; one must "ingest" them through special rituals--the exorcist for the snake possession ritual discussed later in this chapter and in Appendix II, after learning the mantras, had to go to the Ganges and say them while submerged in the river.

13. These genealogical links and the actual characters in them are regionally based. Zahir Pir, for example, exists only in northwestern Uttar Pradesh and the Punjab. In South India, Murugan, the son of Shiva, plays the roles of both Guru Gorakhnath and Zahir Pir. In Bengal, Manasha, the daughter of Shiva, has control of snakes, and the guru-warrior segment of Shiva's character appears to be absent.

14. Gugga is another name for Zahir Pir, the god who controls snakes.

15. Although this version is from an earlier time, I feel justified in using it here. The ritual with which I shall connect it was also partially described by the Wisers, and the ritual sayings concerning Krishna and *kālināga* are almost identical to those which I collected in the summer of 1968.

16. That is, the river of *kālināga*.

17. The author of *Sukh Sāgar* is not given. It is a common version, available in Mainpuri as well as Delhi. Couplets are in Braj, the Hindi dialect of the Mathura region; these are then elaborated in Standard Hindi.

18. I am grateful to Catherine T. Herbert for pointing out these distinctions (see Herbert 1973).

19. This ignores Vishnu's connections with Sesha (Ananta); evidence from the *Bhagavad Purāna* suggests that Vishnu is synonymous with Ananta (Herbert 1973).

20. See Appendix II for a full description of this ritual and the Hindi originals of the texts given below.

21. In the version of this mantra collected by the Wisers in 1925-30, the only variation occurs in this line, which reads, "Taking the form of Narsingh [you] killed Narina Kush."

22. A reference to Guru Gorakhnath, the disciple of Shiva.

23. A reference to Zahir Pir, the heir to Guru Gorakhnath.

24. In the version from the Wisers' collection, this line reads: "Get up snake, Shri Ram Chandra's decree." Other slight variations appear to be due to the methods of recording and transcription.

25. For further discussion of possession in Karimpur, see Wadley 1973.

Chapter VIII: SOME ASPECTS OF RITUAL ACTIVITY IN KARIMPUR

In the preceding pages, I have dealt primarily with the conceptions
that the Karimpur resident has of deities as powerful beings--that
is, with the kinds of powers which he/she believes deities of various
sorts to control; with how these varieties of gods, goddesses, spirits, etc., are categorized in native terminology; with how these deities are related to one another; and with how powerful beings obtain
their portions of the powers of the universe. This discussion has
not, however, been concerned with the Karimpur resident's conceptions
of how he/she should treat these varieties of gods, goddesses, spirits, etc. Not only do men have conceptions of what their gods can
do; men also have conceptions of how they should treat their gods.
The *kathā*, ritual myths, discussed in Chapter IV tell us two things:
the gods are worshiped because of their ability, through their mercy,
to give men boons; and men, through service to the gods and worship
of them, can receive these boons. We have looked at the boons which
the gods can give. Let us now examine the services which men can
offer. This chapter is concerned with how men perceive the correct
forms of interacting with their varieties of deities. The various
classes of deities are defined in large part by their powers, powers
which are embodied in their very nature. Thus the question which
must now be answered is, what men perceive to be proper interactions
with various classes of powerful beings.

Transactions with Powerful Beings

Before we examine men's behavior toward the varieties of gods, goddesses, and spirits in Karimpur, let me suggest another form of understanding power relationships--in this case, power relationships classified by their behavioral implications. As seen in the above analysis, the powers of the gods represent their capacities to act in
various ways, broadly defined as "salvation," "shelter," "rescue,"
and "not rescue." The six classes of powerful beings thus derived
are treated in different ways by men. Examination of the data on
religious observances in Karimpur allows us to infer that the various
kinds of transactions which men have with their gods vary along the

the following dimensions: the value of the transactions (auspicious or inauspicious); the regularity of these transactions; the medium of the transactions (raw food, cooked food, sweets, flowers, leftovers, etc.); the hierarchical relationships expressed in the transactions (does man give, receive, both, or neither); and finally, the agent with whom man is dealing (the deity himself or an intermediary). Let me explain each of these.

In transactions with his gods, man is aware of the value of interacting with them--do the gods represent auspiciousness or inauspiciousness? Those things which are auspicious (*shubh*) can be gods, days, moments, events, items, actions, etc. Those things which are inauspicious (*ashubh*) can likewise be gods, days, moments, events, items, actions, etc. In addition, auspicious (*shubh*) and inauspicious (*ashubh*) both carry a related concept which we must understand if we are to understand Hindu religious activity.

Auspiciousness is closely connected to merit, *punya*, that is, an auspicious moment is an occasion for obtaining merit. When an individual worships an "auspicious" deity or performs an "auspicious" act, he receives merit (*punya*). An auspicious day (*shubh din*) is a meritorious day (*punyāh*). A meritorious "sight" (*punya darshan*) is a "sight" which is auspicious (*jis kā darshan shubh ho*). Lastly, meritorious work (*punyak*) consists of *vrat*, religious performances, and acts of right conduct (*vrat, anushThān dharma kāry*).

The converse is also true. Occasions which are inauspicious are occasions when one cannot acquire merit--actions on these occasions are not merit-making. Those things which are auspicious are "good" (*achchhā*), whereas those which are inauspicious are "bad" (*burā*). Interestingly, bad times (*burā vakt*) are times of distress (*kashT kā samay*) or misfortune (*vipatkāl*). These "bad" times result from acting in bad ways (*burā karnā*, to do bad), that is, acting in ways which are improper (*anucit kām karnā*, to do improper actions) or detrimental (*hānikar kāry karnā*, to act in a detrimental way). Earlier (Chapter VI), when discussing the distinction between sorrow (*dukh*) and distress (*kashT*), I noted that distress (*kashT*) comes from an outside agent. This implication is repeated here--harmful actions (*burā kām*) lead to times of distress (*kashT kā samay*). But man himself has not acted improperly at "bad" times; rather, an outside agent has acted improperly, creating "distressful" times for man that are to man inauspicious times.

A well-known myth illustrates this point. In the second half of the myth of Thursday in which Indra angers Brihaspati, the following episode occurs:

After winning his battle against the demons, Indra performed a sacrifice. However, his priest, Vishvarupa, following the instructions of a demon, offered an oblation in the name of the demons (for his mother was a demon). The sacrifice did not help the gods and Indra became angry and chopped off Vishvarupa's three heads. Eventually with the help of Brihaspati, the sin of Brahman killing was atoned for by splitting it into four parts. One part went to the earth, hence the earth is uneven and not cultivable at all places. But Brahman also gave a boon that wherever a ditch appeared in the earth, it would be filled with water. . . . The third part went to women. Therefore women menstruate . . . but they received the boon of bearing children.

The reader should note that Indra, acting improperly (*hānikar kāry karnā*), has created inauspicious times for all women. Women themselves did not act improperly, but they receive the distress and inauspiciousness of an improper action.

Thus auspicious occasions require action following proper conduct and religious observances, and "inauspicious" occasions (to men) require dealing with a bad spirit who has acted or will act detrimentally. This malevolent spirit must somehow be dealt with in order to cure man's distress. One way one can transform an inauspicious time to an auspicious one is to approach good deities, using them as intermediaries to control the "bad" deity for man himself.

Another factor in man's transactions with his gods is his regularity of contact with them. Does he acknowledge their power regularly or irregularly? Briefly, men's more regular contacts are with their more powerful gods--those who can best aid them on their journey through existence. Men recognize malevolent beings primarily when they have intervened in men's lives, when they have caused distress.

The most important dimensions involved in man's transactions with powerful beings are the types of transactions which occur in his contacts with them. Transactions between men and powerful beings are closely related to the fact that deities represent embodied powers. Because deities are embodied powers, men must not deal with their gods just as "powers" but, rather, as embodied powers, that is, substance as well as power. The fact that power is not distinct from the total substance of a given being is particularly important when discussing transactions with the gods. Along with variation in powers, deities represent variation in substance. Men treat different substances (and therefore powers) in a variety of ways. Thus in order to comprehend men's behavior toward powerful beings, we must take

into account men's concern with transactions of various kinds of
"substance."

Many transactions in the Hindu world involve substance--re-
ceiving substance, giving substance, "exchanging" substance. Transactions of substance require awareness of the bodily substance of
the other being--awareness of the appropriateness of transactions
with him--returning us to our concern for powers as embodied. Recognizing that deities are embodied powers requires us to deal with
certain problems in discussing transactions between man and god.
First, is a given power embodied? Transactions cannot be made with
an unembodied power. Man cannot have interaction with *brahmān*, because *brahmān* is undifferentiated, unembodied power. Likewise the
subtly embodied *bhagvān* of Karimpur must be further differentiated
(and embodied) before transactions of substance can be made with him.

Karimpur transactions with deities are most explicitly stated
in the giving and/or receiving of substance. Because giving is valued over receiving, men must not only give to the gods (in services
and food) but also receive from them. The services which men give
(bathing the gods, removing their polluting bodily substances, providing food) are those which lesser beings give to higher beings.
Men generally give the gods foods which are honorific, i.e., meant
for higher beings or acceptable to higher-status beings.[1] Yet, although these foods are "honorific," men still remain the "givers."
The gods, having eaten their fill, rectify this situation by giving
men their leftovers--which men then consume. Leftovers, *jūThā*, are
a meaningful element in many South Asian contexts and represent the
greatest possible separation between individuals when exchanging
food. The leftovers of the gods, called *prasād*, include all offerings made to the gods and returned to the worshiper after the gods
have taken their share. The consumption of these leftovers reiterates the worshiper's lesser status.[2]

Because *prasād*,[3] as an important element in most rituals,
requires that the gods take their share and return the leftovers to
the worshiper, the god himself must have a "gross" body--not the
subtle body of *bhagvān*, who cannot be manifested in concrete form.
Because he does not have a "gross" body, *bhagvān* cannot return his
leftovers to men. Thus the asymmetrical reciprocity necessary between deity and devotee cannot be stated--man would remain the "giver,"
not the "receiver," and would have greater status. This anomaly, the
impossibility of transactions of substance with *bhagvān*, is resolved
by the use of intermediaries--intermediaries who can be concretely
manifested and who can in some sense convey the message of man's de-

votion and service to *bhagvān* and yet at the same time clearly illustrate their (the gods') superiority to man.

When we are dealing with embodied powers, we must consider
them in their totality. Power is not the only defining feature of a
"being"--he also has qualities, actions, and his own "code of conduct."
Thus features other than power may influence men's perceptions of the
proper transactions with the being. A given deity may, for example,
like meat; because that deity must be offered meat, certain groups
of men are prevented from partaking of that deity's leftovers. Thus,
after considering the "total" being with whom he is dealing, man must
decide whether or not he can receive substance from that being, what
kinds of substance he can take, and if he can take *prasād*. Generally,
men will take *prasād* from those deities whom they consider to be influential and who give men shelter (*prasād* = shelter = solidarity).[4]
Man must acknowledge, through the taking of *prasād*, his commitment
to and sharing of concerns with the more powerful being.

Sometimes men cannot receive substance from a powerful being,
cannot take its *prasād*. They have two options. First, the worshiper
and deity can exchange two different substances, often substances
not heavily loaded with hierarchical meaning, such as clothing,
sweets, perfumes, etc. Some evidence suggests that these "exchanges"
occur when the worshiper in some other contexts is the higher-status
being, so that the worship itself creates an anomalous situation.
Second, men can give to powerful beings without receiving substance
(particularly *prasād*) in return. Since men are the "givers," these
beings are marked in some senses as beings with lower status.[5]

The evil spirits constituting class 6 of powerful beings
present yet another problem. Like *bhagvān*, they lack gross bodies,
and therefore transactions of substance with them are impossible.
If and when these spirits find a body in which to reside, they can
be dealt with, usually with the help of an intermediary--a deity
whose power that spirit acknowledges.[6]

We must know the interrelations among these three factors to
understand the types of transactions which occur in Karimpur: the
"medium" of the transaction (leftovers, *pakka* or *kachcha* foods,
sweets, clothing, etc.); the direction of the transaction (does the
worshiper give, receive, or both); and the agent with whom the transaction occurs (the deity himself or an intermediary). Correlating
these factors plus value and regularity with the classes of powers,
we obtain the results given in table 12.

Examining the religious observances of Karimpur allows us to
penetrate further the relations among types of transactions and the

Table 12

Classes of Powers and Transactions Correlated

Classes of Powers		Transactions				
		Value	Time	Agent	Action of Deity	Medium
Salvation	1	*shubh*	regular	intermediary	give	*prasād*
Shelter	2	*shubh*	regular	self	give	*prasād*
.	3	*shubh*	regular	self	give	*prasād*
Rescue	4	*shubh*	irregular	self	exchange	"goods"
Not rescue	5	*ashubh*	irregular	self (intermediary)	receive give	food *prasād*
.	6	*ashubh*	irregular	intermediary	give	*prasād*

classes of powers. Before discussing these data, I wish to emphasize that perceptions of the powers of a given being are always egocentric: what is a god for individual A may not be for individual B. In the following pages, I give data on some of the religious observances of Karimpur, organized according to the classes of powers of the deities with whom transactions occur.

Transactions with Class 1 Powers

In Karimpur, the most common form of contact between humans and deities is the continually used "Oh Bhagvan" (*he bhagvān*), a call of both despair and hope, used with varying inflections according to whether one is in distress or happy. In situations of distress, it is an immediate, despairing cry for help from the most remote and impersonal yet most encompassing deity in the Karimpur world view. When used before a crisis situation hss been defined, "Oh Bhagvan" is a cry for aid to that ambiguous impersonal *bhagvān* and also a cry for aid to all the varying aspects of *bhagvān*, the marked *bhagvāns* discussed in Chapter VI. Above all, it is a recognition of the constant auspicious relationship present between man and god. The contextual use of "Oh Bhagvan" implies the continual, timely support of a good deity, one who guarantees to shelter his devotee. *bhagvān*, however, is not embodied; therefore there are no transactions of substance with him directly. Instead, men must use intermediaries when physically demonstrating their service to and recognition of the power of *bhagvān*.

Three daily observances in Karimpur serve as the primary intermediate steps in the recognition of *bhagvān*. All three deities
honored are physically manifest in some form (a prerequisite if transactions of substance are to occur). Each morning, part of the food
prepared for the household is presented to the house fire, which
then carries it to the gods in heaven--and thereby their enduring
support is gained. (Agni, the household fire, has been the messenger
between man and the gods since Vedic times.) When questioned about
this practice, the women responded, "We are giving to *bhagvān*," or
"We are giving to the *devatā*." Thus each morning, in making offerings to Agni, the women honor the gods in heaven, particularly
bhagvān. After the offering is made to the household fire, some of
the first food cooked in the house is presented to the cow, whose
feet are then touched. The cow is both a symbol in her own right
(of benevolent power) and a symbol of the ever present *bhagvān*, one
who should guard men at all costs. Moreover, all the food consumed
in the house that day is automatically the *prasād*, leftovers, of the
gods who have first taken their share.

Later, in the houses of the twice-born, the initiated men
perform their daily worship of the sun. First they recite the *gayatrī*
mantra;[7] then they make offerings of water to the sun, drinking the
remaining water (*prasād*); and then they use Mother Earth as an intermediary, touching her "feet" in respectful obedience.[8] In these
ways, men daily acknowledge the presence of their gods. *bhagvān*, as
a deity with class 1 powers, represents auspicious occasions; interaction with him is frequent, although through intermediaries. The
intermediaries for *bhagvān*, the class 2 deities of fire, cow, and
sun, also represent auspiciousness; interaction with them is regular
(daily), and man shares their substance in transactions of food--he
consumes their leftovers.

Transactions with Class 2 Powers

Other auspicious religious observances which occur regularly are the
many *vrat* performed in Karimpur. Men can perform appropriate *vrat*
for each day of the week (see Appendix III) or participate in annual
vrat, monthly *vrat*, or *vrat* for special vows. *vrat* are performed for
deities whom men wish to shelter them--whose special devotee they are.
vrat are most easily distinguished from the dominant ritual form,
pūjā, because they require fasting as well as *pūjā*. Fasting estab-
lishes man's extreme commitment to share substance with the god hon-
ored--only food left over from that deity's meal can be ingested by
the devotee on that day. *prasād*, the taking of leftovers, is a fun-

damental element in the transactions between man and god; in *vrat*,
prasād is accentuated because of the devotee's fasting. Men are acknowledging the deity's power and their desire for his shelter in the
most concrete manner possible.

In Karimpur, the most commonly observed weekly *vrat* are to
Santoshi Mata on Fridays, to Hanuman on Tuesdays and in special seasons, to Shiva on Mondays, and to Ishvar on Sundays. In a few families, *vrat* were observed for auspicious days of the month, especially
the full moon day and sometimes the bright eleventh. The annual *vrat*
are listed in table 13 and are discussed in the following pages.
vrat are generally performed for gods with class 2 powers, that is,
gods with wide-ranging powers--their influence is great and the types
of shelter and rescue asked of them are stated in general, broad
terms.

Table 13

Yearly Rituals Requiring *vrat*

Event	Date	Deity Honored	Theme
Goddess Worship (with a vow)	Chait 2:9	Devi	Family concerns, sons, wealth, health
Marriage Worship	Jeth 2:11	Banyan tree (Devi)	A long married life for women
The Third (sometimes)	Savan 2:3	Parvati	Brother's health
Shiva fasts	Mondays in Savan	Shiva	Shelter and health of family
Krishna's Eighth	Bhadon 1:8	Krishna	General shelter
Lakshmi Worship	Kuar 1:8	Lakshmi "elephant"	Wealth, "fruits"
Pitcher Fourth	Kartik 1:4	Husbands	Husbands' shelter
Kartik *pūranamāshī*	Kartik 2:15	Vishnu, Ram *tulsī*	General shelter of Vishnu
Shiva's Thirteenth	Phagun 1:13	Shiva	General shelter of Shiva

Goddess Worship

Goddess Worship on Chait *sudī* 9 is variously known as *devin kī pūjā*
or *naumī* (The Ninth). This festival is one of the most important of
the year, primarily because it coincides with the district fair and
involves worship at the Devi temple adjoining the fair's site on the
outskirts of Mainpuri, eight miles away. The fair itself lasts for
two weeks and everyone who can afford the time and has any extra pice
attends at least once. The women usually are taken on the ninth of
Chait for their worship of Devi.

Women and children are loaded into bullock carts with at
least one adult male in attendance as chaperon. They while away the
slow ride to town by singing *bhajan* and *kīrtan* (songs in praise of
the gods) and *chhand* (the special songs to honor Devi). When they
arrive at the temple-cum-fair, their first order of business is *devin
kī pūjā*, the worship of the goddesses. Each woman has brought along
purī (wheat cakes fried in *ghī*, clarified butter) and buys sweets and
flowers from the vendors surrounding the temple to add to her offerings to the goddesses. Many women fast until after they have done
their *pūjā*. Those who are offering a special vow to the goddess always fast. (Vows may be offered to provide for the health of a child
or husband, to have a son, to have a good harvest, etc. Included in
the vow is a commitment to have a special *pūjā* for the goddess if
the boon desired is granted.) Note that the goddesses' powers are
wide-ranging (that their *prabhāv*, influence, is great) and they are
appropriate personages from whom to demand shelter. They are embodied, physically manifest (*lakshit ho gayā*), in the Mainpuri temple.
After making their offerings to the goddesses, the women share the
prasād, given them by the temple priest, with their menfolk and children.

Marriage Worship

This ritual is performed on Jeth *badī* 11 and is known in Karimpur as
barok kī pūjā. *barok* means "the gifts given to the groom's family
by the bride's relations at the time of marriage" and has here been
transposed to the name of a ritual in honor of and concerned with
marriage. Married women fast on this day and do *pūjā* to the *bargad*
tree (banyan) in order to obtain a long married life, including the
continued health of their husbands, and many sons.[9] This theme seems
limited until one recognizes the importance of marriage for the women
of Karimpur. Among other things, marriage is a prerequisite for salvation for Hindu women and the honor of one's husband is enjoined as
part of the code of conduct for all women (in this ritual, the women's

concern is with the possibility of performing this honor--without a husband, a woman cannot be faithful). The shelter of the goddess, physically manifest as the banyan tree, is necessary for one's husband's welfare.

The Third

On The Third (*tīj*, Savan *sudī* 3), the women make tiny clay figures of *gauri* or sometimes *gaur-gauri* (that is, Shiva and Parvati). These figures are dressed in "new" clothes (a piece of unused cloth) and *pūjā* is done to them for the purpose of one's brother's having long life and health (and sometimes one's husband's as well).[10] (See figure 11.) Some women fast until after their *pūjā*. At the conclusion of the *pūjā*, they eat the goddess's leftovers, usually on this day *purī*, *dahī* (yogurt), and *simāī* (a milky sweet dish). To the women of Karimpur, a brother's health is important (though less so than a husband's). If things go wrong with a woman's husband's family, her brother is her only protection and refuge. Thus the rewards of a brother's health are a refuge from one's in-laws, a desirable alternative for most Karimpur women.

Shiva Fasts

Throughout the entire month of Savan, many women (and some men) will have a weekly *vrat* to Shiva asking for his shelter and protection against the dangers of the rainy season in progress and during months to come.

Krishna's Eighth

One of the most popular *vrat* in Karimpur is Krishna's Eighth, honoring the birth of the destroyer of Kans and the beloved boy and lover of North India. Krishna's Eighth (*kanhaiyā āten*, more widely known as Birth Eighth, *jamamāshtamī*) occurs on Bhadon *badī* 8. Both men and women consider this a day of *vrat* (one of the two *vrat* days widely recognized by men in Karimpur). They fast until the moon rises, then do *pūjā* to Krishna and break their fast by eating the offerings to Krishna. The *vrat* for Krishna is for general good fortune and aid, not for specific kinds of future aid. After breaking their fast, both men and women (in segregated groups) will gather for songfests lasting far into the night. They sing *bhajan* and *kīrtan* and other songs honoring Krishna and various other deities.

The women in joint family household clusters will often join together for their worship and songfest. Generally the lower-caste women will do their *pūjā* to a design drawn by the women on an inner

Fig. 11. Monsoon rituals:
(a) The Third (b) Elephant Worship

wall of the house. These designs, unlike most ritual drawings in Karimpur, are in vibrant primary colors and are dominated by the black snake on which the boy Krishna danced (see Chapter VII). The upper-caste women and most of the men will do their Krishna *pūjā* either to a picture or at the Krishna altar specially constructed for this purpose at one of the Scribe houses. The birth of Krishna is a very auspicious occasion and is greeted each year with much joy and extreme devotion.

Lakshmi Worship

Lakshmi Worship (*mahālakshmī kī pūjā*, or Elephant Worship, *hāthī kī pūjā*) is not a popular *vrat* and is performed only by the women of one Brahman lineage on Kuar *badī* 8. Again a *vrat* is required, the shelter asked of the deity is broadly defined, and the deities worshiped (Lakshmi and the Elephant) are physically manifested in figures and drawings (see figure 11). The women fast until after the *pūjā* in the late afternoon, at which time the *kathā* is recited. Supposedly this day is the culmination of a sixteen-day observance beginning on Bhadon *sudī* 8, although most of the women involved honored only this day. Nevertheless, everything is done in sixteens-- sixteen *purī* (*ghī*-fried breads) and sixteen *kachorī* (lentil cakes) are offered, sixteen flowers, sixteen lampwicks, sixteen bundles of grass with sixteen pieces in each bundle, sixteen grains of rice, etc. Before the *pūjā*, the women make a largish clay figure of an elephant. At the time of the *pūjā*, a rectangle is cleaned on the floor (with cow dung) and a stylized figure of a woman is drawn on it with *ghī*. A wooden seat is placed over the figure, and the elephant is put on this seat. After these preparations have been completed, the *pūjā* proceeds with the sixteen offerings of everything. The women say that, from the *pūjā* and *vrat*, they obtain wealth and "fruits."

Pitcher Fourth

A major day for married women's *vrat* is Pitcher Fourth, *karvā chauth*, on Kartik *badī* 4. Most of the women fast without food, fruit, or water from sunrise--unlike many fasts where fruit or water are allowed. The fast is not broken until after the moon has risen and the moon and husband have been worshiped.

Pitcher Fourth is a *pūjā* to and for one's husband and only married women participate. The *karvā* is a small clay pitcher filled with *purīs* and/or sweets that is presented to the woman's husband after she has done her *pūjā*.[11] In many households, the women make

an elaborate ritual drawing on a freshly cow-dunged wall with flour
and water. Large figures representing the husband dominate the drawing; other common features are the sun and the moon, the Washerman's
wife (who must bring the clean clothes for the *pūjā*), the Potter's
wife (who must bring the *karvā*), and a girl on a ladder looking for
the moon. (See figure 12.) The *pūjā* cannot begin until the moon
has been sighted, so a daughter of the house is often sent to the
roof as lookout (thus the girl on the ladder in the drawing). In a
few households, the women do their *pūjā* directly to their husbands,
thereby eliminating the necessity of a drawing. After worshiping the
drawings (or their husbands), the women honor the moon and then break
their fast. During both the *pūjā* to their husbands inside and honoring the moon outside, they use *sīnk*, straws of a special grass--first
offering them to the husband, and second throwing them in four directions after honoring the moon with water. I was never clear about
the meaning of the straws, but they are saved and reappear in another
ritual (Cow-Dung Wealth) twelve days later. The food eaten on this
night is that of the marriage feast when the bride first comes to her
hssband's home. This meal, curry and rise (*besan-bhāt*), represents
the reiteration of the marriage tie already acknowledged in the *pūjā*
itself.[12] This *vrat* emphasizes the necessity of a woman's husband's
continuing shelter and treats the husband as a powerful being--which
indeed he is for his wife.

Kartik *pūranāmashī*

On this day, the full moon day of Kartik, Vishnu is worshiped in the
guise of the *tulsī* tree. Again, women are the primary participants:
they fast and do *pūjā* to the *tulsī* trees in their courtyards, con-
cluding with the distribution of *prasād* to their families. No specific kind of shelter is requested in this *pūjā* and *vrat*.

Shiva's Thirteenth

This *vrat* in honor of Shiva occurs on Phagun *badī* 13 and is known in
Karimpur as *shiv teras*. Marking the marriage of Shiva and Parvati,
Shiva's Thirteenth is a major fast day for the women and some men of
Karimpur. Shiva, usually called Mahadeo (the Great God) is worshiped
at various shrines around the village and, after the opening of the
village Shiva temple in 1968, at the temple itself. Shiva's general
shelter is sought in this *vrat*.

Fig. 12. Obtaining protection:
(a) Drawing for Pitcher Fourth
(b) Tying *rakhī* on wheat seedlings

Summary

In all of the *vrat* discussed above, situations of danger, distress, or sorrow are not clearly defined. Instead, the deity's shelter is requested and man's tie to the deity is reaffirmed each year. Interestingly, men are participants in only two of these *vrat*, Krishna's Eighth and Shiva's Thirteenth. These are the two *vrat* with the broadest implications--the concerns involved are very general, as Shiva and Krishna are worshiped on these days for general welfare, to show devotion, and to obtain their shelter. The women in their other *vrat* are always seeking continuing shelter, but the type of shelter (or rescue) is somewhat more specifically defined and revolves around the welfare of their families. The gods honored in these *vrat* are those with whom man has an auspicious, regular relationship. They are felt to be influential gods--that is, their influence (*prabhāv*), based on their powers (*shakti*), is great. Recognition of them involves transactions of substance, and these transactions are made more meaningful by the fast which precedes them. Men confirm their continuing devotion to the gods by eating only the foods of the gods recognized that day. Man not only provides services for the gods by doing *pūjā* to them, by treating them as honored guests in his home; he also marks his devotion (*bhakti*) by eating their leftovers, by ingesting part of their "substance" as transmuted through food and signaling their superiority and their "greater" substance. In addition to those who actually fast and perform the rituals on these days, others receive benefits also. The *prasād* of the gods is consumed by the devotee and is shared with the family and community: everyone can and should benefit from the devotee's transactions with a deity.[13]

Transactions with Class 3 Powers

Another set of religious observances that occur regularly are auspicious occasions which do not involve *vrat*. This set of yearly rituals require *pūjā* and the taking of *prasād*; however, the extreme affirmation of "oneness" with the god found in *vrat* is missing. This set of rituals is given and explained in table 14. Note that, again, the deities honored are always physically manifested in some form before *pūjā* can occur. These deities, however, have less influence than those worshiped with *vrat*--many of them can be categorized as deities with class 3 powers, those who can give men shelter, can rescue him, but their *prabhāv* (influence) is less than that of those deities with class 2 powers. The types of shelter which they can give are most limited--moreover, they cannot give men salvation but can only aid him on his journey through life.

Table 14

Yearly Rituals with *pūjā*

Event	Date	Deity Honored	Theme
Grain Third	Baisakh 2:3	Crops Vishnu	Harvest in the coming months, shelter of Vishnu
Jeth *kā* Dassehra	Jeth 2:10	Ganges	Removal of sins
Asarhi	Asarh 2:15	Devi, guru	Shelter of goddess and guru
The Pot	Asarh	Devi	Protect village from illness
Tying on Protection	Savan 2:15	Wheat Saluno	Shelter for the crops; shelter of Saluno
Eternal Fourteenth	Bhadon 2:14	Hanuman, *ant*	Protection
Ancestor Worship	Kuar 1:1-1:15	Ancestors	Honor of ancestors
Simara-Simariya	Kuar 2:1-2:9	Devi	Good marriages for young girls?
Nau Durga	Kuar 2:1-2:9	Devi	Shelter of the goddess
Divali	Kartik 1:15	Lakshmi	Wealth
Siyao Mata	Kartik 2:1	Siyao Mata	Protection for children (lampblack)
Cow-Dung Wealth	Kartik 2:1	Krishna "mountain"	Shelter for one's family and cattle
Awakening of the Gods	Kartik 2:11	Vishnu, crops	Welcome gods back, worship of harvest
Winter Solstice	. . . .	Sun, moon	Shelter of the sun
Holi	Phagun 2:15	Holika Favorite gods Brahmans	Evil; death Shelter Shelter
Goddess Worship	Chait 1:8	Devi	Shelter in hot and rainy seasons

Grain Third

Grain Third (*akhtīj*) on Baisakh *sudī* 3 is a day in honor of the beginning of the present world age and also Parashuram, the sixth of
the ten avatars of Vishnu. The *tulsī* tree, symbolizing Vishnu, is
sometimes worshiped on this day. But it is more important that Grain
Third marks the new agricultural season and plowing for the next
crops can begin. On this day, clay cups of parched grain are presented to the children and selected *kamīns* (hereditary workers), symbolizing perhaps the parents' and *jajmāns*' (patrons') shelter of less
powerful beings through the medium of the forthcoming crop.

Jeth *kā* Dassehra

During Jeth (May-June), some people go to bathe in the Ganges on
jeth kā dassehra (Jeth *sudī* 10), a day which is particularly auspicious to the *ganga*, itself an embodied deity. The *ganga* gives its
shelter and rescue by removing men's sins, thereby alleviating their
sorrows. Those who bathe in the Ganges return to Karimpur with
prasād in the form of *ganga jal*, water of the Ganges, sweets bought
at the bathing site, and *purīs* taken from home and brought back.
Again, some humans act as intermediaries for others; if a man cannot
go to the Ganges himself, he at least obtains some benefits through
the *prasād* brought by those who did.

Asarhi

Asarhi, also known as *pūrinmānshī*, the full moon day of Asarh (June-
July), is the day for *pūjā* to Devi and also to a person's guru. The
women worship Devi, either at the village Devi shrine (a pile of
stones under a *pīpul* tree near the roadside) or at the Devi temple
near Mainpuri. This worship of Devi is primarily for her shelter
and rescue during the dangerous rainy season in progress. Those people who have gurus will honor them in person whenever possible, and
on *asarhi* the ashram at the far side of Mainpuri is filled with villagers who have come for their yearly *darshan*, "sight," of their
gurus.

The Pot

At the end of Asarh, another ritual is scheduled to occur but seldom
does. This is The Pot (*khappar*), a goddess-oriented cycle of rites
performed by the men to rid the village of illness. I suspect that
its occurrence is dependent upon the presence of the monsoon--if the
rains have begun, it will be performed in Asarh; if they have not
begun, it is put off until Bhadon. Because The Pot requires Devi worship, it cannot be performed during the month of Savan when the goddesses, like all good daughters, have returned to their fathers'
(or brothers') homes for Savan and are not believed to be present in
their village shrines. Devi is manifested in three ways on this
occasion. Initially, *pūjā* and *havan* are done at the *pīpul* tree representing Devi. Later, Devi possesses her oracles (*bhagats*) and is
thus manifested. Finally, one man is dressed as Devi (Kali) and goes
through the village collecting illness in the pot (*khappar*) which he
carries. This pot is finally deposited across the village boundary
on the land of an adjoining village, at which time a pig is killed
for the goddess. *prasād* (puffed sugars and *purīs*) is distributed

after the *pūjā* and the *prasād* of the pig is consumed by the Sweepers, but no one else.

Tying on Protection

Tying on Protection (*rakshā bandan*) takes place on Savan *sudī* 15 and comprises three separate observances performed on one day, united by the common theme of "tying on protection," that is, the tying of *rakhī* (protection), brightly colored threads or tinsel ornaments, on a powerful being from whom the worshiper desires protection or rescue. Two of these observances involve *pūjā* with *prasād*; one does not and will be considered later.

The first observance actually begins on Snake's Fifth (Savan *sudī* 5) ten days earlier, when broken clay pots are filled with dirt in which wheat seeds are planted. The wheat is allowed to grow for ten days and the quality of the "crop" is believed to represent the quality of that household's next wheat harvest. After ten days, on *rakshā bandan*, these pots of wheat, called *bhujaTiyan*, are worshiped and *rakhī* are tied on to the seedlings, with the obvious implication of "tying on protection." In this instance, the protection is that of a food supply (see figure 12).

A second observance is the worship of Saluno (Silano or Sona), to whom *pūjā* is done and *rakhī* are tied. Using a mixture of flour and water, the women of the household draw Saluno on a wall or doorframe (figure 13). Explanations of his powers and character are sparse, but he is considered a good god who gives protection and shelter. *prasād* is distributed in the household after these two rites are concluded.

Eternal Fourteenth

This rite, *anant chaudas*, on Bhadon *sudī* 14, requires no *vrat* and only a minor *pūjā*. On this day, *ant* (end or endless?), string armlets procured from the bazaar are tied on one's upper arm for protection. Each *ant*, armlet, is composed of fourteen strings and fourteen knots. These are put on the right arms of men and the left of women. Before the *ant* are tied on by the eldest woman of the household, she does *pūjā* to them and to Hanuman,[14] after which *prasād* (puffed sugar) is distributed to members of the family.

Ancestor Worship

The first fortnight of Kuar (September-October) is that of *kanāgat*, Ancestor Worship (also called *shraddha*). Ideally, remembrances are made to the ancestors daily, although in fact only those days when a

Fig. 13. Ritual designs: (a) Saluno
(b) Figures for the marriage of
Simara-Simariya

recent ancestor has died (dated by the day of the fortnight on which
he died) are usually recognized. Generally, a small rectangle is
freshly cow-dunged and five lines are drawn on it with flour. Flowers
are then sprinkled on it. Many families will feed Brahmans on the
last day of *kanāgat* in honor of their ancestors (who are functioning
here as intermediaries). It is hoped that the ancestors will protect
the family in the following months.

Simara-Simariya

Starting on Kuar *sudī* 1, the girls' play (*khel*) begins. This play
is variously known as *neothar* (Nine Days), *simara-simariya*, or *niyarta-
niynetar*. A large figure of a woman called *neutariya*, the Ninth One,
is made on the wall of the house, and below her are two clay figures,
Simara and Simari (Simariya). Before dawn, the girls from various
houses or joint family clusters gather together to "play" with and
worship the goddess with songs and games. In addition, each day the
girls make tiny clay figures called *gauri* (Parvati) and do *pūjā* to
them, using flowers as offerings. All the *gauri* are kept, and on the
last (ninth) day they are immersed in a pond along with the other
images.[15] On the last day (Kuar *sudī* 9), smaller representative
images of Simara and Simariya are "married" to each other, with accompanying songs, fireworks, and hoopla. For the marriage itself, the
girls make tiny clay dishes to be offered to the groom figure--as is
proper in a "real" marriage--palanquins for the bride and groom to
ride in, and processional figures. In one compound, a three-foot
male figure with a real torch was made by the young boys to lead the
marriage procession (figure 13). The Barber's wife visits the leading families of the village to help the girls properly perform the
marriage of Simara and Simariya.

Nau Durga

During the same nine days that the girls are "playing," their mothers
are honoring the goddess Durga, although most of them will only worship her once on the ninth day, at either the village Devi shrine or
the Mainpuri temple. The women do *pūjā* and distribute *prasād* to
their families.

Divali

The days surrounding Kartik *amavas* (Divali) are happy, joyful days.
The fall harvest of corn and cotton is in and Divali, the Festival
of Lights, and its accompanying rituals are here. Houses damaged by
the monsoon rains are repaired, new clothes are bought for everyone,

sweets and special foods are prepared, and the excitement slowly
builds up. Divali is in part a harvest festival and in part a New
Year festival (and by some Hindu calendars still is considered the
New Year) and has become one of the major festivals in all of India.
In Karimpur, it is also a time for recognizing one's complete circle
of *jajmān-kamīn* ties, the hereditary patron-client relationships more
widely known as the *jajmānī* system. As noted in Chapter II, many
kamīns no longer fulfill their worker functions in Karimpur, yet for
Divali all the old or almost nonexistent ties are remembered and acted upon. The Cotton Carder comes to each house with his small bundle
of cotton for wicks for the lamps for which Divali is named. In return, he receives a small payment of grain offered on the winnowing
basket (*sūp*), the ever present symbol of household prosperity and
togetherness. The Potter brings both new pots for the year and the
clay lamps for Divali itself. The Tailors are busy making the new
clothes which are as much a part of Divali as the lamps. The Barber's
wife is going from house to house to help the women decorate their
feet with henna or a bright red dye bought in the village store. On
the night of *chotī divālī*, the day preceding Divali, one lamp made
of flour and water is lighted in each household. This day is extremely inauspicious, and all members of the household are put to bed with
lampblack (*khajal*) on their eyes and oil (*tel*) in their ears as pre-
ventive measures against the evil spirits out that night.

During the day of Divali itself, the women cook the last special foods. Many of them are distributed to their *kamīns*, who come
by the house at some time for their handouts (including some *kamīns*,
like the Oil Presser, who no longer have a true *kamīn* function, but
who still in some sense "belong" to their *jajmān*'s household).[16]
These gifts of food from the *jajmān* are comparable to the *prasād* of
the gods: the *jajmān* provides shelter (and food); the *kamīn* provides
service and "devotion." The wicks for the lamps to be used at night
must be made. Everyone must bathe and dress in his or her finery.
The children must collect their fireworks from the village shops.

Some of the women will do *pūjā* to their favorite deities during the day, but this day is also one when the men act for the household. The main *pūjā* is done by the head of the household at the time
of the lamp-lighting. After dark, the head of each household worships Lakshmi and other favorite gods. Then the mother passes out
prasād to the family members. Then the lamps used in Lakshmi *pūjā*
are used to light the many clay lamps which are carried off on a
winnowing basket to be placed in windows, along rooftops, and around
cattle compounds until the whole village is aglow with tiny flicker-

Fig. 14. Divali: (a) Lighting the lamps (b) *pūjā* to a brother

ing lights. The children joyously do their part by using up their
precious supplies of fireworks. After the lamps have burned themselves out and the popping of firecrackers ends, sleep descends, only
to be broken in the middle of the night as each mother wanders through
her home brandishing her winnowing basket to chase away poverty, illness, and evil spirits.

The reasons given for *pūjā* at Divali are the wealth of a person's family and the removal of illness from the household. The goddess's shelter is asked, but for limited reasons.

Siyao Mata

This early-morning ritual is performed on Kartik *sudī* 1, jointly by
all the women in an extended family group (all women related three
to four generations back, generally in groups for about five or six
households, or ten to twelve women). The women do *pūjā* to Siyao
Mata, a goddess concerned with the welfare of their children. While
the women sit together singing *bhajan* and *kīrtan*, they make a figure
of a cow out of cow dung. *pūjā* is done to this cow and lampblack is
prepared as a particularly auspicious protection for one's children
in the coming year.[17]

Cow-Dung Wealth

Cow-Dung Wealth (*gobardhan* on Kartik *sudī* 1) involves a *pūjā* to
Krishna and the mountain Gobardhan (see Chapter VII). No fasting
takes place on this day, but *prasād* is distributed after the *pūjā*.

Awakening of the Gods

On Kartik *sudī* 11, the gods are awakened from their four-month sleep,
after which marriages can again take place. The women draw complex
designs on their courtyard floors and make a path leading to the door
of the house. In the center of the design, two figures are drawn
and then covered with a brass tray. Around them are drawn many agricultural implements and other valued objects (cots, weights, pots,
a woman's toe rings which symbolize marriage, shoes, etc.). Before
the *pūjā*, the men bring in sugarcane stalks and handfuls of a nutlike
fruit (*singhare*), just harvested from the village ponds. The women
then do *pūjā* to the figures under the tray, "awakening" them by lifting the tray. The sugarcane and nuts are also worshiped and then
distributed as *prasād*.

Winter Solstice

This day, *makar sankrānti*, welcomes back the sun after its long decline. It is a relatively minor rite, involving *pūjā* to the sun and moon.

Holi

Phagun, the month preceding Holi, is a time of preparation and enjoyment. Holi concludes the month's festivities. While Holi is perhaps not the most important festival of the year in the influence of the gods worshiped, it certainly provides the most gaiety. The full moon day of Phagun is Holi itself, and the following day, Chait *badī* 1, is known as *rangdhul*, "Color Cleaning."

Seven days before the full moon, the women of each household begin their preparations for their courtyard Holi fires. Each evening a small square is cow-dunged and a figure representing Holika, the evil aunt of Prahlad, is drawn on it. It is Holika who is eventually burned in the bonfires while Prahlad, because of his devotion to *bhagvān*, is saved from the fire. Meanwhile the men's bonfire preparations[18] are also proceeding, as the three village bonfires increase in size each day.[19]

Like Divali, Holi is a time of cleaning and repairing and of buying new clothes. For several days, it seems as if mud is everywhere, as houses are repaired, courtyards replastered, and walls rebuilt. Special foods must be cooked and clothes bought--keeping everyone busy and the excitement growing. Early in the month, *phāg*, the songs of Holi, begin to be heard throughout the village, although the Brahman men and women generally do not participate in singing them, since these songs are "beneath" them. Several troupes of Farmers and Water Carrier men are noted for their singing, as are some of their women, who are often called to Brahman houses to entertain the secluded Brahman women during this period. The play of Krishna dominates the themes of *phāg*, with the color-throwing aspect of Holi often mentioned. Krishna, in fact, becomes the color thrower par excellence in these songs.

Finally, the evening before Holi itself arrives and everyone remains awake to see the bonfires lighted by a "low-caste Brahman" (*bhadri*) from a nearby village. As the fire lighter has several villages to visit that night, no one knows exactly when he will come. Meanwhile, the women have prepared their small courtyard bonfires, which must be lighted the next morning with embers from the main fires. The men's fires are eventually lighted, with little fanfare, and everyone sleeps in preparation for the following day. In the morning, the women gather around their fires with their bundles of green barley, brought by the men from the fields. Singing *bhajans*, they roast the heads of their new barley crop. Later the men gather around their respective bonfires and, circling them, loudly shout "long live Holika Mother" (*jai holika mātā*). They, too, toss barley into the fire and roast the new crop. At the conclusion of their circling, some dust and mud are thrown, but the tone of the day remains rather somber. At some time during the day, *pūjā* is performed to some deity and *prasād* is distributed in most houses, by either the men or the women.

Returning home from the bonfires, everyone bathes (including all the cattle, which are driven to the village ponds) and dons clean, preferably new, clothes for the second event of the day, the Holi greeting (*holī milānā*). Large mats are spread before the doors of the major houses of the village and *pān* is prepared for the expected visitors. Suddenly the village is filled with long lines of men going from house to house to greet the inhabitants, some men even going inside to greet the women, particularly their village sisters. The "big men" (mostly Brahman) remain at their doors until the main influx of guests has come and gone before they proceed on their own visits. Each man of the village is expected to visit every house in the village--including or excluding the untouchables' homes, depending on his own feelings.[20] Furthermore, some of the leading Brahman families have a tradition of feeding the men of particular castes on this day, one caste to each family, so for a while their courtyards are filled with lines of feasting men. In addition, Holi is a day when *kamīns* can expect food from their *jajmāns*, so their house is deluged with women and children seeking their share of the day's goodies. The feasting of the men from lower castes and the giving of food to one's *kamīns*, both acts of influential *jajmāns*, reiterate yet again the *kamīns*' claim to the shelter of his *jajmāns*, a claim which is characterized by these gifts of food on auspicious occasions. This theme is found in one other aspect of Holi, the Holi greeting itself.

One aspect of the Holi greeting is worth special notice. Most of the non-Brahman men greet the Brahman men of whatever age with a hug and also by touching their feet. Normally a person only touches the feet of higher, more powerful beings and, in the everyday routines of Karimpur, the men would not touch the feet of younger Brahman males. On Holi they do. On this one annual occasion, caste, or rather "Brahman," dominates age, and the fact that Brahmans are powerful beings deserving of the kinds of honor due the gods is clearly recognized.[21]

The second day of Holi, *rangdhul*, Color Cleaning, manifests the older aspects of Holi, although these do not reach the level of upheaval noted elsewhere in India (see especially Marriott 1966).

Considered in terms of interaction with powerful beings, Holi represents the destruction of malevolent beings by more powerful ones, man's recognition of some deities normally residing in heaven, and man's recognition of those powerful beings (in this case, Brahmans) who reside on earth.

Goddess Worship

Another ritual to the goddesses occurs on Chait *badī* 8. Some of the women travel to the Mainpuri temple to do *pūjā* to the goddess there, to obtain her protection during the hot and rainy seasons just ahead.

Summary

The rituals discussed so far have been concerned with powerful beings of classes 1 through 3 and the corresponding principles of religious categorization. These deities can provide shelter to lesser beings who show them devotion and can rescue lesser beings from the distress caused by malevolent spirits. There are regular transactions with these gods and the transactions always involve the sharing of substance, either through an intermediary or through *prasād* from the god himself.

Transactions with Class 4 Powers

It is not always desirable to partake of the substance of other beings, even those who have recognized powers. For dealing with auspicious beings with whom an individual does not desire to share substance, man has several options. One of these is a form of mutual exchange, enacted with those beings who are auspicious but who can only rescue man, not provide him with shelter. Their influence is less than that of the deities of classes 1 through 3, and more limited kinds of aid are demanded of them. Transactions with them are correspondingly less regular.

There are only a few yearly rituals with this characterization, as table 15 shows.

Tying on Protection

In contrast to the two other rites performed on this day, the "tying of protection" on brothers by sisters and on *jajmāns* by Brahmans does not involve the taking of *prasād*. Instead, the brother gives his sister money or clothes and the *jajmāns* of the Brahman priests or Bards give them uncooked food or clothing.

Table 15

Yearly Rituals of Mutual Exchange

Event	Date	Deity Honored	Theme
Tying on Protection	Savan 2:15	Brothers	Brother's aid
Brothers' Second	Kartik 2:2	Brothers	Brother's aid
Spring Fifth	Magh 2:5	*jajmān*	?

Brothers' Second

Taking place on Kartik *sudī* 2, Brothers' Second (*bhaiyā dūj*) is a popular rite. Sisters do *pūjā* to their brothers and male cousins (on their father's side), either directly to their brothers (figure 16) if they are in their natal homes or to designs symbolizing the brothers drawn on the courtyard floor if they are in their husbands' villages. The brothers acknowledge their sisters' *pūjā* by presenting them with small gifts. In one household, the women also made a figure out of cow dung that they claimed was the brother's enemy. Crowning this figure with thorns, they took it to the door of their house, placed it on the ground, and destroyed it with a thrust of a rice pestle, thus demolishing their brother's enemy for the year. Then the day was over. Brothers and sisters again enact a mutual exchange, with the sister's asking for the brother's protection--but protection in the sense of rescue, since it is not his long-term responsibility to provide her with shelter. *prasād* cannot be taken from a girl's brothers, as it can from more powerful beings (including husbands).[22]

Spring Fifth

Spring Fifth (*basant panchmī*) is a minor rite on Magh *sudī* 5. Marking the approach of spring and the beginning of the preparations for Holi, it also emphasizes the present fertility of the fields. Those who feel like it wear yellow, a color found at this season in the mustard flowers rampant in the fields. Some Brahmans present their *jajmāns* with barley shoots and receive uncooked grain in return. Lesser *kamīns* receive gifts of food when honoring their *jajmāns* with the barley shoots. The higher-status Brahmans cannot be given the food of the *jajmāns*, although lower-status *kamīns* can be.

All three of these rituals involve transactions in which the worshiper is in fact the "higher"-status being, but recognition of the powers of the "lesser" being is necessary.

Transactions with Class 5 Powers

Another way men deal with powerful beings is through a one-way transaction in which men present the powerful being with offerings but receive no substance in return. (Again, men do not desire to share substance with lesser, more inauspicious powerful beings.) Instead, they hope that the offerings will be reciprocated by services, especially the cooperation of that being. Deities whose powers put them in class 5 are often treated in this way. In Karimpur, only one yearly ritual suggests this behavior, Snake's Fifth on Savan *sudī* 5. On this day, *pūjā* is performed by the women to a stylistic design of snakes drawn on their household walls and the snakes are begged to leave the family alone. *prasād* does not seem to be taken from the snakes.

Transactions with Class 6 Powers

Powerful beings of the lower classes--deities with whom it is not desirable to exchange or share substance--are dealt with less frequently than the more powerful gods who give men shelter as well as rescue them. The former deities represent inauspiciousness, and various ways of coping with them are available, as the following examples illustrate.

1. A middle-aged shepherd woman has a severe toothache. Eventually her arm also becomes sore. One of the village oracles is approached and, through the aid of his possessing spirit, is able to diagnose the cause as the spirit of her dead husband, who had been a "bad" person and is now a ghost, *bhūt*, and is returning to cause her harm. She is told that if she does *pūjā* to Devi daily, the toothache and soreness in the arm will go away.

In this example, the woman deals with the goddess (honoring her with *pūjā* and taking *prasād* from her) who in turn will cope with the inauspicious class 6 powerful being harming the woman. No transaction occurs directly between the woman and the ghost.

2. A Brahman woman's daughter suffers from a severe eye infection. The woman does *pūjā* daily to the *nīm* tree (*azidirachta Indica*) at her door and at the household Devi shrine. Meanwhile, her daughter must carry a branch of the *nīm* tree with her constantly.

Leaving nothing to chance, this woman copes in two ways. She honors the *nīm* tree (whose leaves are also a cooling substance) and the spirits who are believed to reside in it. She also pays respect

to the goddess, who either may have something to do with the illness
herself or may be able to control the evil spirit causing the illness.

3. A snake has been seen in the fields near the east side
of the village. A group of women from nearby houses go to a hillock
in a garden where they believe a snake lives and make offerings of
milk to him, asking him please to keep away from their families.

The snake, an inauspicious lesser power, is treated with respect, but no *prasād* is taken from him. The people hope that their
acknowledgment of his powers and their offerings of food will please
him and keep him away from their relatives.

4. Preparations for a wedding are under way. Some days
(usually three) before the beginning of the ceremonies, the mother
of the house performs *tāī*, a ritual in which she gathers up into her
sari all the evil spirits residing in the house and then plasters
them under a piece of cloth in the back room of the house. They will
remain there, where they cannot injure the family, until after com-
pletion of the wedding ceremonies (*tāī* is performed in the houses of
both bride and groom).

Here the evil spirits are averted by being removed. Avoidance
of evil spirits is a common theme.

5. There is illness in a house or in the village. Believing
it to be caused by evil spirits, the women of the village take care
that their children are protected by putting lampblack on their eyes
and often on their hands and feet.

Again, class 6 powerful beings are avoided or warded off,
through the power of a more auspicious powerful being, Siyao Mata.
This avoidance is also seen on inauspicious days (e.g., *chotī divālī*).

Conclusion

The principles by which men order their religious thoughts are reflected in their religious actions. In Karimpur, one of the primary
factors underlying both thoughts and actions is the villagers' recognition of deities as embodied powers. Men then regulate their transactions with their various deities according to the powers which
these deities embody. Many other facets of Karimpur religious activity still need to be explored. Nevertheless, we can begin to see
some order within the apparent chaos of Karimpur religious activity.
Understanding that deities are powerful beings allows us to have new
insight into men's actions toward their gods and spirits. Recognizing that these deities represent *embodied* powers permits us to discern further aspects of the nature of man-god transactions, transactions which relate man and god substantively and which state clearly
the level of man's concern for a given deity.

1. The problem of which foods are acceptable to whom has been considered elsewhere (see Marriott 1968; Babb 1970b). Briefly, *pakka* foods (foods cooked in *ghī* or milk) are more acceptable to higher-status beings than foods cooked in water. The lowest-status beings often cannot give any cooked foods to higher beings. Sweets are apparently the most widely accepted cooked foods.

2. See Babb 1970b for further discussion of the meaning of food in Hindu ritual.

3. *prasād* also carries the connotations of "mercy" (*kripā*) (by the gods) and "happiness" (of the worshiper), returning us again to the questions raised in Chapter IV.

4. Varma reports that the *naivedya*, food offering, has the meaning of "realization of the identity of the worshipper with the worshipped" (Varma 1956:462).

5. Note that "status" does not equate with "power." "Status" derives from and is related to the "total" being, not merely that aspect of him which is his powers. A given being may have lower "status" but much "power."

6. As in the ritual discussed in Chapter VIII and Appendix II.

7. "Let us meditate on the most excellent light of the Creator [the sun]; may he guide our intellect" (Pandey 1968:39).

8. The sun must be "manifested"--on those days when it cannot be seen, worship of it cannot take place.

9. Under another name, *vat-Savitri*, this festival is found elsewhere in North India. See Babb 1968:140-42.

10. This ritual is performed only by married women, not by the young girls, although they participate in other rituals honoring their brothers.

11. According to one informant, the *karvā* must be made of brass the first year after marriage; thereafter it can be clay.

12. Not only is *besan-bhāt* the first meal offered a bride in her husband's home; it is also prepared as the first meal whenever a wife returns to her husband's home after a long absence.

13. This aspect of Karimpur religious activity needs further investigation. What benefits does the child given *prasād* by its mother receive? The child (and anthropologist) are not devotees of that god, but *must* take its *prasād*. Does the worshiper act in some way as an intermediary, thus allowing the sharing of substance to be more widely distributed among human beings? If this is the case, then the transaction of substance becomes almost more important than the devotion of an individual--perhaps not a startling development. There are limits, however--one teen-age boy refused to take *prasād* from the village midwife (government-placed--she claimed to be of a Kshatriya caste), as he thought she (not her god) was a "bad" (immoral) person.

14. Hanuman is a deity commonly associated with protection. It is also possible that the armlets (with their fourteen knots and strings) represent protection for the fourteen dangerous days ahead--the fortnight of the ancestors.

15. Most images, which are "the deity," are destroyed at the conclusion of the ritual, either by "cooling" them by immersion in water or (if drawn) by replastering the wall with cow dung.

16. One interesting aspect of these handouts of food is that the anthropologists' distinctions between households, on the basis of

chūlhā or actual house or coownership of land, are ignored by the
kamīns. Whatever they feel is a household is treated as one and in
any of the anthropologically questionable cases about whether a household is or is not joint, they treat it as joint. This happens most
often for households where the mother and father are still living
but whose sons have broken away. To the *kamīns*, it is still a joint
family. Other evidence also suggests this interpretation.

17. See LaBrack 1969 and Lewis 1965:218-21 for discussions of a
similar ritual called Hoi, and Marriott 1955:195 for one called Lampblack.

18. These preparations have begun on Spring Fifth, *basant panchmī*,
over a month earlier.

19. The peculiar social structure of Karimpur seems to be the
reason for three fires. There are two fires in the main village,
one for the West Pandeys and one for the East Pandeys. The other
castes attend one of these two fires, depending on where they live
(East or West) in the village. The Dube lineage of Brahmans can
attend either fire and often the men attend both, a symbol perhaps
of their neutrality. The third bonfire is near the Farmer settlement on the *kherā* and everyone not resident in Karimpur *khās* goes to
it. Even at the various bonfires, caste formality is observed. The
lowest untouchables (Leatherworkers, Midwives, and Sweepers) are not
allowed to circle the fire until the other castes are finished. In
1967 the Sweepers insisted on joining the high-caste men--who abrupt-
ly left and did not return until the Sweepers had departed. This
incident was not repeated in 1968.

20. The younger Brahman men claim that they visit untouchables'
houses after dark to avoid repercussions from their elders.

21. The men of the Sweeper caste, "really" untouchables, do not
touch the feet of their Brahman superiors; rather, they raise their
hands in the traditional Hindu greeting and *say* "I touch your feet."

22. Sisters are in an ambiguous social position in North India,
in part owing to hypergamy. At marriage a sister obtains a status
higher than her natal family's. Nevertheless, her natal family continues to represent a refuge in times of distress and is therefore
important. Brothers become the most important members of the natal
family, in part, I suspect, because of the high incidence of early
deaths of the parents.

Chapter IX: POWER IN HINDU SOCIETY

Ritual behavior in Karimpur provides us with a viewpoint complemen-
tary to that of the gods' actions toward men--men's actions toward
the gods. Taking both views--that of powers over men and that of
men's actions with regard to the powers--we find a set of relationships that are also fundamental to social relationships in Karimpur.
One major concern in anthropological studies of Hinduism has been
the interrelationships of religion and social behavior. Having found
that power is a fundamental idea in Hindu society, I contend that
conceptions of power also operate in man-man relationships in Karimpur. It cannot be denied that men are also powerful beings of one
sort or another. They, too, are born with their share of the powers
of the universe; they, too, can alter their substance and thereby
their powers through various means.

        The ritual specialists of Karimpur manifest these facts.
The Brahman priests (and Brahmans in general) obtain their powers by
birth (actions in their previous lives), although they must continue
to maintain and increase these powers by correct actions in this
life. The Brahman priests serve as intermediaries between men and
some gods. Brahmans in general are also intermediaries in some instances, e.g., men feed them so that the offerings will reach either
bhagvān or their ancestors. In contrast, the village oracles (*bhagat*,
"devotee") obtain their powers through their actions in this life.
Because they are extraordinarily devoted to their chosen deity, that
deity rewards them with the boon of manifesting the deity--of becoming possessed.[1] Likewise, the village exorcist is taught mantras
(magical ritual sayings) by his guru; when he is sanctified by re-
peating them while immersed in the Ganges, these mantras provide him
with the power to call on powerful gods for their aid in crises. Men
call on one of these various "specialists" when his particular extraordinary powers are needed. The individual faced with a crisis may
not be able, because of his lack of devotion, to coerce a given deity
to aid him. By approaching that deity through an intermediary whom
the deity recognizes as a devotee, he can obtain the deity's aid.

        Actions based on perceptions of power are found elsewhere in

Karimpur social life. As mentioned in Chapter IV, the worshiper's attitude of devotion (*bhakti*) which is reciprocated by the deity's mercy (*kripā*) is remarkably similar to the *kamīn*'s attitude toward his *jajmān*. Further, we know that some deities can give shelter, symbolizing a long-term commitment to their devotees. In a similar fashion, the patron-client relationship is hereditary and is recognized twice yearly on the threshing floor of the patron, when the client is given his share of that harvest. Moreover, those deities who have enduring relationships with men have commitments to aid men when they are in danger. Likewise, the patron has a commitment to aid his worker in times of crisis--by providing milk for an infant, giving grain when the crops have failed, supplying wood for a new house, etc. The patron-client ties are also demonstrated on festival days, when the client is able to claim food from his patron (who, of course, wishes to give him food and thus clearly establish his superiority). In return for physical aid and symbolic "shelter," the client provides services for his patron--the same types of services which men often provide for their deities in *pūjā*, services which are primarily concerned with the removal of the deity's polluting bodily substances. *kamīns* in Karimpur include the Washerman, the Sweeper, and the Barber (whose wife comes on festival days to decorate the feet of the women in her *jajmān*'s household, just as the women themselves will adorn the god or goddess whom they will worship that day). Other services are given by *kamīns*. However, it is noteworthy that, with the changes which have occurred in the past forty years, the *kamīns* most concerned with the bodily welfare of their clients have continued in service, whereas those more concerned with general welfare (e.g., Goldsmith and Oil Presser) have tended to lose their hereditary jobs.[2] However, on major festival days, present and past *kamīns* are expected to claim food from their *jajmāns*. The *jajmāns*, like the gods, give food; the *kamīns*, like the devotees, receive it. From the viewpoint of the *jajmān*, the *kamīn* is a lesser, inauspicious being (though the degrees of "lesser" and "inauspicious" vary, of course); from the *kamīn*'s viewpoint, the *jajmān* is an auspicious being who provides shelter.

If we recognize that men think of and act toward their gods on the basis of the gods' powers, and that men also have powers and are treated in various ways because of these powers, some of the apparent inconsistencies in caste-ranking in the villages of India can be understood. An example from Karimpur is relevant here. Over forty years ago, a poor *mahājan* woman (a caste of Shopkeepers with very lowly status in many places) came to Karimpur with her sons. By the

mid-1960s, these sons and their sons had prospered. They now own a
large shop by the roadside, run a mill for grinding grain, and have
bought land. In addition, they are moneylenders. As a symbol of
their increased prosperity, they built a large brick home. At the
time of the opening of their home, they gave a feast for the whole
village. There was much consternation about this event, because the
Brahmans of Karimpur had never before taken cooked food from this
group or eaten in their homes. In the idiom of Hindu transactions,
the Brahmans would be admitting some kind of increased status for the
Shopkeepers by being given food by them. Eventually, the Brahmans
did decide to eat in the new home; and the Shopkeepers gained points
in the ranking system of Karimpur. In explaining these events to me,
the Brahmans were explicit about the fact that they had had to eat
in the Shopkeepers' home because of their new wealth.

Material prosperity is clearly closely tied to people's perceptions of someone's powers. Yet this connection should not be surprising, because the attainment of *artha*, wealth, is a justifiable
pursuit under most codes for conduct--as long as that wealth is used
correctly (when it is not, as in *kathā* 4 in Chapter IV, disaster results). Wealth, then, can be interpreted as an indication of the
family's or person's correct actions, indicating that his embodied
powers have increased. A Brahman family whose wealth and position
in Karimpur had been drastically cut in recent years presents the opposite picture. As the grandson of this family explained to me, "My
father and grandfather and uncles have acted badly. Because of this
we have no money now and it will be very hard to find wives for my
brothers because our family does not act right and people think that
we are bad. People were glad to marry a daughter to me [three years
previously]."

Another type of man-man relationship found in Karimpur is the
baTāi system of sharecropping. These relationships seem to be based
on the same kind of "mutual" exchange previously associated with class
4 powers. *baTāi* is a contract settled yearly; the landowner usually
provides the land and 50 percent of the seeds and fertilizer. In return, the sharecropper supplies labor and the other 50 percent of
the seeds and fertilizer. When the harvest is in, each receives 50
percent of the crop. Other relationships based on the two concerned
individuals' varying powers are those between shopkeeper and buyer
(goods in exchange for money); tailor and housewife (skill in exchange
for cash or grain); farmer and day laborer (money in exchange for
physical labor); rickshaw driver and passenger; and so on. In all
these, there is a type of mutual exchange. Each individual needs
the services of the other--the "rescue" by the other individual.

Power relationships are also expressed among kin. The wives' worship of their husbands has already been mentioned; in addition, wives daily eat their husbands' leftovers. A wife, even though she is incorporated into her husband's lineage at the time of marriage, continues to be subordinate to him. During the marriage ceremony, the new husband and wife exchange food. However, all later transactions mark the woman's inferiority. Moreover, the wife's membership in her husband's lineage is continually restated in a variety of ways, suggesting some of the ambiguity of her position. The first meal served by her in her husband's home is *besan-bhāt*, symbolizing her rise in status--hers now equals that of her husband's lineage.[3] This same meal is served whenever a wife returns to her husband's home after a long absence, thus reiterating her "solidarity" with her affines through meaningful transactions of food.

Other affinal relationships are marked by equally meaningful food transactions. A woman's husband, who has by birth greater powers than his wife's family, must be fed "honorific" foods whenever he visits his wife's village, and, naturally, he is fed first. In addition, all his male affines are required to touch his feet in respect. Foot-touching--taking bodily substance from the lowest part of the other's body--is a sign of extreme humility, devotion, and lower status. In contrast, a woman's parents should never accept food from her husband's family, particularly in his village.

There are many other instances of similar behavior: a wife touches the feet of her husband's mother, as well as those of his older brothers' wives, sisters, and brothers. A son touches the feet of his parents and older relatives. Sisters eat before sisters-in-law; mothers before their sons' wives; etc. I must repeat that, given the definition of "supernatural" developed in this monograph, there is no "bounded" domain of the "religious" or "spiritual" in Karimpur. Thus any behavior toward any being which is based on the fact that that being has power is "religious" behavior.

In the Introduction, I mentioned several areas of concentration by anthropologists concerned with Hinduism. To illustrate the kinds of questions which we can and should answer, assuming that deities are power-filled, let me suggest the ways in which this study is related to these areas.

One general area of interest has been the relationships existing among the great and little traditions. Here my contribution is slight. However, we should recognize that intermediaries (often considered to be little-tradition deities) are not separated from the great tradition. Rather, through various sorts of "genealogical"

bridges, they are tightly incorporated into it. More research needs
to be done in genealogical bridges which are created, the corresponding separation of powers, and their mythological justifications.

Scholars concerned with differences between the great and
little traditions should also move in the direction of more systematic studies of the variations in the components of these traditions.
The kinds of texts available in villages like Karimpur have not yet
been contrasted to the corresponding great-tradition texts. Through
comparative studies of the works of the literary elite and the village storytellers and priests, we can begin to cope with problems of
reflectiveness and refinement. A first step is the collection and
translation of the local texts--a task which has, even today, barely
begun.

Related to the problem of great and little traditions is an
aspect of Karimpur religion which has continually intrigued me
throughout this study--the pervasiveness of *bhakti*, of ideas of devotion and the necessity of devotion. Even the pre-*bhakti* Vedic sacrifice (*havan*) has been transformed into a *bhakti* rite in Karimpur.
Yet *bhakti* as perceived in Karimpur is not the *bhakti* of the South
Indian poets or even of Kabir and Mirabai. It, too, has been transformed in interesting ways. *kripā* has an element of causality. The
god must be worshiped as an image and not, as Kabir and others have
stated, in the individual's mind. The gods provide shelter, not
just because of men's love, but also because of men's service and
faith (in fact, *prema*, "love," seems to be absent in most Karimpur
religious thought). Last, the deities' abilities to give shelter
and perhaps their most important powers--those which men most desire
the gods to use.

Previous works have been concerned with examining the attributes and characteristics of village and local gods and rituals.
Our analysis is relevant to this concern, particularly for understanding the structure of local pantheons. Many studies of local
pantheons have used the analytical device of great and little traditions, or Sanskritic and non-Sanskritic deities. Harper (1959)
classifies the gods of his South Indian pantheon as Sanskritic (good),
local (good-bad), and malevolent (local?). The data from Karimpur
would not allow such a classification. Some Sanskritic gods, such
as Basuk Dev, are malevolent gods. Some local gods, such as Khan
Bahadur, are good. Babb (1968) makes a distinction similar to Harper's. He develops a three-level typology for "supernatural" order-
ing--"high" supernatural beings, those most pure and Brahmanically
oriented; "intermediate" supernatural beings, those concerned with

purity but not the Brahmanical priesthood; and malevolent, polluting deities, the spirits of the dead. In his analysis, the critical factors are (a) the associated ritual specialist, and (b) the role of purity in ritual practice. Yet in Karimpur a non-Brahmanical ritual specialist (the exorcist) uses the powers of "high" deities to deal with an "intermediate" god. In another Karimpur rite, the Sweeper cuts the head off a pig as an offering to the goddess Kali.

That village Hinduism is complex, no one will deny. However, Sanskritic, non-Sanskritic, all-India, and local schemes have not yet aided us in penetrating the complexity. Purity and Brahmanical orientations are certainly factors in ritual behavior to be considered, but the powers of the gods must also be examined. We need much more work along the lines of the "semantics" of village Hinduism, as illustrated by Babb (1970a) and Beck (1969), especially about the relationship between the character of a given deity and the kinds of power which he/she represents.

Continuously, I find myself returning to the question of power. If men "think" about their deities in terms of power and if cultural principles for relationships among gods-gods, men-gods, and men-men are based on perceptions of powers, then surely power and the principles by which it is understood are fundamental to Hindu society.

Power, although it is a fundamental factor in the ideology of Hindu society, is not generally considered a dominant theme. Yet power underlies two of the most important concepts which aid Hindus in defining action--*dharma* and *karma*. Right action, *dharma*, guarantees that an individual's fate, *karma*, will be good and that his status in the next life will be higher than in this one. With a higher status--perhaps even that of a *devatā*--comes an increase in power, the ability to control, to command, the lives of other beings.

It is in his perception of power that I disagree most strongly with Dumont (1970). He maintains that purity, or the principle of pure-impure, is dominant in Hindu society. I contend that purity and power are two inseparable factors of any ideas of "being" or action in Hindu thought. Power in human affairs is always embodied and is a characteristic of the state of any being. In addition, all being is in some state of purity. An individual's quantum of power in this life and his quantum of purity are both based on his actions, that is, his fate (*karma*) as derived from the correct or incorrect following of his *dharma*, code for conduct, in previous lives. Thus Brahmans are both the most powerful beings and the most pure beings. And, in Karimpur at least, Sweepers are the least powerful men and are the most impure. Moreover, in this life, as an individual's bodily substance changes through various transformations and transactions, his or her power and purity likewise change. The Brahman male, after the sacred-thread ceremony, has an increase in both power and purity (and a corresponding new code for conduct). The woman at marriage receives the power and purity of her husband's family--she becomes one with them in bodily substance (and has a new code for conduct). The Shopkeepers mentioned earlier illustrate an increase in both power and purity--the Brahmans, in deciding to take food from them, were also making a judgment of purity and were careful to take only the most "honorific" foods, i.e., those least contaminated by the Shopkeepers' lesser purity. Even the gods' powers are connected to their purity--those with the most influence tend to be the most pure. Both power and purity are used jointly in determining hierarchical relationships. Thus any being is at one and the same time purity and power. Action changes both purity and power.

Previous works on village Hinduism have been concerned largely with behavior as manifested in ritual action, that is, with the physical transactions between man and deity (Marriott), but insufficiently with the meanings of the transactions which that ritual represents. I suspect that the tendency to overemphasize purity as the "dominant" theme in South Asia is due in part to our paying inadequate attention to the meanings of transactions. Ideas about purity are more readily "seen" in ritual actions; ideas about power are not so easily "seen" in ritual action but must instead be "listened" to. Functionalist nonliterate anthropology, and its apparent fixation on actual, preferably certain visible, behavior, and materialist anthropology, with its attention to nonhuman substance, have created unnatural biases in our studies and led to culturally erroneous interpretations of our natives' societies. The trend is beginning to change--functionalism and materialism no longer have exclusive sway. I hope that this monograph, in which I have sought to delineate the major conceptual categories which give meaning to actual behavior, has shown that we can gain more comprehension of the meaning of behavior by attending to the words used in ritual and myth.

Action (behavior) and substance (nonhuman as well as human) cannot, however, be denied. Thought, substance, and action are interrelated. Because power, and its complement purity, are so closely connected in Hindu thought to men's past and future actions, let me close by returning to the verbal statements with which I have been so concerned. The words of the great god Shiva himself are appropriate:

This world's field of rules is such that those seeds that a farmer sows in the fields, those fruits he cuts; and in this world, such acts as are done, that fruit is tolerated.

NOTES

1. Not all possession, however, is a "boon." Possession by malevolent spirits is definitely inauspicious.

2. I do not wish to suggest that treating the *jajmān* as a god is the only factor in these changes. Obviously, other economic factors are important. Further research needs to be done both on attitudes involved in the *jajmāni* system, particularly various groups' perceptions of the necessity of "shelter," and on the economic positions and advantages of the various groups.

3. Only members of the family can share in this meal.

Appendix I: TRANSCRIPTIONS OF SONGS IN HINDI

Song #1

jasodā lālan jāyā ānand gokul men chhāyā
āyī-āyī bāhar dāī kī pukār
dāī ne nār chhidāyā ānand bhavan men chhāyā
ab rānī lālan jāyā ānand gokul men chhāyā
āyī-āyī bāhar sāsuli kī pukār
sāsuli ne charuā dharāyā ānand bhavan men chhāyā
jasodā lālan jāyā ānand bhavan men chhāyā
āyī-āyī bāhar nanadī kī pukār
nanadī ne satiyā dharāyā ānand bhavan men chhāyā
āyī-āyī bāhar jiThānī kī pukār
jiThānī ne pīs pisāyā ānand bhavan men chhāyā
devar ne tīr marāyā ānand bhavan men chhāyā
āyī-āyī bāhar paNDit kī pukār
paNDit ne rāsi gināyī ānand bhavan men chhāyā
sakhiyān ne mangal gāyā ānand bhavan men chhāyā
jasodā lālan jāyā ānand bhavan men chhāyā

(*lorī* sung by Scribe women, at the birth of a Bard child,
July 1968.)

Song #2

mujhe kyā kām duniyān se merā shrī kriShNa pyārā hai
tuhī gangā tuhī yamunā tuhī sarayū kinārā hai
mujhe kyā kām duniyān se merā shrī kriShNa pyārā hai
tuhī chandā tuhī sūraj tuhī ākāsh tārā hai
mujhe kyā kām duniyān se merā shrī kriShNa pyārā hai
tuhī mātā tuhī bhrātā tuhī sab sahārā hai
mujhe kyā kām duniyān se merā shrī kriShNa pyārā hai

(*bhajan* sung by a Brahman girl, age 23, 19 July 1968.)

189

Song #3

> *terī sattā ke vinā he prabhū mangal mūl*
> *pattā bhī hiltā nahīn khilai na ekhu phūl*
> *rām nām lī ho nahīn kiyo na hari sai hetu*
> *vo nar yaise jāyege jyo mūlī kā khet*
> *prabhū bhajan hari ko bhūl jānā jindagānī men*
> *aur rahe is hisāv se jaise kamal rahtā hai pānī men*

(*sher* sung by a male Brahman, age 26, March 1968.)

Song #4

> *gangā ke khaRe kināre bhagvān māngi rahe naiyā*
> *mallāh naiyā idhar ko lāo*
> *moy jānā hai pallī pārā*
> *gangā ke khaRe kināre bhagvān māngi rahe naiyā*
> *mallā kyā terī utaraiyā*
> *mujhe jaldī se dev bataiyā*
> *naiyā bīch bhavar me āyī*
> *jaya bolau gangā maiyā*
> *bhagvān na merī kuch utaraiyā*
> *ham karte gangā pārā*
> *tumhe karnā bhavse pārā*

(*kīrtan* sung by Brahman women at the *lagun*[1] of a Brahman boy, April 1968.)

Song #5

> *bhagvān tumhāre dvāre par ek dās bhikhārī āyā hai*
> *prabhū āp kī darshan bhikshā ko do*
> *merī bīch bhavar me naiyyā hai*
> *prabhū tere bin kaun khivaiyyā hai*
> *mai dār pe khaRe, mai vintī karu*
> *prabhū āp hī pār lagaiyyā ho*
> *dhan daulat kī kuch chāh nahīn, ghar vār chhuTe parvāh nahīn*
> *jag se yah dil dhavarāyā hai*
> *yah dās sharaN me āyā hai*
> *bhagvān āp ke darshan ko ek dās bhikharī āyā hai*

(*gānā* sung by a Brahman girl, age 23, July 1968.)

Song #6

> *kriShNā līnhīn na khabariyā kaise saparī*
> *parso kī manmohan kahi gae nahīn lauT kar āe*
> *rādhā soch kartī hai nit uTh nīr bahāe*
> *chhalke nainan kī gagariyā kaise saparī*
> *din na chain rain na nidiyā hardam birah satāe*
> *varNan kī pyāsī hain āṅkhīyān darshan ko lalavāe*
> *kāhe bhūle re sāvariyā kaise saparī*
> *tum bin shyām aur na koī jis kī ās lagāun*
> *kise sunāun dukh kī vatiyān kis bidhi man samajhāū*
> *tum bin ho rahī babariyā kaise saparī*
> *sānvarī sūrat mohanīn mūrat ab dikh lājā*
> *chintāmaNi kī bīch bhavar se naiyā pār lagājā*
> *kāhai bhūle ho sāvariyā kaise saparī*
> *kriShNā līnhīn na khabariyā kaise saparī*

(*kīrtan* from the pamphlet *shāntī-sarovar*, used by Brahman men.)

Song #7

> *he mere bhagvan batlā do kahān DhūNDhe tumhen*
> *sāre jag men DhūRh hārā par na pāye tum hamen*
> *mujh adham kī nāv bhav se pār kar do he prabhū*
> *kyonki tum tāraN sune ho tār kar jānā hamen*
> *tum ne hī ākar bachāyo ham sunon prahlād kī*
> *tum ne gaNikā aur ajāmil gotamī silnāri ko kyā*
> *yah gāthā satya hai yā jhūTh, batlā do hamen*
> *path vo batlā do prabhū tum tak jā pahunche sīRiyān*
> *gyāna mere kī prabhū ab khol do sab khiRakiyān*

(*kīrtan* sung by Farmer men from the pamphlet *chacha Nehru*.)

Song #8

> *mere jīvan kī naiyā majhadhār kanhaiyā pār karo*
> *pāp bhār te Dūbat naiyā tum bin koī nahīn khivaiyā*
> *bas āp hī mere patavār kanhaiyā pār karo*
> *kabi vinod vinavat karjorī āshā pūr karo prabhū morī*
> *ab mohin līno ubār kanhaiyā pār karo*

(*kīrtan* sung by a Brahman male from the book *kīrtan sāgar*, May 1968.)

Song #9

> *tumha tau shrī kriShNa janam ke kapTī*
> *sab kī gauen āp charāte*
> *sab kī gāye āp charāte*
> *merī gauen van kyo bhaTkī*
> *sab kī gāgar āp bharata hai*
> *merī gāgar kyon jamunā jal paTkī*
> *sab kī naiyyā prabhū pār āp lagāte*
> *merī naiyyā kyon bhamar vīch aTkī*
> *tumha tau shrī kriShNa janam ke kapTī*

(*gānā* sung by upper-caste women at the birth of a Bard child, July 1968.)

Song #10

> *jāgo jāgo bhārat ke vīr*
> *jāgo jāgo bhārat ke vīr*
> *gāndhī bābā kī leti balaiyā*
> *sab kī pār lagāy dev naiyā*
> *sab kī pār lagāy dev naiyā*

(*gānā* sung by Brahman men, April 1968.)

Song #11

> *naiyā lagā do pār kanhaiyā morī naiyā lagā do pār*
> *Dūb rahī hai jīvan naiyā tum vin koī nahīn khivaiyā*
> *bhav sāgar majhadhār kanhaiyā*
> *pāp kī naiyā Dagamag Dole bīch bhavar men khāt hilore*
> *tumhīn ho khevan hār kanhaiyā*
> *āyā sharaN prabhū main terī vinay karūn doū kar jorī*
> *tumhīn gaho patvār kanhaiyā*
> *tum bin koī nahīn hamārā kabi vinod ko tero sahārā*
> *vinay karata har bār kanhaiyā*

(*kīrtan* sung by a Farmer male from the book, *kīrtan sāgar*.)

Song #12

> *Dag mag Dag mag Dole merī naiyyā*
> *pār lagā do to jāne khivaiyyā*
> *chāron taraph se yah pāpon kā dherā*
> *chhāyā huā hai jag men andherā*
> *lāj ko āke bachā lo kanhaiyā*
> *pār lagā do to jāne khivaiyyā*

Dag mag Dag mag Dole merī naiyyā
pār lagā do to jāne khivaiyyā
bhakton ne tum ko bhajan se pukārā
mai bhī pukārungī tum ko us man se
girte ko āke uThālo kanhaiyā
pār lagā do to jāne khivaiyyā
Dag mag Dag mag Dole merī naiyyā
pār lagā do to jāne khivaiyyā

(*bhajan* sung by a Brahman girl, age 23, July 1968.)

Song #13

are o muralī vāle muralī bajaiyo ek bār
shyām tumhe rādhā tāre re
are o muralī vāle rās rachaiyo ek bār
shyām tumhe narasī tāre re
are muralī vāle bhāT bharaiyo ek bār
shyām tumhen dropadī tāre re
are o muralī vāle chīr baRaiyo ek bār
shyām tumhe ham sab tāre re
are o muralī vāle darshan dikhay jāv ek bār

(*kīrtan* sung by a teen-age [and blind] Farmer boy, July 1968.)

Song #14

bhagvān hamen kab tāroge
bhagvān tumne dropadī tārī karke chīron kā vahānā
hamen kab tāroge
bhagvān tumne mīrā tārī karke pyāle kā vahānā
hamen kab tāróge
bhagvān tumne shivajī tāre karke Thamru kā vahānā
hamen kab tāroge
bhagvān tumne arjun tāre karke vasho kā vahānā
hamen kab tāroge

(*kīrtan* sung by Brahman women at the *lagun* of a Brahman boy, April 1968.)

Song #15

terī khātir kanhaiyā main jogin banī
khāk tan pai ramī kī ramī rah gayī
intajārī thī āne kī āp nahīn
terī rāhon men ānkhe

terī khātir kanhaiyā main jogin banī
khāk tan pai ramī kī ramī rah gayī
   dil men āyā ki chiTThī likhu shyām ko
   phasāna adhik thā par kāgaj thā kam
   jab se ānkho se pānī kādariyā vahā
   par kalam to rukī kī rukī rah gayī
terī khātir kanhaiyā main jogin banī
khāk tan pai ramī kī ramī rah gayī
   prīti ku kuvjā kī dil men vasī āpke
   mujh ko chhoRā akelā na āyā raham
   lauT kar vakht danā gabārā nahīn
   mere man men pasī kī pasī rah gayī
   āj dil men lagī kī lagī rah gayī
terī khātir kanhaiyā main jogin banī
khāk tan pai ramī kī ramī rah gayī
   tum ne tāre hai pāpi adham se adham
   mai hūn pāpin magar un se jyādā nahīn
   phir kyo ruThe ho mujh se samajh men nahīn
   mere sevā men sāyad kamī rah gayī
terī khātir kanhaiyā main jogin banī
khāk tan pai ramī kī ramī rah gayī

(*kīrtan* sung by Brahman women, February 1968.)

Song #16

vah shakti hame do dayā nidhe kartā dimāg par rah jāve
par sevā par upkār men ham jam jīvan saphal vamā jāve

ham dīn dukhī nivalon vikalon kaise bhagvān kantā pālan
jo hain aTake bhūle bhaTke un ko tāre sab tar jāven
chhal dabhm drep pākhanR phūT anyāy se nis din dūr rahen

jis dās jāti me janm liyā validān usī par ho jāven
vah shakti hame do dayā nidhe kartā dimāg par rah jāve
par sevā par upkār men ham jam jīvan saphal vamā jāve

(*gānā* sung by a Brahman girl, age 23, July 1968.)

Song #17

to bin bhagban merī nāv adhpar aRī tu na āyā
nāth tumne hī sab ko bachāyā
tumne hī gautam silā kaisī tarī
dukhī dropadī bhī tumne ubārī
nāth tum ne hī āj lāj us kī bachā nām pāyā

gaj graha jab laRā thā jal men gaj gayā hār
nang pairon hī ā gaj grah se chhuRā ā bachāyā
*nāth nām prahlād ne jab liyā thā harNānkush ne manā tab kiyā
thā*
rūp narsinh dhar harNānkush mār kar jā bachāyā

(*kīrtan* sung from the pamphlet *chacha Nehru* by a Farmer
male.)

Song #18

tumhī ho mātā pitā tumhī ho
tumhī ho bandhu sakhā tumhī ho
tumhī ho sāthī tumhī sahāre
koī na apnā sivā tumhāre
tumhī ho naiyyā tumhī khivaiyyā
tumhī ho bandhū sakhā tumhī ho
jo khil sakenā vah phūl ham hai
tumhāre charaNon kī dhūl ham hai
sharaN tumhārī ham ā paRe hai
tumhī ho mātā pitā tumhī ho
kar do apnī dayā kī hīShT
bhar do ham men mahān shakti
sharaN tumhārī ham ā paRe hain
tumhī ho bandhū sakhā tumhī ho

(*gānā* sung by schoolgirls, July 1968.)

Song #19

he prabhū ānandadātā gyāna ham ko dījie
sīdhradhrasāre durguNon ko dūr mujh se kījie
lījie ham ko sharaN men ham sadā chārī vanen
brahmachārī dharmrajhak vīr vrat dhārī vanen

(*kīrtan* sung by a Brahman male, age 26, February 1968.)

Song #20

bhagvān kā jis men nām nahīn
vah gānā gānā nā chāhiyā

(*gānā* sung by Scribe girls at the birth of a Bard child,
July 1968.)

Song #21

> *chāhe sārī duniyān van vigaRe*
> *bhagvān vigaRnā nā chāhiye*
> *chāhe kitnā pyārī laRkī ho*
> *galiyon men Dulānā nā chāhiye*
> *chāhe kitnā pyārā laRkā ho*
> *par sir pai chaRānā nā chāhiye*
> *chāhe kitnā dushman bhaiyyā ho*
> *par dil se haTānā nā chāhiye*
> *chāhe sārī duniyān van vigaRe*
> *bhagvān vigaRnā nā chāhiye*

(*gānā* sung by a 10-year-old Brahman girl, July 1968.)

Song #22

> *merā kriShNa kanhaiyā bhagvān*
> *kināre se lagā do naiyā*
> *merā vīr vah dekho vanshī ko bajaiyā*
> *yah vakt ab ā gayā hai*
> *ab kī nibhā lenā*
> *ab tere vinā kaun hai merā vanshī kā bajaiyā*
> *he shyām salone merī*
> *he shyām salone tujhe mīrā pukārtī*

(*bhajan* sung by Brahman women, April 1968.)

Song #23

> *chāhe rām kaho kriShNa kaho*
> *matlab dono kā ek hī hai*
> *shrī rām ke hāth men dhanuSh vāN*
> *shrī kriShNa ke hāth men muralī hai*
> *shrī rām ke mātā koshilyā*
> *shrī kriShNa ke mātā jasodā hai*
> *chāhe rām kaho kriShNa kaho*
> *matlab dono kā ek hī hai*
> *shrī rām ke pitā dasharath hai*
> *shrī kriShNa ke pitā Nand bābā*
> *chāhe rām kaho kriShNa kaho*
> *matlab dono kā ek hī hai*
> *shrī rām ne ravaNa mārā thā*
> *shrī kriShNa ne kansh pachhārā thā*

(*gānā* sung by Brahman girls [ages 10-13], February 1968.)

Song #24

> *kriShNa kī muralī van pāyī*
> *shyām kī vanshī van pāyī*
>> *uTho tau jasodā maiyā khaulo kivariya*
>> *mai vanshī ghar den ko āyī*
>> *bachan sunat mohan uThi dhayo*
>> *lavo sakhī morī mohan muralī*
>> *vanshī ke sang merī gayī pahuchiyā*
>> *hāy so sakhī moy dev vataī*
> *shyām kī muralī van pāyī*
>> *ham to kahī kuchhu prem vaDhaigo*
>> *hay ulTī chorī shyām lagāī*
> *shyām kī muralī van pāyī*

(*gānā* sung by a Brahman woman, age 35, February 1968.)

Song #25

> *toRi dhanuSh varnā janakī ko vyāhi lahiyai*
> *āj mere varnā jī ne dhanuSh uThāy līyo*
> *nānā ko līyo māmā ko sāth līyo*
> *sir pai eR kare kī pīrā*
> *dekho kaise sundar rām vanen varnā*

(*varnā* sung by Carpenter women at the *lagun* of a Carpenter boy, April 1968.)

NOTES

1. The ceremony preceding a marriage by about two weeks in which the marriage date and dowry transactions are finalized.

Appendix II: *Dank*: A RITUAL OF SNAKE POSSESSION

The ritual described in the following pages is *Dank*, a snakebite-curing rite also used to cure other illnesses and to cause possession of an "oracle" of the snake king. I am concerned here with the possession of the oracle, not snakebite.[1] On Snake's Fifth, *Dank* is played throughout the day. The snake king's oracle is repeatedly possessed and answers questions from the villagers gathered around. *Dank*, as translated by the villagers, means "snake," though the word also refers to the whole rite. I will use the expression "playing *Dank*"--it could be "snake playing"--as a direct translation of the village expression *Dank khelte hai*.[2]

   Dank takes place outside, usually during the monsoon season, when Snake's Fifth occurs and snakebite and boils are most common. It is a rite conducted by men alone, although it can be played for a woman if she is bitten by a snake. Women are allowed to be present at the far edges of the crowd or on nearby housetops, but no pregnant woman is allowed near the site of *Dank*, as one could anger the snakes. Actual participation in the playing of *Dank* is limited to those who know the ritual songs, but the audience is composed of any interested man or boy who happens along.

   The Participants: *Dank* as played on Snake's Fifth requires a variety of participants. The most important two are the oracle himself, who is also considered a *bhagat*, and the leader or master, who is in actuality the exorcist.

   The snake king's oracle is a young Farmer, an extroverted, active man who is also famous for his storytelling. According to village legend, this man had been bitten by a snake three or four years earlier and recovered, after becoming possessed by the snake king. The villagers also say that, when he was bitten by the snake, he instantly leaped upward to a tree limb and was almost dead. Some time after his first possession, the snake king came to him in a dream and said that he should take food for two and put aside the first serving for the snake king. Then he could eat the second. Also he should not eat from others' pots and should never sit in a chair. If he followed these rules, he would become rich. The vil-

lage folk conclude this telling of his dream by saying that a similar incident happened in another village and the man there became
rich. I also heard several times that the oracle does not follow
the rules laid down by the snake king and that his powers are de-
creasing because of his misbehavior. Nevertheless, there is always
a snake over him (*us ke ūpar sānp hamesha hai*).[3] And in his words,
he "plays snake very well."

The master is a Shepherd about thirty-five years old. He
became the master, *astīk*, for the Karimpur area at the death of his
gūrū, a Water Carrier from Karimpur, some years ago. He believes
that he too will one day take on disciples and be a *gūrū*, but he is
still too young for that position. His *gūrū* taught him the *mantras*
for *Dank* and other curing rites. After learning them, he went to
the Ganges where, putting his head in the sacred waters, he said
each of them, thus guaranteeing their power.

In addition to the master and oracle, a group of men called
baigī are necessary to play the drums and sing the songs of *Dank*--
songs which please the snake king and prompt him to possess his oracle. Untouchables are not allowed to be part of this group, but all
other men are eligible once they have learned the songs.

The men of Karimpur also play *Dank* in nearby villages--usu-
ally for curing illnesses, not for snakebite. They play outside of
Karimpur primarily because the snake king's oracle is well known in
the area, and men from other villages come to question this oracle
on Snake's Fifth. The oracle can tell how to cure illness of humans
or of beasts, name thieves, and provide other kinds of information.

The Setting: Any large open area is suitable. On Snake's
Fifth, *Dank* occurs in the open area in front of a Potter's house. A
large, new clay pot like those used for cooking milk is brought to
the site. One side of it is rubbed with *ghī*, then ashes from a milk
stove are sprinkled on it and seven to nine snakes are drawn in the
ashes. Twenty *annas* and some leaves from a betel nut tree are put
inside it "to make it work truly." The pot is then set upon a flour
sieve, and a brass tray is placed upside down on top of the pot.
During the rite itself, the tray is treated as a drum. The snakes
are drawn so that the oracle will see them and feel pleased. Meanwhile, a small brass pot is filled with water and *nīm* leaves and a
ghī-filled clay lamp are placed on its top. A folded blanket is
placed on the ground with the clay pot-tray in front of it and the
waterpot to one side. Barley seeds are then sprinkled on the blanket.

As the men gather, they align themselves at the two sides

and back of the pot-tray combination. No one is allowed to sit at
the front of the pot-tray, because the snake king enters from that
direction. In addition, the opening to the front must always be toward the Ganges. There is a constant battle to keep observers at
the sides near the front seated so as to not block the passage.
Those who know the songs of *Dank* sit along the sides of the blanket,
the oracle between them, seated with his legs folded under on the
blanket, the master to his right. One of the men has a drum and another a wooden stick with which to beat the pot-tray combination.
(See figure 15.)

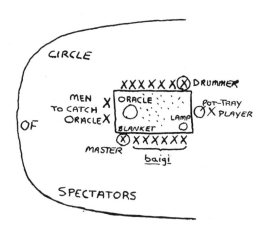

Fig. 15. *Dank* layout

The Rite: After much commotion, discussion, and shoving
around, the singers begin *kārikh*, songs to make the snake king happy
and come to possess the oracle. First, the men at one side sing,
then those on the opposite side repeat the line. Gradually the drum
player begins and the man by the pot-tray begins to beat it on the
top with one hand and on the side with the wooden stick, setting up
a fierce ringing din sounding rather like a collection of tin cymbals
being beaten continuously.

The song continues until the oracle is possessed by the snake
king or the song ends. If possession does not occur, the singers
will rest briefly, then begin again. When the oracle does become
possessed, he begins a circular movement with the upper half of his
body, slowly at first, with little forward movement, then faster and
faster until his hair lock is standing straight out because of his
speed and his head is almost touching the ground on each forward movement (one or two men sit behind him in order to catch him if he

should topple over that way). Suddenly, he collapses onto the ground,
bent forward from his hips. The song stops and the master takes over,
beginning with a prayer (*prāthnā*) while dipping a grain of barley in
the *ghī* of the lamp and throwing it at the possessed oracle. From
now until the end of the rite, the oracle is addressed as Maharaj,
"Great King." The master then recites a series of *bāchā*, ritual say--
ings which praise the gods. Next he recites a series of ritual questions, *pūchonī*, which establish the real identity of the spiritual
being possessing the oracle. The possessed oracle is required to
answer these questions. After the identity of the possessing deity
has been established, questions are asked by the men gathered around
and the oracle answers them. The men asking the questions give one
or two rupees to the oracle after their answers are given (the oracle
is told the amount and if it is not enough he will demand more).
One or more questions are asked during each possession, and the master periodically asks the oracle if he is tired and wishes to stop.
The oracle's answers are discussed by the audience and further veri-
fication is often required. When the questioning is over, the master again dips a grain of barley in *ghī* and throws it at the possessed, at the same time reciting an *uThonī*, or ritual saying, to
bring the oracle out of the possession.

The oracle at this time has two alternatives. He may sit up
and stare about in a dazed manner; or he may go into a kind of spasm,
leaping (with a very rapid movement) to his feet to be caught by
five or six men standing ready behind him (the oracle may warn them
before the *uThonī* that he will require this service and, in any case,
they are prepared). Covering his mouth, ears, and nose with a cloth
and holding his feet down and his body securely, they shout *khūn*,
sayings to make the snake king return home.[4] The people of Karimpur
say that at this moment the possessed oracle may die--that his spirit
is with the gods and, if they do not hold him securely, his body will
fly heavenward. At this point, the oracle has a completely rigid,
arched body and in his spasmodic movements is capable of moving the
whole group of men holding him down two or three feet in any direction. One or more *khūn* may be necessary before the snake king leaves
and the now unpossessed oracle relaxes and drops in a sitting position
on the ground. There are different types of *khūn*, some more
powerful than others. I have seen it take ten minutes of *khūn* before
the spasm ceases.

The whole cycle takes from fifteen to forty-five minutes,
depending on the number of songs necessary to induce possession, the
number of questions asked, and the number of *khūn* required to force

the snake king to leave. On Snake's Fifth, the whole cycle is repeated again and again until all the questions are asked or until
everyone is exhausted.

The Oral Components of Dank

Dank is composed of the following named oral components which structure the events of the ritual: kārikh, songs to make the snake king
happy and come and possess his oracle; a prāthnā, prayer; bāchā, ritual sayings invoking various gods; pūchonī, ritual questions; uThonī,
sayings to cause the possessed oracle to rise; and khūn, sayings to
make the snake king leave. Of these, the first and last are known
and recited or sung by a group of men, usually of middle-ranked
castes. The other four are known by the master and can be used only
by him. The functioning of these components is intricately tied to
relationships between the various deities involved and the purpose
and structure of the rite as a whole. In order to comprehend Dank
fully, we must examine closely the texts of the various named oral
components.

The kārikh are the songs to make the snake king happy. kārikh
is probably derived either from the word karish, "to draw" or "pull,"
or from karita, "to cause to occur." There are many songs called
kārikh. They deal with two topics--songs specifically about Raja
Basuk, the snake king, or songs about Zahir Pir, a regional god who
controls snakes.

"Basuk" is a derivation of the name Vasuki, king of the
snakes, or nāgas, lord of the nether world in the Sanskritic literature. In the Mahābhārata and Purānas, Vasuki is listed second, after
Sesha Naga, in the catalogue of snakes.

> But as Sesha, the first-born among the snakes is absorbed by his
> ponderous duty of carrying either the earth or the supreme deity,
> it is Vasuki who acts as the sovereign ruler of the serpent
> tribe whenever an active leadership is required (Vogel 1926:199).

So it is Vasuki (Basuk), the great king, who is appealed to for possession and who does possess, rather than Sesha Naga, who does not
actively participate in mundane affairs.

Zahir Pir is also known as Gugga. He is known and worshiped
in the Punjab and western Uttar Pradesh. He is an intermediary god,
one who mediates between the high gods and the world of men. By analyzing his various legends, we see that his powers are derived from
Shiva, via his gūrū, Gorakhnath. He is known for being a warrior and
a loving husband, but most important is his power over snakes--be-
cause he gained control over them, they now serve him as, in Sanskritic works, they serve the great god Shiva (Wadley 1967).

The songs about Raja Basuk and about Zahir Pir are not fully
comprehensible to the outsider until the local stories about these
two figures are known. In a rather cryptic fashion, the songs relate
to or refer to incidents in the legends of these two deities. Although not specifically songs of praise, they are about Basuk and
Zahir Pir. And certainly the change in meaning from *jas*, songs sung
to the same melody and for the same purpose for Devi (the goddess),
to *kārikh*, is relevant. *jas* means "fame" or "praise"; *kārikh* means
"to pull" or "to cause to occur." Devi is made happy by the singing
of *jas* and thus possesses her oracle; Raja Basuk is made happy and
is also induced to possess his oracle. The songs about Zahir Pir
can be understood in light of his controlling the snake king; if he
is pleased by *kārikh*, he can make Raja Basuk possess the oracle.

The prayer, or *prāthnā*, which follows the possession of the
oracle is often omitted in the cycle of *Dank* and is not particularly
important or enlightening. Essentially, it is a reminder to the
higher, more powerful gods of their presence at *Dank*. Much of the
message of the prayer is repeated in the *bāchā* which follow.

The *bāchā*, "saying," is the first step in gaining control of
the possessing deity once he is "riding" on his oracle. *bāchā* begin
with the master's saying:

Master:	Oh, God, as Bavan you deceived Bali;
	Becoming Krishna [you] destroyed Kans;
	Har Nar Kush was killed.
	Being Ram, Ravan was ridden.
	The black [snake] was subjugated.
	Mathura was full of light.
	Do you hear the words of the master?
	Oh Basudev, say yes.
Oracle:	Yes.
Master:	Yes, the snake comprehends.
	The companions met and sang *mangal*.
	Ganga, Gauri, Gayatri, the three gave blessings.
	The snake is safe.
	Very happy is the snake.
	King Basuk who is here, the king is happy?
Oracle:	Yes.
Master:	His horse is happy?
Oracle:	Yes.

Hindi Version:

Master:	*are gusāī bāman huī van chhale*
	kān huy kans pachhāre

hirnarkush huy mare
rām huyi rāvan tāre
kāre nāye paij pai
mathurā bhaye ujiyāre
āstik ke bachan suni
are bāsudev, hūn karo

Oracle: *hūn*

Master: *hūnk nāth pāī sakin mili mangal gāye*
gangā gaurī gāyatrī tīnon dey asīs
kun Dalet kushalāt hai
kharī kushal hai Dank
rājā bāsuk ke yahān mahārāj kushal hai

Oracle: *hūn*

Master: *jā ghoRā kushal hai*

Oracle: *hūn*

Now the master knows that the possessing deity is well and that the oracle, or horse, is also fit. Note that the image is that of riding, as shown by the use of "horse" for the oracle himself. This series concludes the *bāchā*.

At this point, the master moves immediately into the *puchonī*, "questioning." These also are memorized, required *mantras*, and the questioning gives the master further control of the snake king.

Master: You are fine, I am fine, the horse is fine.
These things are true things.
Why is there such laziness in your head that you bite this man?
I am asking you why.
Why do you not put out your hand?

Oracle: Am putting out hand.

Master: The king is giving his hand for one second or for all life?

Oracle: For life.

Master: Extending my hand, catching your arm, I'll repeat to you the words of the guru.
To you the guru's words, the warrior's words, the strong words.
If you hide your *jat* [caste], you will become a leper.
King, who are you?

Oracle: Black.

Hindi version:

Master: *kushal to ko kushal mo kon kushal jā pinD ko*
DhiTTi DhiTTi satti bhāv champai laRe kai
au chhape kul joye subhāv
kai phan men āras bhao pūnchhat pyo aur rāy
pūnchhat pyo aur rāy kin dharo so
kyon na pasorā hāth

Oracle: *hāth pasār detā hai*

Master: *mahārāj hāth dharī ko dao hai kai janm ko*

Oracle: *janm ko*

Master: *hāthu pasāri bānh daī moy gūrū ke bachan sunaūn toy*
gūrū bachan so pīhar bachan aur bachan balvīr
jāti chhipaiyo āpnī tau koRī hoy sharīr
mahārāj kon ho

Oracle: *kāre*

After the *puchonī*, the real business can commence--question-
ing the snake king. Questions from the men in the audience are related to the snake king through the master, who repeats the snake
king's answer. However, during this questioning period, the master
not only requests advice from the snake king but also asks him about
his behavior during possession of the oracle and about his desires.
Although he does not use *mantras* during this section of the rite,
the master attempts to maintain his control. At times he even scolds
the snake king. For example:

Master: Great King, today you have given much trouble.
You took too much *khūn* today. What is wrong?

Oracle: Nothing.

Master: There is something. You are angry with me.

Oracle: Yes.

Master: Speak the truth.

Oracle: You did not give 13 *khūn*. [13 is the most powerful
khūn.]

Master: If 13 *khūn* you would be oversatisfied. So many
words all together at one time will burst out. So
why are you again and again giving trouble? 13 is
nothing.
Great King, you are not angry? How many times will
you play?

Oracle: Many.

. . . .

Master: So we should bring milk, Great King? Will you
drink milk?

       Oracle: Yes, will drink.

       Master: Will drink?

       Oracle: Yes, will drink.

(The oracle is questioned further to discover whether he will drink during play or during the questions or after the whole cycle is over. He chooses to drink during "play.")

       Master: O.K. I am giving *uThonī*. Don't do *khūn*. Don't
                  cheat. Take my words. When I say them, then. You
                  deceive me, then I will become angry.

Thus we see that, during the more informal (not bound by ritual sayings) portion of the ritual, the master coerces and controls the oracle, now Maharaj, the Great King. However, the oracle's words are believed and he is pacified with milk, given him during "play" as he requested. After the question period is completed, the master returns to the use of his magical formulas.

       The *uThonī*, "lifting," is used to make the oracle rise. There is only one:

       A bangle of conch shells,

       A garland of pearls.

       Feet like a lotus,

       Lanka was destroyed.

       The ditch of Lanka was as wide as the sea.

       Get up snake,

       Hanuman the Great's decree.

Hindi: *shank chūri kī eRurī*

       gajmotini ko hāru paiyān

       padmen lankā kare

       lankā koT samud sī khaī sī

       uTho Dank hanumant vīr kī duhāī

       As noted, the cycle may end with the *uThonī*. However, the oracle may require *khūn*. *khūn* can mean "blood," but it is more likely to mean "murder." In this case it is the murder of the snake king, that is, his removal from the oracle's body so that he himself does not murder the oracle. With the master leading, the men shout the *khūn*, repeating each line twice. It is necessary to shout the *khūn* until the oracle comes out of his spasm. There are a variety of *khūn*, and their efficacy depends in part on the deities referred to in them. It is best not to use a powerful *khūn* unless it is absolutely necessary to remove the snake king and return the oracle to life.

       All of the *khūn* have the same two lines at the end:

> If life is in the edge of nails or cells of hair,
> Arise, awake, be conscious.

In Hindi,

> *jo jiy hoy naha kī kor bār kī sor*
> *uThi jāgu chetu subhmār ho*

In about half of the *khūn*, these lines are followed by a third:

> Shri Guru Param Hans. Ram says.
> *shrī gūrū param hans rām kahte*

The rest of each *khūn* is concerned with episodes from the mythological cal repertoire of the North Indian villager and with references to various powerful beings. In the following frequently used *khūn*, the episode is a favorite for the Karimpur storytellers and the god, though Muslim, is still powerful.

> Earthen pot, clear water, golden spout,
> So Raja Basuk's daughter filled.
> Taking the pot in the hand, all poison was removed.
> That poison Mahmada cleansed.
> Make without poison Khuday.
> If life is in the edge of nails or cells of hair,
> Arise, awake, be conscious.

> *jhanjhal gaRuā jhalā nīr sone kī TonTī*
> *so bhari lāī rājā bāsuk kī beTī*
> *gaRuā līnau hāth men sab biSh lao utāri*
> *jo biSh achay mahāmadā nirabiSh kare khudāy*
> *jo jiy hoy naha kī kor bār kī sor*
> *uThi jāgu chetu subhmār ho*

Other *khūn* can be used, but if the snake leaves, *Dank* is over.

Appendix III: THE KARIMPUR CALENDAR

The Hindu calendrical system has been admirably described and discussed by Ruth and Stanley Freed (1964), and I refer the reader to
their article for detail beyond that given below.

The Yearly Calendar

The calendrical system used by Hindus is lunisolar. The North Indian
version of the Hindu calendar is known as the *pūrinmānta* system.
The annual cycle of festival activity is based primarily on a cycle
where one lunar month is one complete lunar cycle, from full moon to
full moon. Each lunar month consists of 29.5 solar days (Freed and
Freed 1964:68). There are twelve lunar months per year. Periodic
adjustments are made by adding or deleting lunar months to make the
lunar year accord with the solar year. The New Year begins on the
new moon day (approximately the sixteenth day) of the lunar month
Chait. Following is a list of the lunar months as they are named in
Karimpur, with their approximate Western counterparts.

chait	March-April
baisākh	April-May
jeth	May-June
āsārh	June-July
sāvan	July-August
bhādon	August-September
kuār	September-October
kārtik	October-November
aghan	November-December
pūs	December-January
māgh	January-February
phāgun	February-March[1]

Each lunar month is divided into two fortnights, or *pāk*, of
about fifteen days. Under the *pūrinmānta* system, the first fortnight,
that of the waning of the moon, is called *badī*, or the dark fortnight.
The second fortnight, that of the waxing of the moon, is known as
sudī, or the bright fortnight. Festivals and other ritual dates in
the annual cycle are then noted by their lunar month, their fortnight

(*badī* or *sudī*), and the lunar day (*tithi*) of the fortnight on which
they occur, with the days of the fortnight being named by Hindi der-
ivations of the numbers 1-14, as follows:

first	*ekam*	eighth	*āten* or *ashtmī*
second	*dūj*	ninth	*naumī*
third	*tīj*	tenth	*dassehrā*
fourth	*chauth*	eleventh	*ekādashī*
fifth	*panchmī*	twelfth	*dvādash*
sixth	*chhat*	thirteenth	*teras*
seventh	*saptamī*	fourteenth	*chaudas*

The days of no moon (the fifteenth day of the dark fortnight) and of
the full moon (the fifteenth day of the light fortnight) are specially designated as *amāvas* (no moon) and *pūrinmāshī* (full moon). The
yearly festivals of Karimpur (discussed in Chapter VIII) are given
in table 16. For convenience, I have used "1" in place of *badī*,
the first fortnight of the month, and "2" in place of *sudī*, the second fortnight of the month.

The Weekly Cycle

The weekly cycle of Karimpur ritual activity represents another aspect of man-god relations. Each day of the week is associated with
different powerful beings and different problems of man. Named after seven of the nine *grahas* (certain heavenly bodies and events),
each day is associated with corresponding deities and problems/
rules.[2] The days of the week, with their *grahas* and Western counterparts, are:

Day	*graha*	Western Day
iTvār	Sun	Sunday
somvār	Moon	Monday
mangalvār	Mars	Tuesday
budhvār	Mercury	Wednesday
brihaspativār	Jupiter	Thursday
shukravār	Venus	Friday
shanivār	Saturn	Saturday

Sunday is perhaps most notable, because it is a government
holiday and there is no school. But it is also an auspicious day,
since it is astrologically associated with the sun. Many men in Karimpur worship the sun on this day before their first meal.

Monday, *somvār*, is the day associated with the moon. How-

Table 16

A Table of the Karimpur Ceremonial Year

Lunar Month/Date	Event (Hindi)	Deity Honored	Form of Ritual	Theme
Chait 2:9	Goddess Worship (*devin kī pūjā*)	Devi	*pūjā* (*vrat*)	protection of family, *vrat* if a vow is given
Baisakh 2:3	Grain Third (*akhtīj*)	grain, Vishnu	*pūjā*	new crops, general shelter
Jeth 1:15	Worship of Marriage (*barok kī pūjā*)	banyan tree Devi	*vrat*	long marriage, long life of husband
Jeth 2:10	The Tenth (*dassehra*)	Ganges	*pūjā*, bathing	removal of sins by bathing in the Ganges
Asarh 2:11	The Eleventh (*ekādashī*)	. . . .	. . .	Gods go to sleep for 4 months--no marriages can occur until Kartik 2:11 (see *deothan*)
Asarh 2:15	Asarhi	Devi, guru	*pūjā*	protection and shelter, especially during rains
Asarh 2:?	The Pot (*khappar*)	Devi	*pūjā* possession	rid the village of illness
Savan 2:3	The Third (*tīj*)	Gauri (Parvati)	*pūjā* (*vrat*)	protection of one's brothers
Savan 2:5	Snake's Fifth (*nāg panchmī*)	snakes	*pūjā*	that they will not harm one's family
Savan 2:15	Tying on Protection (*rakhī bandan*)	Salune	*pūjā*, tying *rakhī*	protection, shelter
		wheat	*pūjā*, tying *rakhī*	protection, shelter
		brothers	tying *rakhī*	protection

Date	Festival	Deity	Type	Purpose
Savan (every Monday)	. . . .	Shiva	vrat	guard and shelter families
Bhadon 1:8	Krishna's Eighth (kanhaiyā āten)	Krishna	vrat	Krishna's love and protection
Bhadon 2:14	Eternal Fourteenth (anant chaudas)	ant (strings of protection) Hanuman	pūjā	protection
Kuar 1:1-15	Ancestor Worship (kanagat)	ancestors bhagvān	pūjā	general honor of ancestors, and happiness for them
Kuar 1:8	Worship of Lakshmi (mahālakshmī kī pūjā) Worship of the Elephant (hathī kī pūjā)	Lakshmi Ganesh	vrat	wealth and "fruits"
Kuar 2:1-9	The Nine Nights (neothar)	Gauri (Parvati)	pūjā	happiness for young girls and a successful marriage and children
Kuar 2:9	Durga Ninth (nau durga)	Durga (Devi)	pūjā	honor to the goddess
Kuar 2:10	Victory Tenth (bījā dasehrā)	Ram	. . . .	Ram's victory over Ravana
Kuar 2:10-15	Teshu-Sanjhi	Teshu-Sanjhi	children's play	. . .
Kartik 1:4	Pitcher Fourth (karva chauth)	husband, Moon	vrat	protection for husband and self
Kartik 1:14	Small Divali (choṭī dīvālī)	. . . .	lighting one floor lamp	. . .
Kartik 1:15	Big Divali (baRī dīvālī)	Lakshmi Ganesh, etc.	pūjā lamp-lighting	guide the goddess of wealth to one's house
Kartik 2:1	Lampblack (or Necklace) (sihayo or siyao)	Siyao or Sihayo Mata	pūjā	protect children for the year and make lampblack

Table 16--*Continued*

Lunar Month/Date	Event (Hindi)	Deity Honored	Form of Ritual	Theme
Kartik 2:1	Cow-Dung Wealth (*gobardhan*)	Krishna cow dung mountains	*pūjā*	ask Krishna's protection for one's family for the New Year just begun
Kartik 2:2	Brother's Second (*bhaiya dūj*)	brothers	*pūjā*	honor one's brother and obtain his shelter in exchange for your power
Kartik 2:11	Gods' Awakening (*deothan*)	Vishnu harvest	*pūjā*	wake the gods after their 4-month sleep and honor the new sugarcane harvest
Kartik 2:15	*kārtik puranamshī*	Vishnu, Ram *tulsī*	*pūjā* (*vrat*)	obtain general shelter and protection
Pus/Magh	Winter Solstice (*makar sankranti*)	Sun, Moon	*pūjā*	welcoming back the sun, coming of spring
Magh 1:3(4)	*sakat**	. . . .	. . . .	. . . .
Magh 2:5	Spring Fifth (*basant panchmī*)	. . . .	. . . .	honoring of spring, beginning of Holi season
Phagun 1:13	Shiva's Thirteenth (*shiv teras*)	Shiva	*vrat*	obtain protection of Shiva, honor his marriage to Parvati
Phagun 2:15	Holi	barley household gods	*pūjā*	the new harvest, burning of Holika, sport of Krishna
Chait 1:1	Color Cleaning (*rangdhul*)	. . . .	. . . .	sport of Krishna, levity, throwing color

| Chait 1:8 | Goddess Worship (*devīn kī pūjā*) | Devi | *pūjā* | Devi's protection in the hot weather |

*I was not in Karimpur at the time of this festival. It was named by the villagers when they were asked about yearly rituals. I was never able to get more information about it.

ever, it is most important because of its association with Shiva;
any devotee of Shiva should worship him every Monday, as indeed the
women of Karimpur do during Savan. Shiva is also associated with
the dark days of the month (Shiva's Thirteenth is in the dark half
of the month), and the conjunction of Monday and a no moon day
(*amāvas*) is particularly auspicious. It is called *somvatī* and many
women will fast and worship Shiva on such special days.

In Karimpur, Tuesday, *mangalvār*, is associated with Hanuman
worship.[3] The day of Mars, it is sometimes considered an inauspicious day on which one needs protection. However, *mangal* itself
means auspicious, and *mangal dev*, the deity named for this day, is
benevolent, although sometimes capricious. Devotees of Hanuman will
have his *vrat* on this day.

Wednesday, *budhvār*, is the day on which one should worship
budhdev. Astrologically associated with Mercury, Wednesday is a day
of peace and knowledge (*budh* means both "Mercury" and "knowledge").
It is a good day to begin a journey or to start plowing one's fields.
No one in Karimpur has *vrat* on this day.

Thursday, *brihaspativār*, is astrologically associated with
Jupiter, a benevolent planet. However, its primary association is
with *gurū* worship, particularly worship of the *gurū* of the gods themselves, Brihaspatiji. *vrat* on this day is particularly popular with
women because they will find beautiful husbands by doing it.

Friday, *shukravār*, is associated with the planet Venus. It
is an auspicious day and is sometimes described as being "like Monday." Although some people do worship Shiva on Friday, the more
popular *vrat* is to Santoshi Mata, a benevolent goddess considered to
be the daughter of Ganesh. Several women in Karimpur regularly do
the *vrat* of Santoshi Mata.

Saturday, *shanivār*, is a very inauspicious day associated
with the planet Saturn (*shani*). It is a day of no ritual importance
in Karimpur, although its extreme inauspiciousness was recognized
and no one would plow fields or begin journeys on this day.[4]

The weekly ritual cycles are important primarily to people
with an *ishtā devatā* (chosen deity). If a person worships his chosen
deity, it is for that deity's shelter and general aid. The deities
worshiped in the weekly ritual cycle are benevolent, ones who will
give shelter and aid. As chosen deities, they are type 1 or type 2
powerful beings.

NOTES

1. Hereafter, I shall use the normal transliterated equivalents of these months without Hindi diacritics.

2. The weekly religious cycle for Chattisgarh has been described by L. A. Babb (1968:107-21), and I refer the reader to that work for more details than those given below. There are also important variations between Chattisgarh and Karimpur which I shall try to note.

3. Babb's data indicate that Mars's is a very inauspicious day in Chattisgarh. It did not seem to be in Karimpur.

4. See Babb 1968 for a thorough discussion of Saturday in an area where it is ritually important.

REFERENCES

Babb, Lawrence A.
  1968   Systemic Aspects of Chhattisgarhi Religion: An Analysis of
         a Popular Variant of Hinduism. Unpublished Doctoral Disser-
         tation, University of Rochester.

  1970a Marriage and Malevolence: The Uses of Sexual Opposition in
         a Hindu Pantheon. *Ethnology* 9:137-48.

  1970b The Food of the Gods in Chhattisgarh: Some Structural Fea-
         tures of Hindu Ritual. *Southwestern Journal of Anthropology*
         26:287-304.

Bahl, K. C.
  n.d.   Project of a Medium Sized Doctionary of Hindi Verbs. Part 1:
         Synonymous Action Noun Phrases with *Kar-*. Department of
         South Asian Languages and Civilizations, University of Chica-
         go, Mimeograph.

Beals, Alan R.
  1962   *Gopalur: A South Indian Village*. New York: Holt, Rinehart
         & Winston.

Beck, Brenda E. F.
  1969   The Vacillating Goddess: Sexual Control and Social Rank in
         the Indian Pantheon. Paper presented at the Association for
         Asian Studies Meetings, Boston, March 1969.

Berreman, Gerald D.
  1963   *Hindus of the Himalayas*. Berkeley: University of California
         Press.

Briggs, George W.
  1920   *The Chamars*. London: Oxford University Press.

Burling, Robbins
  1969   Linguistics and Ethnographic Description. *American Anthro-
         pologist* 71:817-27.

Carstairs, G. Morris
  1967   *The Twice-Born*. Bloomington: Indiana University Press.

Chomsky, Noam
  1965   *Aspects of the Theory of Syntax*. Cambridge: MIT Press.

Cohn, Bernard S.
  1959   Changing Traditions of a Low Caste. In *Traditional India:
         Structure and Change*. Milton Singer, ed. Philadelphia:
         American Folklore Society.

Cohn, Bernard S., and McKim Marriott
  1958   Networks and Centers in the Integration of Indian Civiliza-
         tion. *Journal of Social Research* 1:1-9.

Conaghey, M. A. Mc.
  1869   Karimganj Settlement Report, 1869. Reprinted in Wiser 1933.

Conklin, Harold C.
 1955 Hanunco Color Categories. *Southwestern Journal of Anthropology* 11:339-44.

 1962 Lexicographical Treatment of Folk Taxonomies. Work paper for the Conference on Lexicography, Indiana University, Nov. 11-12, 1960. In *Problems in Lexicography*. Fred Householder and Sol Saporta, eds. Supplement to *International Journal of American Linguistics*, vol. 28, no. 2.

 1964 Ethnogenealogical Method. In *Explorations in Cultural Anthropology*. W. H. Goodenough, ed. New York: McGraw-Hill.

Crooke, William
 1896 *The Popular Religion and Folklore of Northern India.* Westminister: Archibald Constable & Co.

Dumont, Louis
 1959 A Structural Definition of a Folk Deity. *Contributions to Indian Sociology* 3:75-88.

 1970 *Homo Hierarchicus: An Essay on the Caste System.* Translated by Mark Sainsbury. Chicago: University of Chicago Press.

Dumont, Louis, and D. Pocock
 1959 Pure and Impure. *Contributions to Indian Sociology* 3:9-40.

Durkheim, Emile, and Marcel Mauss
 1963 *Primitive Classification.* Translated by Rodney Needham. Chicago: University of Chicago Press.

Frake, Charles O.
 1969 The Diagnosis of Disease among the Subanun of Mindanao. *American Anthropologist* 63:113-32.

 1962 The Ethnographic Study of Cognitive Systems. In *Anthropology and Human Behavior*. T. Gladwin and W. C. Sturtevant, eds. Washington: Anthropological Society of Washington.

Freed, Ruth S., and Stanley A. Freed
 1964 Calendars, Ceremonies, and Festivals in a North Indian Village: Necessary Calendrical Information for Fieldwork. *Southwestern Journal of Anthropology* 20:67-90.

Freedman, Maurice
 1967 *Rites and Duties, or Chinese Marriage.* London: G. Bell.

Geertz, Clifford
 1957 Ritual and Social Change: A Javanese Example. *American Anthropologist* 59:32-54.

 1958 Ethos World View and the Analysis of Sacred Symbols. *Antioch Review*, Winter (1957-58):421-37.

 1966 Religion as a Cultural System. In *Anthropological Approaches to the Study of Religion*. Michael Banton, ed. London: Tavistock.

Gombrich, Richard F.
 1971 *Precept and Practice: Traditional Buddhism in the Rural Highlands of Ceylon.* Oxford: Clarendon Press.

Goodenough, Ward H.
 1956 Componential Analysis and the Study of Meaning. *Language* 32:195-216.

Goody, Jack
 1962 *Death, Property and the Ancestors.* London: Tavistock.

Harper, Edward J.
 1959 A Hindu Village Pantheon. *Southwestern Journal of Anthropology* 15:227-34.

1964 Ritual Pollution as an Integrator of Caste and Religion. In *Religion in South Asia*. Edward J. Harper, ed. Seattle: University of Washington Press.

Herbert, Catherine T.
1973 The Nagas in Vaishnavite Art, Ritual and Myth. Unpublished Honors Thesis, Department of Anthropology, Syracuse University.

Hubert, Henri, and Marcel Mauss
1897-98 Essai sur la nature et la fonction du sacrifice. *Année Sociologique 2*.

1902-3 Esquisse d'une théorie générale de la magie. *Année Sociologique 4*.

Johnson, Donald, and Jean Johnson
1970 Looking behind Mud Walls. (Filmstrip.) New York: Industrial Media Associates.

Kellogg, S. H.
1972 *A Grammar of the Hindi Language*. New Delhi: Oriental Books Reprint Corporation.

Kolenda, Pauline M.
1964 Religious Anxiety and Hindu Fate. In *Religion in South Asia*. Edward J. Harper, ed. Seattle: University of Washington Press.

Kroeber, A. L., and C. Kluckhohn
1952 *Culture: A Critical Review of Concepts and Definitions*. Papers of the Peabody Museum. Cambridge: Harvard University.

Kroeber, A. L., and T. Parsons
1958 The Concepts of Cultural and of Social System. *American Sociological Review* 23:582-83.

LaBrack, Bruce W.
1969 Calendrical Rites of a North Indian Village as a Mechanism in the Perpetuation of Hinduism. Unpublished Master's Paper, Department of Anthropology, University of Arizona.

Langer, Suzanne
1951 *Philosophy in a New Key*. New York: Mentor Books.

Leach, Edmund
1963 Pulleyar and the Lord Buddha: An Aspect of Religious Syncretism in Ceylon. *Psychoanalysis and Psychoanalytic Review* 49:80-102.

Lehman, F. K.
1972 Doctrine, Practice and Belief in Theravada Buddhism. *Journal of Asian Studies* 31:373-80.

Levi-Strauss, Claude
1963a The Structural Study of Myth. In *Structural Anthropology*. New York: Basic Books.

1963b *Structural Anthropology*. New York: Basic Books.

Lewis, Oscar
1965 *Village Life in Northern India*. New York: Knopf, Vintage Books.

Lupton, Walter
1904 Karimganj - General Inspection Note, 1904. Reprinted in Wiser 1933.

Lyons, John
1963 *Structural Semantics*. Oxford: Basil Blackwell.

Lyons, John
 1968 *Introduction to Theoretical Linguistics*. Cambridge: Cambridge University Press.

Mahar, Pauline
 1960 Changing Religious Practices of an Untouchable Caste. *Economic Development and Cultural Change* 8:279-87.

Mandelbaum, David
 1964 Introduction: Process and Structure in South Asian Religion. In *Religion in South Asia*. Edward J. Harper, ed. Seattle: University of Washington Press.

 1966 Transcendental and Pragmatic Aspects of Religion. *American Anthropologist* 68:1174-91.

Maranda, Pierre, and E. K. Kongäs Maranda, eds.
 1971 *Structural Analysis of Oral Tradition*. Philadelphia: University of Pennsylvania Press.

Marriott, McKim
 1955 Little Communities in an Indigenous Civilization. In *Village India*. McKim Marriott, ed. Chicago: University of Chicago Press.

 1966 The Feast of Love. In *Krishna: Myths, Rites, and Attitudes*. Milton Singer, ed. Chicago: University of Chicago Press.

 1968 Caste Ranking and Food Transactions: A Matrix Analysis. In *Structure and Change in Indian Society*. Milton Singer and B. S. Cohn, eds. Chicago: Aldine Publishing Co.

Marriott, McKim, and Ronald B. Inden
 1972 An Ethnosociology of South Asian Caste Systems. Paper read at the American Anthropological Association Meetings, Toronto, December 1972.

Miller, Robert
 1966 Button, Button . . . Great Tradition, Little Tradition, Whose Tradition. *Anthropological Quarterly* 39:26-42.

Monier-Williams, Sir Monier
 1956 *A Sanskrit-English Dictionary*. Oxford: Clarendon Press.

Neave, B. R.
 1913 *District Gazateers of the United Provinces*, Vol. X, *Mainpuri*. Allahbad: Government Press, U.P.

Nicholas, Ralph W.
 1968 Structures of Politics in the Villages of Southern Asia. In *Structure and Change in Indian Society*. Milton Singer and B. S. Cohn, eds. Chicago: Aldine Publishing Co.

Opler, Morris
 1959 The Place of Religion in a North Indian Village. *Southwestern Journal of Anthropology* 15:219-26.

Pandey, Dr. Raj Bali
 1968 *Hindu Samskaras*. Delhi: Motilal Banarsidass.

Planalp, Jack W.
 1956 Religious Life and Values in a North Indian Village. Unpublished Doctoral Dissertaion, Cornell University.

Platts, John T.
 1968 *A Dictionary of Urdu, Classical Hindi, and English*. London: Oxford University Press.

Propp, V.
 1968 *Morphology of a Folktale*. Houston: University of Texas Press.

Raghavan
1956   Variety and Integration in the Pattern of Indian Culture.
        Far Eastern Quarterly 15:497-507.

Redfield, Robert
1955   The Social Organization of Traditions. *Far Eastern Quarterly*
        15:13-23.

Robinson, Marguerite S.
1968   "The House of the Mighty Hero" or "The House of Enough Paddy"?
        Some Implications of a Sinhalese Myth. In *Dialectic in Prac-
        tical Religion*. E. R. Leach, ed. Cambridge: Cambridge
        University Press.

Schneider, David
1968   *American Kinship: A Cultural Account*. Englewood Cliffs:
        Prentice-Hall.

Singer, Milton
1955   The Cultural Patterns of Indian Civilization. *Far Eastern
        Quarterly* 15:23-37.

1961   Text and Context in the Study of Religion and Social Change
        in India. *Adyar Library Bulletin* 15:274-303.

1972   *When a Great Tradition Modernizes*. New York: Praeger.

Spiro, Melford
1966   Religion: Problems of Definition and Explanation. In *Ap-
        proaches to the Anthropological Study of Religion*. M. Banton,
        ed. London: Tavistock.

Srinivas, M. N.
1952   *Religion and Society among the Coorgs of South Asia*. Bombay:
        Asia Publishing House.

Staal, J. F.
1963   Sanskrit and Sanskritization. *Journal of Asian Studies* 22:
        261-76.

Tambiah, S. J.
1968   The Magical Power of Words. *Man*, New Series 3:175-208.

Varma, L. A. Ravi
1956   Rituals of Worship. In *The Cultural Heritage of India*. H.
        Bhattacharyya, ed. Calcutta: Ramakrishna Institute of Cul-
        ture.

Vogel, J. Ph.
1926   *Indian Serpent Lore*. London: Arthur Probsthsin.

Wadley, Susan S.
1967   Fate and the Gods in the Panjabi Cult of Gugga: A Structural
        Semantic Analysis. Unpublished Master's Paper, Department
        of Anthropology, University of Chicago.

1973   The Spirit "Rides" or the Spirit "Comes": Possession in a
        North Indian Village. Paper presented at the Ninth Inter-
        national Congress of Anthropological and Ethnological Sciences,
        Chicago, September 1973.

Whitehead, Henry
1916   *The Village Gods of South India*. London: Oxford University
        Press.

Wiser, William H.
1933   Social Institutions of a Hindu Village of North India. Un-
        published Doctoral Dissertation, Cornell University.

1958   *The Hindu Jajmani System*. Lucknow: Lucknow Publishing House.

Wiser, William H., and Charlotte V. Wiser
1971 *Behind Mud Walls: 1930-1960.* With a Sequel--The Village in 1970. Berkeley: University of California Press.

Yalman, Nur
1964 The Structure of Sinhalese Healing Rituals. In *Religion in South Asia.* E. J. Harper, ed. Seattle: University of Washington Press.

1967 *Under the Bo Tree: Studies in Caste, Kinship and Marriage in the Interior of Ceylon.* Berkeley: University of California Press.

Hindi-Language References

Anonymous
brihaspati vār vrat kathā. Mathura, bhāshā thok pustakalay, n.d.

saptvār vrat kathā. Delhi, goyal bradars, n.d.

saptvār vrat kathā. Delhi, anand prakāshan, n.d.

saptvār vrat kathā. Haridvar, arju nrsinh amarjīt sinh bukselar, n.d.

shrī satya nārāyan vrat kathā. Delhi, anand prakāshan, n.d.

shukrvār vrat kathā. Mathura, mital eraDkuthok pustakālay, n.d.

shukrvār vrat kathā. Delhi, anand prakāshan, n.d.

dīkshit, rajesh
vrat, parv aur tyohār. Kanpur, dīp prakāshan mandir, n.d.

mishra, cintāmaNi and prabhākar mishra
shānti-sarovar. Mainpuri, mishra pustak bhaNDār, n.d.

prasād, kālika; rājvallabh sahāy and mukundīlāl shrīvāstav, eds.
brihat hindi kosh. Varanasi, gyanmaNDal limiTeD, n.d.

sharmā, ramesh chandra
chacha nehrā. Mainpuri, mishra pustak bhaNDār, n.d.

"Winod," gangā sevalc shakla
kīrtan sāgar. Kanpur, nyū dargesh printars, n.d.